Faizal

The Makkan Crucible

ZAKARIA BASHIER

The Islar

First published FOSIS 1978

ISBN 0 86037 203 0 (Hardback)
ISBN 0 86037 204 9 (Paperback)

Cover Design: Zafar Abbas Malik

Published by
The Islamic Foundation,
Markfield Dawah Centre,
Ratby Lane,
Markfield,
Leicester LE6 0RN,
United Kingdom.

Quran House,
P.O. Box 30611,
Nairobi,
Kenya.

P.M.B. 3193,
Kano,
Nigeria.

British Library Cataloguing in Publication Data
Bashier, Zakaria
The Makkan crucible.–Rev. ed.
1. Islam, history
I. Title II. Islamic Foundation
297.09

ISBN 0-86037-203-0
ISBN 0-86037-204-9 pbk

Printed and bound by
Cromwell Press Ltd., Broughton Gifford, Wiltshire.

Dedicated
to my senior colleagues and friends
Professor ‘Abdullah al-Ṭayb – former vice-chancellor
of the University of Khartoum
and
Professor ‘Abdullah al-Naṣīf – former deputy
vice-chancellor of King ‘Abdul ‘Aziz University
and presently Secretary General,
Rābiṭa al-Ālam al-Islāmī, Makkah.
Both men have encouraged and supported me
during the course of writing this book.

بسم الله الرحمن الرحيم

Contents

Acknowledgements

I acknowledge with deep gratitude the assistance extended to me by my friends and colleagues, Dr. Ibrāhīm Aḥmad Omar and Sayed az-Zubair b. Ṭāhā of the Department of Philosophy, University of Khartoum.

To my wife, 'Umm Ayman, I am indebted for the untiring help and most patient attendance on almost every demand I made in connection with preparing references and draft manuscripts.

I would also like to thank Qurashi Muḥammad 'Alī, Jamīl Sherīf and the Executive of the Federation of Students Islamic Societies in the U.K. and Eire for their efforts in seeing the work through the press. In particular, I am grateful to 'Abdul Wāḥid Ḥāmid who suggested several improvements in the text and who has done much work in editing and preparing the manuscript for publication. My thanks are also due to Mr. A.T.V. Wolton of Ithaca Press who kindly read the typescript and suggested many improvements in the language.

During the extended period of writing this book, I received helpful assistance from many people whom I cannot acknowledge by name. To all of them, I accord my sincere gratitude.

My greatest and ultimate debt and gratitude is due to Allah, the Creator of the heavens and the earth. May He pardon and forgive my failings and weaknesses, strengthen and enliven my faith in Him and endow me with knowledge and wisdom.

17 August 1977 **Zakaria Bashier**
3 Ramaḍān 1397

Preface

This book is not a comprehensive narrative of the life of the Prophet of Islam. Some aspects of his life during the Makkan period are discussed and highlighted. These aspects have been chosen either because of their intrinsic interest or because they relate to issues which have evoked controversy or misgivings in the ever-increasing literature on Islam.

Care has been taken that the book should express a Muslim point of view on the subject. While Orientalists have written extensively on the life of the Prophet, *ṣallā Allāhu 'alayhi wa sallam,* at times displaying a degree of objectivity and even of sympathetic sensitivity, their writings invariably reflect Western attitudes. They have failed to give due recognition to two central themes of the Islamic faith – the Qur'ān as the infallible, Divinely revealed word of God and Muḥammad, *ṣallā Allāhu 'alayhi wa sallam,* as a Prophet and Messenger of God sent after Jesus to all mankind.

No attempt has been made to make the approach of the book excessively rational. The theme clearly transcends the ordinary categories of rational discourse. A significant aspect of the life of any true Prophet inevitably touches upon the mystical and the metaphysical. The prophetic miracles, for instance, is a topic which does not admit of hard-headed, rigorous analysis. Our line is therefore to accept and acknowledge accounts of miracles whenever they are given in credible versions by our sources.

I have attempted to strike a balance between the demands of narration and analysis. If this attempt is judged successful, even in a small measure, it will hopefully contribute to a better understanding of a life that has inspired and will always inspire millions of people till the end of all time.

Hendon, London
August 1977

Zakaria Bashier

Preface to the Revised Edition

Although numerous books have been written on the life of the Prophet, *ṣallā Allāhu 'alayhi wa sallam,* highlighting different aspects of his life and mission, none can claim to be exhaustive. More studies are therefore bound to appear and many hitherto unexplored dimensions brought into focus by new generations of authors who will continue to inspire people to follow the Prophet's *Uswah ḥasanah* (the excellent example) by presenting studies on multi-dimensional aspects of the life of the Prophet. Dr. Zakaria Bashier by writing *The Makkan Crucible* has tried to add his name to the illustrious list of the Prophet's biographers. While, on the one hand, it is a great honour to pen something on the life of the Blessed Prophet, on the other it is a great responsibility and indeed an exceedingly difficult task to present the life of the Prophet from the right perspective. In paying homage and showing reverence to the Prophet some authors have exceeded proper limits while others have not been able to adequately highlight the multi-dimensional aspects of the Prophetic life. Dr. Zakaria Bashier however has succeeded in striking a balance and presenting a graphic and inspiring picture of the *Sīrah* of the Prophet.

He has not only breathed a new freshness into the subject but has focused on the *Sīrah* in the context of the Prophet's mission as reflected in the Qur'ān. In portraying the major events of the Prophetic era he has delved deeply into the reasons and consequences of such events not only for the Prophet's generation but for all generations to come. 'The focus moved', as Professor Khurshid Ahmad puts it, 'beautifully and meaningfully from man to mission, from individual to movement, from past to the present and the future, from chronicle of events to ethos of society and history'. The result of Dr. Zakaria Bashier's research based on original Arabic sources and modern writings on the *Sīrah* is a powerful restatement of the Makkan life of the Prophet and a searching analysis of the *Jāhiliyyah* environment in which the blessings of Islam produced a generation of people who not only became the finest embodiment of human conduct but typified the highest virtues of faith and endurance.

Dr. Zakaria Bashier in this pioneering work also challenges some of the popular assumptions about the *Jāhiliyyan* society and suggests that many of them possessed great qualities of head and heart which under divine guidance and the leadership of the Prophet transformed them into individuals of exemplary strength and moral worth. The book lists and discusses some of these qualities in some detail. The study is marked for its patient unravelling of the tribal and clanish allegiances and tensions of the Arab society which often played a crucial role in the career of the Prophet and his *Ṣaḥābah* (Companions). The details of the lives of these *Ṣaḥābah* give an important dimension to *The Makkan Crucible,* demonstrating no doubt that 'it is in the regime of rigour and even hardship rather than in the lap of ease, comfort and plenty that immortal deeds are wrought'. Because of his unique style and masterly treatment of the subject, I am sure, both the general reader and the specialist will find *The Makkan Crucible* quite informative and stimulating.

The first edition of this book was published by the Federation of Students Islamic Societies in the UK and Eire (FOSIS) in 1978 and received wide acclamation from all quarters. The book has been out of print for many years and the need to bring out a new, revised edition was felt keenly. I am extremely grateful to my able colleague and brother, Dr. Zakaria Bashier, for giving permission to bring out this edition from the Islamic Foundation. Not only have certain editorial changes been made, two very useful appendices have also been added. The first appendix, by Dr. Zakaria Bashier, highlights the significance and lessons of the Prophet's *isrā'* and *mi'rāj* and the second one, by me, provides a sharp rebuttal of the Orientalists' obsession with the so-called story of the 'Satanic Verses' – a concoction which has been turned into blasphemy and profanity in Salman Rushdie's outrageous publication of the same name. A proper anatomy of the 'story' and exposure of its preposterous nature was once again very much called for. The Foundation has had the pleasure of publishing two of Dr. Zakaria Bashier's outstanding contributions on the life of the Prophet: *Hijra, Story and Significance* (1983) and *Sunshine at Madinah: Studies in the Life of the Prophet Muḥammad* (1990). *The Makkan Crucible* will now become the first and essential volume in the series. The fourth and concluding volume, when ready, will *Inshā' Allāh* add further lustre to an already excellent series on the *Sīrah* of the Prophet.

I am grateful to Mawlana Iqbal Azami and other colleagues in the Foundation for going through the text and suggesting improvements. Mr. Eric R. Fox deserves my special thanks for his assistance at various stages of the publication of the book. May Allah, *subḥānahū wa ta'ālā,* accept our humble effort, forgive our lapses and make it a source of inspiration and guidance for all.

Leicester
October 1990
Rabī' al-Awwal 1411

M. Manazir Ahsan
Director General

CHAPTER 1

Pre-Islamic Arabia

In the strip of arid land running parallel to the Red Sea and extending eastward for perhaps less than a hundred miles, the world witnessed the flowering and perfection of Islam. This narrow strip of land is the Ḥijāz. Herein lies Makkah, the birthplace of the last of the Prophets, *ṣallā Allāhu ʻalayhi wa sallam.* Here also lies al-Madīnah, the political capital of the state which he founded and where he died and was buried.

With the exception of a few of its cities which are situated in rather green oases, the bulk of the Ḥijāz is arid desert. A sample of this can still be seen by the pilgrim as he journeys from Jeddah to Makkah. The landscape is strikingly hilly and bare – even desolate – and there is nothing to catch the eye as he moves along breathlessly, and in great awe and expectation, to have the first glimpse of the Kaʻbah in the most sacred of sanctuaries. Here in the valley of Makkah itself, the vegetation is but sparse and for miles around the terrain is scorched and barren. Yet from this very area arose men and women who, under Divine guidance and the leadership of the Prophet, *ṣallā Allāhu ʻalayhi wa sallam,* became the finest examples of human conduct and behaviour, typifying the highest virtues of faith and endurance that the world has known.

Was there, we might well ask, a sudden transformation from a primitive, fragile and debased society (as pre-Islamic Arabia is often depicted in popular accounts) to one of exemplary strength and moral worth? Or was there something in the desert and its oases of sedentary life, in the disposition of its inhabitants and the values of its society, that caused this transformation and rendered it more possible? In what follows we will in fact suggest that it is partly at least in the interplay between the sea of desert and the disposition and aptitude of the Arab that we must seek to understand the phenomenal speed with which Islam arose in Arabia and covered the face of the then known world, changing it for all time to come. We will suggest that it is in the regime of rigour and even hardship rather than in the lap of ease, comfort and plenty that immortal deeds are wrought. This is not a romantic approach and will not preclude us from taking a close, critical look at the composition of Makkan society in particular and the tensions and conflicts which characterized it at the turn of the sixth century C.E. But for the moment we suggest that if the Arabian personality of the desert catches the imagination at all, it could open up a whole field of research for the sociologist and the philosopher of social studies. It is into this field that we now venture.

The population of the Ḥijāz was both nomadic and sedentary but there was considerable interaction, as we shall see, between the two types. The nomadic bedouin roamed the large desert and semi-desert terrain and formed a vast network of tribes and clans which characterized the Arabian scene just before the rise of Islam. The sedentary folk inhabited the cities of Makkah, Yathrib (later to be known as al-Madīnah) and aṭ-Ṭā'if, towns which had grown out of the bedouin desert. These towns in fact were places where bedouins and sedentarized folk mixed freely for trade and pilgrimage, and for marriage and cultural pursuits particularly during the famous fairs which attracted poets from all over Arabia. If the bedouin were not totally free from the pull and influence of the towns, neither were the Makkans or Yathribites ever quite distant from the 'deep' desert. Many of the latter were former nomads or descendants of nomads and it was the practice of wealthy Makkans to send their youth (as the Prophet, *ṣallā Allāhu 'alayhi wa sallam,* himself was sent) to the surrounding desert to grow up healthy, tough and self-reliant and to speak the pure, uncorrupted Arabic of the bedouins. We should be justified in saying that a sedentarized-bedouin type was common in Makkah at the time.

Of the bedouin and the sedentary forms of social organization, the former was no doubt the earlier and the more fundamental. 'Umar ibn Al-Khaṭṭāb is reported to have said that the bedouins were the raw material of Islam. Perhaps he meant simply that they, or some of them at any rate, were potential converts to Islam. Or perhaps he meant that they were naturally disposed to become personifications of Islamic ideals and virtues, if only they could be persuaded to accept Islam. Here, his statement may be understood as alluding to the pure, natural state of the bedouin's psychical make-up. This state tends to be neutral (as to its receptiveness of either good or evil). It is like a blank tablet ready to be imprinted by whatever the scriber wishes to imprint on it.

A third way of interpreting 'Umar's statement is that the bedouins, although they led a life which knew no inhibitions or great moral constraints were, if somehow won over to Islam, potentially its major striking force. Their tremendous physical and psychical powers, their considerable capacity to endure hardships and their phenomenal fortitude and personal initiative, made them naturally disposed to become the vanguard of a fighting force. However 'Umar's statement is interpreted, the bedouin form of social association certainly possesses some basic characteristics which set it apart from some of the acquired habits of a sedentary life. Ibn Khaldūn, in his celebrated *Muqaddimah,* expressed this notion as follows:

> We have mentioned that the bedouins restrict themselves to the necessities in their conditions (of life) and are unable to go beyond them, while sedentary people concern themselves with conveniences and luxuries in their conditions and customs. The (bare) necessities are no doubt prior to the conveniences and luxuries. (Bare) necessities, in a way are basic, and the luxuries secondary and an outgrowth (of the necessities). Bedouins, thus, are the basis of, and prior to, cities and sedentary people. Only after he has obtained the (bare) necessities, does he get to comforts and luxuries. The toughness of the desert life precedes the softness of sedentary life.[1]

Let us now consider in some detail the influences of the desert mode of life which constituted the major single influence upon the pre-Islamic Arabian personality.

The Bedouin Mode of Life

Life in the desert is such that it produces a man whose major characteristic is that of the tough fighter. The main features of this life are the following:

(1) excessive scarcity of food;
(2) the great effort needed to produce it;
(3) the need to undertake lengthy travels in the desert and the need of the bedouin to be his own guide on these travels;
(4) the need to provide for all the requirements of his own security.

Of these dominant conditioning influences on the character of the bedouin, the scarcity of food is perhaps the most dominant. It results in a healthier body and a stronger physique. Although the bedouin's meal is small in quantity, it is not lacking in proteins, consisting as it does of milk, meat (sometimes) and dates. Cereals are a luxury and sweets are unknown.

Ascetics of all schools of mysticism believe that eating very little is part of a training which results in the expansion of the inner consciousness of a person. It is believed to foster and develop certain psychical powers in the person who follows a scheme of systematically decreasing the amount of food and drink which he takes. Eventually the ascetic training is supposed to result in a clearer and healthier complexion, a greatly increased power of perception and well-developed faculties of understanding. Those who eat to excess become slothful, unimaginative and dull. The habit of eating little may help a person to endure hunger for longer periods. This develops fortitude in the bedouin and enables him to survive when he is totally without food.

The other three needs are also conducive to the development of fortitude, courage and self-reliance. They greatly develop the well-known bedouin qualities of vigour, strength, vigilance and the ability to act swiftly in self-defence when he is ambushed or exposed to sudden danger. These traits enable him to retain his personal initiative and his personal independence. He does not submit easily and is not easy to control. He is brash and uninhibited. He is free to come and go, free in his personal style of eating, talking and dressing. He is not encumbered by the niceties of etiquette and he instinctively and violently resists and resents any attempt to bring him under the jurisdiction of town etiquette. The bedouin cherishes this freedom and highly values it. To him, it is an inseparable part of his dignity *(karāmah)* and honour. A serious loss of it is tantamount to humiliation which he would rather die than suffer. So the bedouin never yields his freedom nor does he survive in an environment in which it is missing.

While appreciating the above qualities we should not lose sight of some of the inadequacies or negative characteristics of the bedouin way of life. The hardened bedouin is not noted for sensitivity, affection and human deference to others. His language may be pure and uncorrupted but he is not noted for his ability to appreciate elegant linguistic expressions, nor is he immediately capable of grasping abstract concepts and ideas that require a speculative mentality. All these qualities were needed for a deeper understanding and appreciation of the ideological message of Islam. These incapacities of the bedouin were recorded, in strong terms, in the following Qur'ānic revelations:

> The desert Arabs are more confirmed in unbelief and hypocrisy, and more fitted to be uninformed about the commands which Allah hath revealed unto His messenger. But Allah is all-Knowing, all-Wise.[2]

This is a strong denunciation, but it must not be taken to have universal application to all bedouins that were then living, let alone bedouins of all times; because in the very same *sūrah* (*At-Tawbah* – Repentance), we find the following qualifying verse:

> And of the desert Arabs there is he, who believes in Allah and the Last Day, and takes that which he expends (in the way of Allah) and also the prayers of the Messenger.
> As pious gifts bring them nearer to Allah.
> Indeed they bring them nearer (to Him). Soon will Allah admit them into His mercy,
> For Allah is oft-Forgiving, Most Merciful.[3]

Thus, although verse 97 does not imply that all bedouins are confirmed unbelievers and hypocrites, it nevertheless makes a general characterization of the psychological make-up of bedouins. This psychological attitude must be understood in the context of the conditioning of environmental and sociological conditions of bedouin desert life; it is not something intrinsic to them as a racial group. It can be said that whenever a group of people live under these bedouin conditions, they invariably tend to develop modes of feeling and behaviour conducive to unbelief and hypocrisy. It may be that tough living conditions bordering on poverty and starvation tend to harden the hearts of men, rendering them cruel and quite devoid of love and mercy. A heart which is so devoid is a heart which is, *prima facie,* not disposed towards generosity, deference to others or general moral excellence.

Ibn Khaldūn, however, maintains that bedouins are more disposed towards goodness than sedentary people:

> The reason for it is that the soul in its first natural state of creation is ready to accept whatever good or evil may arrive and leave an imprint upon it . . . Muḥammad[4] said:
> 'Every infant is born in the natural state. It is his parents who make him a Jew or a Christian or a Magian.' (al-Bukhārī, *Ṣaḥīḥ*).
> Bedouins may be as concerned with worldly affairs as (sedentary people are). However, such concern would touch only the necessities of life and not luxuries or anything causing or calling for, desires and pleasures. The customs they follow in their mutual dealings are, therefore, appropriate. As compared with those of sedentary people, their evil ways and blameworthy qualities are much less numerous. They are closer to the first natural state and more remote from the evil habits that have been impressed upon the souls (of sedentary people) through numerous and ugly, blameworthy customs.[5]

What can we make of Ibn Khaldūn's view as stated in this last quotation, in view of the strong Qur'ānic denunciation of the bedouin as 'more confirmed in unbelief and hypocrisy'?

Perhaps the best way to understand Ibn Khaldūn's remark is to put it in its true context. The context is one in which the bedouin is compared to the city-dweller with respect to his readiness to accept new ideas and new beliefs in general. The bedouin is pronounced by Ibn Khaldūn to be more prone to receive new ideas because his mind is quite empty of them. On the other hand, the city-dweller is more indoctrinated, so to speak. If the dweller of Makkah or aṭ-Ṭā'if happened to be uninfluenced by the Jewish or Christian ideas, he was nonetheless greatly influenced by Arab paganism. Arab paganism was considerably less pronounced in Yathrib than it was in either Makkah or aṭ-Ṭā'if. For this reason, it may be argued, the new religion, Islam, won considerably fewer converts in Makkah and aṭ-Ṭā'if compared with the great success it encountered in Yathrib.

But even here, with this sympathetic interpretation, Ibn Khaldūn's remark seems to land us in difficulties. If the bedouins who were living on the outskirts of Yathrib are compared with their town counterparts, then the former were certainly more disposed towards unbelief and hypocrisy than the latter. Perhaps the Prophet's saying which states that newly-born infants are in the natural state with respect to religion does not fit where Ibn Khaldūn wants it to fit. The bedouins could not be said to be, like the newly-born infant, undeveloped psychically and sociologically. On the contrary, the bedouin's personality tends to be very well developed due to the trying conditions of living in the desert. And it is by no means inconsistent to say that those conditions do produce some positive and praiseworthy qualities.

The Town-Dwelling Folk

As we have remarked before, Makkah, Yathrib and aṭ-Ṭā'if were not completely sedentarized communities. They still retained many positive and praiseworthy bedouin traits. They were still a vigorous people comparatively unspoilt as yet by soft living habits. In particular, the Makkans, owing to the nature of their valley, had to depend for their livelihood on the long-distance trading which they actively pursued in Syria and Egypt to the north, and with the Yemen and Abyssinia to the south. No doubt the traders were men of fortitude, courage and self-reliance. They must have been of such physical and mental powers as enabled them to endure the harshness of the long desert journeys and survive the dangers inherent in them.

To these qualities they must have added the shrewd acumen necessary for the success of every trader. Some of them became extremely rich due to the large profits of their long-distance trading. Unlike their bedouin kinsmen they could afford to enjoy some of the luxuries of the civilized world with which they came into contact in the course of their trading activities. They had more and varied food, and they possessed softer and more attractive clothes and beddings. Their sedentarized social setting enabled them to reap the benefits of mutual help and collective organization. The existence of specialized crafts and the division of labour which was made possible by the development of those crafts gave the Makkans and Yathribites time and leisure to enjoy these benefits. Thus the Makkans had more time to spend in speculative activities and to attend to the higher needs of the soul and the intellect. They had more time to socialize and more time to enjoy poetry and literature, two things in which the pre-Islamic Arab had achieved a very high level of excellence and distinction. Admittedly, the vast majority of these Arabs were illiterate. But they possessed exceptional powers of memory, and were able to memorize entire poems consisting of hundreds of well-knit beautiful verses. Long pieces of prose, usually full of proverbs and wise sayings, were also committed to memory.

Although the Makkans and Yathribites were subject to social rules, these did not encroach upon the personal liberties of the pre-Islamic Arab. These rules were inherent in the social system which he had adopted and with which he identified himself. They were rules and laws that were, in some sense, entailed by the tribal *'Aṣabiyyah* (group solidarity) which was deeply ingrained in his psychical make-up. They were thus rules that were freely accepted and obeyed. The Arab who was a citizen of Makkah or Yathrib never felt encumbered by them. Nor did they, in any way, encroach upon his dignity *(karāmah)* or his personal liberties. Thus these Makkans were largely free from those political and social ills which one finds in societies governed by stern, unjust and inhuman laws.

Characteristics of the Pre-Islamic Arab

If the foregoing analysis is generally correct, it would seem that the Arab citizen of Makkah, Yathrib or aṭ-Ṭā'if, combined the advantages of the bedouin and the sedentary environment. The pre-Islamic Arab who was confronted with the invitation to adopt

Islam thus had some remarkable characteristics that made him potentially an outstanding person. These characteristics have often been obscured by the application of the term *Jāhiliyyah* which is taken to imply a blanket condemnation of pre-Islamic Arabian society, and of the term *Jāhil* to imply a totally debased individual in that society. The literal meaning of *Jāhiliyyah* is ignorance. Islamic society refers to pre-Islamic Arabia as the age of *Jāhiliyyah* or the Age of Ignorance. It is also described as the Age of Darkness and the Qur'ān describes the mission of Muḥammad, *ṣallā Allāhu 'alayhi wa sallam,* as bringing people from darkness into light. The most striking feature of this Ignorance is moral ignorance or *ḍalāl* (the state of going astray or being lost). A good account of the nature of that *Jāhiliyyah* is afforded by the eloquent ambassadorial address of Ja'far ibn abī Ṭālib (see pp. 165–71) in front of the Negus of Abyssinia.

> 'O King,' he said, 'We were a people of *Jāhiliyyah,* worshipping idols, eating the flesh of dead animals, committing abominations, neglecting our relatives, doing evil to our neighbours and the strong among us would oppress the weak . . .'[6]

Essentially, the Arabian *Jāhiliyyah* was a state of moral ignorance which manifested itself in practical behaviour and attitudes. It does not necessarily imply intrinsic badness of character. Two of the most prominent heroes of Islam, namely 'Umar and Ḥamzah, were both known for their indulgence in *Jāhiliyyah* ways before they were converted to Islam. Their basic psychological make-up was potentially good and ready to exhibit that goodness if they were taught the way of truth and right. The Prophet, *ṣallā Allāhu 'alayhi wa sallam,* referred to people as having various basic 'metals'; those who are strong in *Jāhiliyyah* are also strong in Islam if they become wise and are rightly-guided. Thus there seems to have been intrinsic goodness even in *'Jāhil'* persons which could be brought out and developed by the high demands of Islamic moral standards.

A more detailed and specific investigation will now be made into some other characteristics which the pre-Islamic Arabs possessed and by virtue of which they had outstanding potentialities despite their *Jāhiliyyah.* That is to say, they possessed the basic psychical and sociological properties which, given certain further stimuli, were readily convertible into great human virtues and characteristics. Moreover, such a group of people possessing these basic properties will in any place or at any time, be a vigorous, energetic group that is naturally qualified, in the logical nature of things, to become the dominant leader of society. Its energy renders it outward-looking and dynamic and it naturally seeks to perpetuate and extend its world-view. It is easily seized by a sense of mission which irresistibly induces it to undertake a process of expansion in the course of which other less active groups come under its domination. This sense of mission persuades the more energetic group that it has a moral and civic duty to fulfil by educating those who are less energetic. This they were quite qualified to do. By virtue of possessing the qualities and characteristics we are about to consider, the pre-Islamic Arabs were well qualified to become staunch adherents and supporters of the new, militant faith with its universalistic, revolutionary call and vigorous activist programme.

Karāmah (Dignity)

Perhaps *karāmah* (or dignity) is, in a nutshell, the source of all the great qualities which the pre-Islamic Arab possessed. It is also the reservoir of all that is noble and praiseworthy in him. And like a reservoir, if the *karāmah* of a person is exhausted, those subsidiary qualities which contributed to it cease to exist in the person concerned. These subsidiary qualities are, in this respect, like tributaries and rivulets that flow into the reservoir and keep it from drying up. In fact the simile of the reservoir is perhaps more appropriate, because *karāmah* is increased in a particular person when he acquires certain particular virtues and faculties. It was and still is, the essence of a good, traditional Arab upbringing. The cultivation of the right degree of courage, physical and moral honesty, fortitude, self-restraint and generosity, naturally culminates in the cultivation of *karāmah*. So, *karāmah* is the most consummate virtue an Arab (or any other person for that matter) can possess. Lacking any of these particular virtues, a person's *karāmah* becomes eroded. Thus *karāmah* is the highest of all virtues.

To the Arab of Makkah and Yathrib, his *karāmah* is his ultimate dignity and human worth. It is his honour which is the highest ideal of his life. If this *karāmah* is destroyed, he no more sees any meaning or purpose in life. Loss of *karāmah* is tantamount to spiritual and moral death. It is the death of the soul, while the body still drifts on, soulless and worthless. To him, this is a state of affairs to which death is preferable. So pre-Islamic Arabs were quite willing and prepared to risk their lives in defence of their *karāmah* without any doubts or scruples.

Karam (Nobility)

A person is *karīm* if he is noble at heart, of great integrity and of unmistakable *karāmah* or dignity. Such is a man of moral worth who is naturally qualified for leadership and authority. He is an enterprising person, capable of wielding considerable influence in the affairs of the group to which he belongs. For this reason he is held in great esteem, honour and respect (sometimes even awe) by members of this group. He is loved and greatly honoured by his family and close associates. And for the whole clan and the tribe at large, he would perhaps be recognized as a *Shaikh.*

Such a person, if he is truly *karīm,* is expected, by virtue of his *karam,* to render help to others, especially to those with whom he shares a clan or tribal *'aṣabiyyah* (group solidarity). Thus the word *'karam'* has (a) a generic sense and (b) a derived sense which is more associated with *giving* and *rendering* help to others. The original, generic *'karam'* is the unseen, indefinable basis or cause, while the derived one is the more tangible result or effect. The following are some of the tangible effects of *'karam'*:

(i) *Jūd (Generosity)*

The Arabs had always been, and still are to the present day, a good example of this virtue. They, and people who are influenced by their cultural values, are remarkable for their *jūd* or generosity. They give away much more than the prospective recipient, who is unfamiliar with them, initially expects. Not only are material things given away but they are given without *'mann'* or reproachful reminder; sympathy and personal care are also readily given. It is perhaps this unselfish and immaterial component of *jūd* which is especially attractive, and even very fascinating. In an age which is fast becoming more and more materialistic and in which *everything* tends to have a price tag attached to it, this immaterial component becomes closer to every human heart. The more scarce these things relating to spontaneous and sincere feelings become in this world, the more they are valued and sought after. This *jūd* is no doubt related to that other great Arab characteristic – hospitality. The Arabs have a way of making the guest feel quite at home in the first few moments and this is no doubt the result of an ancient tradition that has been cultivated for very many centuries.

(ii) *Muruwwah (Chivalry)*

This is another way of rendering help. It is a great human virtue, because it makes a great demand on the person who is rendering it. Quite often, the person who seeks to render it not only has to suffer loss of money, property or time, or all three at once, but he may be forced to confront hostile and unjust forces. The Arab's *Muruwwah* makes it imperative for him to render help to weak or oppressed parties, and this brings him face to face with their oppressors. For instance, an Arab's *Muruwwah* is greatly perturbed if a woman is threatened with assault or if a gang of men attack a peaceful man who is unable to defend himself. The Alliance of the Virtuous *(Ḥilf Al-Fuḍūl)* was a pledge undertaken by Banū Hāshim and their allies in Makkah just before the advent of Islam. This alliance condemned injustice committed against persons who did not enjoy strong tribal *'aṣabiyyah* in Makkah. The immediate cause for concluding the alliance was that a Yemeni failed to recover a sum of money which he had lent to a man from the powerful clan of Sahm. He complained to Banū Hāshim and their allies about his grievance, and this complaint must have deeply shaken these Makkans. It must be remembered that Sahm was an old adversary of Banū 'Abd Manāf, who were parties to the *Fuḍūl* Alliance. (See pp. 66–7.)

Muruwwah is also associated with chivalry. An Arab who possesses *Muruwwah* may feel called upon to stand against injustice and in defence of the weak and the oppressed even if this involves risking his own life. It thus entails a great deal of personal courage and fighting skill. This *Muruwwah* is a very noble kind of *giving*. It is a kind of generosity which sometimes means giving one's own life for the sake of relieving the sufferings of others.

(iii) *Najdah (Deliverance)*

This is rendering help to others, when they are in severe distress or in great danger. Quite often, *Najdah* is a life-saving operation or act, which a person who possesses it feels compelled to perform in aid of someone in distress despite the great risks to his own life. The person with *Najdah* performs the act out of moral duty, and with no expectation of any personal benefit.

Najdah is a kind of *Muruwwah* which is rendered in an emergency. It is a kind of help that must be rendered, if at all, very quickly to a person who is in immediate peril of death. Both *muruwwah* and *najdah* formed part of a strong unflinching *'aṣabiyyah* of the pre-Islamic Arab to his clan, tribe or confederate. This *'aṣabiyyah* can be a sort of blind solidarity among members of a group in all circumstances whether right or wrong. It can lead to a narrow ethnocentricity or racialism and nationalism. But, as Ibn Khaldūn has pointed out, *'aṣabiyyah* is not purely evil nor is it wholly negative or monstrous. It has a positive aspect as a force for internal cohesion of the group possessing it. In this sense, *'aṣabiyyah* is not necessarily a blood relationship and can encompass ethnically diversified groups. This *'aṣabiyyah* made it possible for the Arabs to initiate and develop a whole system of alliances which provided for the collective security of the Society. They took these alliances very seriously. An ally would be defended even if it would lead to total war. The Fijār war (see pp. 63–5) is a good example of the Arabs' commitment to the safety and security of their allies. Admittedly, the wars were instances in which this system of security failed to function. But the fact that everybody suffers when war breaks out is a reasonably strong inducement for everybody to maintain and observe this system.

Even the characteristic vindictiveness for which the Arabs were famous was often a device for deterring and preventing injustice and aggression. Blood can only be compensated for by blood, and the deliberate, cold-blooded killer ought not to be allowed to feel that his own life could not be taken in retaliation and retribution. A human life taken unjustly can only be redressed as an injustice by taking the life of the killer. For them, the law of retribution in this respect must be absolutely just and firm. The fact that the Arabs operated this law is indicative of the profound sense of justice which they possessed. This is *karāmah* of a high order and related to it is the famous Arab ideal of *'irḍ* or chastity and honour, in particular sexual chastity. A prostitute has no *'irḍ* nor has a man or woman who commits adultery or fornication. The idea that fornication was widespread in Makkah and other towns of pre-Islamic Arabia must be understood in a new way which does justice to the fact that the Arabs were known to have possessed a very high sense of *'irḍ*. Fornication was probably widespread only among women who belonged to a certain social class. They were mostly women who were brought to Makkah as slave-girls, or women who belonged to poor families or clans who, for the most part, did not belong to the Quraysh. Hind bint 'Utbah ibn Rabī'ah, wife of Abū Sufyān, was sought by the Muslims after the conquest of Makkah, because she had mutilated the corpse of the Prophet's uncle Ḥamzah who was killed in the Battle of Uḥud. However, she managed to find her way to the Prophet's home and without revealing her identity asked to become a Muslim. In the course of teaching her the fundamentals of the new religion, he remarked that it is illegal for Muslims to commit fornication, to which she immediately retorted:

'But, Prophet of Allah, could a freewoman (who is not a slave) commit fornication?'[7]

So the idea that fornication was a common practice in Makkan society must be revised. It would seem natural to suppose that marriage rather than *laissez-faire* sexual behaviour was the predominant mode of sexual association in Makkah. The Arab sense of honour and *'irḍ* cannot possibly be reconciled with the existence of unrestrained fornication. The strong sense of *'irḍ* which the Arabs enjoyed, must have led to strong and coherent families. Family ties must have been very strong, since these are the ultimate foundation of the clanish or tribal *'Aṣabiyyah* which was a fundamental phenomenon of the Arabian scene. Our sources indicate that strong affections existed between members of Arab families. We shall later on talk about the practice of burying girls alive. It would seem that this practice was restricted to certain tribes, and even here was not widespread.

Outstanding Individuals

Apart from the Prophet himself, *ṣallā Allāhu ʻalayhi wa sallam,* one can point to his supporters and Companions who perfectly exemplified the virtues which we have been discussing in the previous section. Not only do we find persons of competence and integrity in the Muslim camp, but we also find them in the opposing camp of the Jāhilīes. Their existence in the latter camp is not inconsistent with our supposition that even before the advent of Islam, these Arabs were actually or potentially remarkable human beings.

We have already mentioned the example of Hind bint ʻUtbah ibn Rabīʻah and how the Prophet, *ṣallā Allāhu ʻalayhi wa sallam,* said that illicit sexual relations were taboo for Muslim women. Her husband, Abū Sufyān, was not only a prominent trader and financier but, moreover, was one of the important leaders of the Quraysh in times of peace and war. Abū Sufyān's competence and political genius was demonstrated when the Prophet's forces victoriously entered Makkah. Abū Sufyān managed to maintain his social status as one of the leaders among the nobility of Makkah, despite the fact that he actively and vigorously opposed the Prophet to the very last. Being a pragmatic and cool calculator, perceptive and well-informed, he realized, just before the Prophet's entry into Makkah, that the Prophet could not be stopped at that point. It was pointless to oppose him. So he quietly joined the Muslim ranks. Other events indicate the competence of this man. At Badr, he skilfully managed to evade the Muslim forces and escape with the huge commercial caravan which belonged to the Quraysh and which was under his command. He was the master-mind and the driving force behind the success which the Quraysh achieved at Uḥud. He must also be credited with the initial successes which brought the forces of the Quraysh, the Jewish generals of Banū an-Naḍīr and the bedouin tribes of Ghaṭfān, Sulaym and others, pounding ruthlessly at the doors of al-Madīnah at the battle of Khandaq. Again, being a naturally gifted statesman he was quick to realize the political implications of the breach of the Ḥudaybiyyah pact by the Quraysh. He hurried to al-Madīnah to meet the Prophet and to save what he could.

His mission achieved absolutely nothing and he was received

very coldly. Ibn Isḥāq reports that Abū Sufyān's daughter, Umm Ḥabībah who was married to the Prophet, *ṣallā Allāhu 'alayhi wa sallam,* quickly rolled up the Prophet's linen when she saw that her father was going to sit on it during his brief call at her home in al-Madīnah. When he angrily asked what she was doing, she bluntly told him that, as an unbeliever, he was *najis* (impure) and thus could not sit on the Prophet's bed. Nonetheless, Abū Sufyān is still to be credited with having made the attempt to avoid military confrontation with the Prophet. In view of the disastrous consequences which this breach of contract brought upon the Quraysh, one cannot help but commend the far-sightedness and excellent diplomatic perception of this Arab notable of pre-Islamic times.

'Abū Jahl', meaning a man of ignorance, was a nickname for the arch-enemy of nascent Islam. His real name was 'Amr ibn Hishām ibn al-Mughīrah. He belonged to the powerful Quraysh clan of Makhzūm. He was at the head of those who opposed the Muslims. He ruthlessly led the wicked campaign of torture and persecution which the Quraysh relentlessly launched against them. There could be little doubt that Abū Jahl was a man of courage and the foremost custodian of the legacy of the Quraysh and pagan Arabia. That legacy was no doubt seriously endangered by the inception of the new religion of Islam. He was also the guardian of the Quraysh aristocracy. That aristocracy was also seriously jeopardized by the new revolutionary message of Islam. Abū Jahl was noted for the resolve and energy with which he vainly tried to suppress the emergence of Islam. He was also noted for his great military courage and his great arrogance. The Muslim who killed him at Badr was a humble shepherd before becoming a Muslim. His name was 'Abdullāh ibn Mas'ūd. 'Abdullāh had been severely persecuted by Abū Jahl before he made his way to al-Madīnah as a *Muhājir* (emigrant). When Abū Jahl fell on the battlefield, 'Abdullāh, who was a small man clambered onto his chest. Abū Jahl opened his eyes and when he recognized 'Abdullāh sitting on his chest, he said bitterly, 'You have made a difficult ascent, little shepherd of the sheep,' meaning that, had the circumstances been different, it would have been very hard indeed for 'Abdullāh to sit where he was sitting. Thus Abū Jahl did not lose his faith in himself and what he stood for, to the very last moment. Nor did he lose his spirit under the awful pressures of a bitter defeat and of death itself. This is no doubt indicative of great personal strength and tremendous personal integrity. Perhaps in recognition of this, the Prophet once prayed (just before the conversion of 'Umar, see pp. 161–4) that God should strengthen Islam with whichever of the two men were more dear to Him – 'Umar ibn al-Khaṭṭāb or 'Amr ibn Hishām (Abū Jahl).

Abū Jahl's son 'Ikrimah was a great general and also a bitter enemy of Islam who led the Quraysh opposition to the Prophet until the last moment. Having failed in defending the capital of the Quraysh (i.e. Makkah), he fled to Yemen only to return when his wife obtained an amnesty for him from the Prophet. Belonging to the same group of Makhzūm was Abū Jahl's uncle, al-Walīd ibn al-Mughīrah. He was a man of great wealth with a widespread family. Al-Walīd devoted his wealth and organized his family in conspiring against the Prophet. He is reported to have been greatly impressed by the stylistic beauty and the glorious meaning of the Qur'ān but, being the chief propagandist of the Quraysh, he had to make unfavourable criticism of it. Al-Walīd was no fool; he knew that for that criticism to be effective it had to be reasonably credible. So he rejected suggestions that the Qur'ān was the sayings of a soothsayer or a poet. Being a man of wit and experience, he knew quite well that these were not tenable suggestions. At this point, the Quraysh who were making such suggestions demanded that he give his own evaluation of the Qur'ān. This incident is beautifully portrayed in the Qur'ān itself. Al-Walīd ibn al-Mughīrah is denounced in strong terms, and his intrigues in connection with the Qur'ān fully exposed:

> Leave me (to deal) with him whom I created lonely,
> And then bestowed upon him ample means,
> And sons abiding in his presence,
> And made (life) smooth and easy for him,
> Yet he greedily desires that I should give him more.
> On him I shall impose a fearful doom.
> For lo! he did consider; then he planned. Self-destroyed
> Is he, how he planned!
> Again (self-) destroyed is he, how he planned!
> Then looked he,
> Then frowned he and showed displeasure.

Then turned he away in pride,
  And said:
This (Qur'ān) is nothing but magic
Handed down (from old times)
This is nothing but the speech of mortal man.[8]

There are many examples of great Arabs who joined the Prophet, *ṣallā Allāhu 'alayhi wa sallam*. Names like Abū Bakr, 'Umar and Ḥamzah readily come to mind. As for the greatness of Abū Bakr, it is enough to say that many leading Muslims adopted Islam at his suggestion; that he spent most of his wealth for the cause of the new religion and that he was the right hand of the Prophet until his last days. But perhaps we can obtain a glimpse of his noble personality by remembering that he was the father of two great women who played tremendous roles in the history of Islam. They were 'Ā'ishah, the young, attractive and most favoured wife of the Prophet and Asmā', wife of az-Zubayr ibn al-'Awwām, and mother of 'Abdullāh ibn az-Zubayr.

As for 'Ā'ishah, she is so well known as to require no introduction. But perhaps the traditional image which many people have of her is rather misleading. This is the image of an attractive, very young girl, who was favoured by her husband for her youth, beauty and the great friendship which linked him with her father, Abū Bakr. But this image does her an injustice. 'Ā'ishah possessed many qualities which endeared her to the Prophet. Outstanding among these was her very affectionate nature and her great capacity for love. She was very well educated and had a wide knowledge of Arab culture. And despite her very young age, she had a profound understanding of the needs of a husband who was leading a chequered life, full of great dangers and endless troubles. It was a great tribute to her that the Prophet judged her competent to enjoy his confidence, and found her company attractive and delightful.[9] In view of the fact that she later became a leading jurist, and one of the fundamental and most reliable sources of the history of early Islam in general, and of the sayings and deeds of the Prophet in particular, she must have possessed a very high degree of intelligence and intellectual maturity. Her memory, too, must have been exceptionally retentive.

The other daughter of Abū Bakr, Asmā', was the person who

helped the Prophet during the days of emigration to al-Madīnah. She actually played a crucial role, displaying tremendous courage, considering the fact that she was no more than a young girl at the time. Her role was to bring in food and news during the three days when the Prophet and her father were in hiding just outside Makkah, waiting for events to cool down, before they could make their way to al-Madīnah. Asmā' was a very old women, approaching her hundredth year, when her son, the brave 'Abdullāh, was engaged in a decisive battle with the Umayyads for the control of Makkah and the sacred sanctuary. The battle was clearly turning against him and many of his supporters, including some of his close relatives, defected to his adversaries. Moreover, he was offered money and the governorship of the city by the Umayyads if he would give up fighting. He sought the advice of his ageing mother who was also blind. She firmly advised against surrender despite her great love for 'Abdullāh. When he pointed out that he was not afraid to meet his death, which was almost certain, but was only worried that his dead body would be maltreated, she retorted:

'What harm is it for the goat to be skinned after being slaughtered?'

'Abdullāh, against his better judgement, continued fighting only to be killed by the cruel tyrant al-Ḥajjāj ibn Yūsuf ath-Thaqafī, who was the commander of the Umayyad army. After killing him, al-Ḥajjāj ordered his body to be crucified in a public place. His body was left there for several days. People implored Asmā' to make an appeal to al-Ḥajjāj to let them take down his body for burial. But she adamantly refused. One day she went past his crucified body and, knowing that the body was still there, she only said, 'Is it not time yet for this knight to dismount?' When this was reported to al-Ḥajjāj he ordered the body to be taken down and buried. The reason for this change of heart on the part of al-Ḥajjāj is uncertain. At any rate, the body might have been left hanging there forever, but some sources have it that he considered this last remark of 'Abdullāh's mother as a kind of appeal.

The list of these outstanding early Arabs is long and includes such names as Ḥamzah, 'Umar ibn al-Khaṭṭāb, Muṣ'ab ibn 'Umayr, Ja'far ibn Abī Ṭālib, Sumayyah, Bilāl, 'Ammār, Yāsir, Abū Bakr, Abū Sufyān, 'Uthmān ibn 'Affān, Az-Zubayr ibn al-‘Awwām, ‘Abd ar-Raḥmān ibn ‘Awf, and so on. Some of these figure prominently later in our narrative. Here one point needs to be made: that the personal greatness of these Arabs was not to be attributed to considerations relating to their race or to any specific factors confined to them as a racial group. It has been our contention that this greatness derived essentially from the natural environmental and cultural factors then prevailing. Probably any race of people living in the same circumstances would have acquired the same characteristics. Whatever greatness these Arabs possessed was *ipso facto,* human greatness produced and developed by what was best in both the bedouin and sedentary forms of life in pre-Islamic Arabia.

Notes and References

1. Ibn Khaldūn, *The Muqaddimah,* trans. by Franz Rosenthal (3 vols.), Dollingen Foundation Inc., New York, vol. I, p. 252.
2. Qur'ān, 9 (*At-Tawbah*): 97.
3. *Ibid.,* verse 99.
4. There is a discrepancy in Rosenthal's rendering of the Arabic text. The name Muḥammad does not occur in the original Arabic. Moreover, there is an unwarranted omission of the religiously significant, from the Muslim viewpoint, phrase, ‘May Allah's peace and blessings be upon him’. See *Muqaddimah ibn Khaldūn* (Arabic), Dār iḥyā' at-turāth al-‘Arabī, Beirut, p. 123.
5. Franz Rosenthal, *op. cit.,* p. 253f.
6. Ibn Hishām, vol. I, p. 336. For full text of address, see below, p. 167.
7. Qur'ān, 84 (*Al-Muddaththir*): 11–25.
8. See ‘Abbās Maḥmūd al-‘Aqqād, *‘Abqariyyat aṣ-Ṣiddīq,* Cairo, p. 179f.

CHAPTER 2

Makkah and the Quraysh

The Ancient Sanctuary

When Ibrāhīm entered the valley of Makkah, with his Egyptian wife Hagar and her two-year-old child Ismā'īl, it was quite barren and empty. Indeed the history of Makkah, prior to the advent of Ibrāhīm and his family, is very obscure. All that the cautious historian can assert with any reasonable degree of certainty is that Makkah, as an important station on the ancient commercial route between the ports of Arabia Felix on the Indian Ocean and the Syrian ports of the Mediterranean sea, had been operative since time immemorial. However, the valley did not at first contain any permanent settlement. Perhaps the caravans used the valley only as a resting place and were not encouraged to settle by the excessive ruggedness and dryness of the locality.

The uniqueness of Makkah, however, derives essentially from the fact that it contains the 'Ancient House' *(al-bayt al-'atīq)* which is one of the expressions used in the Qur'ān to refer to the Ka'bah or the sacred sanctuary of Arabia. The word 'Ka'bah' refers to the cube-like shape of this ancient 'house of God' *(bayt-Allāh)*. It is so ancient that the Qur'ān describes it as 'the first house ever to be established for mankind, for worship of God':

> Verily, the first house (of worship) established for mankind was that at Bakkah (Makkah) full of blessing and guidance to all mankind. Wherein are plain signs . . . Whoever enters it is safe.[1]

Ibrāhīm and his celebrated son Ismā'īl are credited with the building of the Ka'bah. But it is not clear whether they built it originally, or whether they found an earlier structure which they demolished or used as a foundation to build on. I am inclined to believe that some kind of building was in existence long before the advent of Ibrāhīm and his son to Arabia. The evidence for this can be found in the Qur'ān itself.

First, we have already quoted the verse (3: 96, 97) which unambiguously describe the Ka'bah as the first sanctuary appointed for mankind for the worship of God. In view of the absence of any indication that the truth of this verse was either doubted or contested by anyone, it must have been taken by the Arabs as stating a well-known fact.

More significantly, the verse which reports the building of the Ka'bah by Ibrāhīm and his son, does not at all imply that they were the original builders. If anything, it rather implies just the opposite:

> And when Ibrāhīm and Ismā'īl were raising the foundations of the House, (they prayed): 'Our Lord, accept from us (this service) for You are the All-Hearing, the All-Knowing'.[2]

It should be noted that the words 'raised the foundation' used in this verse imply the prior existence of some kind of foundation on which the rest of the building was erected. This interpretation of the verse agrees more readily with verse 96 of *Sūrah* 3 quoted earlier. It is also in harmony with the description of the sacred House as 'Atīq'.[3]

The existence of the 'Ancient House' which was an object of profound veneration for those pre-Islamic Arabs, must have provided a very strong motive for halting the caravans at this place. It was, however, the coming of Ibrāhīm's family that formed the germ of what eventually became a permanent, urban centre. Our sources[4] have it that the well of Zamzam gushed forth, with clear, sweet and plentiful water, as a blessing from God to the thirsty little boy Ismā'īl, and his mother Hagar, when Ibrāhīm had to leave them in that arid, and unpopulated spot in fulfilment of God's command. Ibn Hishām[5] also has it that the Arab tribes of Amalekites and Jurhum, as they were moving northward in the course of their emigration from Arabia Felix to the southern confines of Syria, stopped at Makkah to rest and perhaps visit the ancient sanctuary. To their great delight, they unexpectedly found pure and sweet running water, and the company of the family of Ibrāhīm. They decided to stay, and Ismā'īl is reported to have first married a girl from the Amalekites, but the marriage was neither fruitful nor enduring. He divorced her to marry a girl from the tribe of Jurhum. This marriage proved very successful, and led to the founding of the celebrated Arab tribe of Quraysh.

The Tribe of Quraysh

The ancestry of the Quraysh goes back to Ismā'īl, son of Ibrāhīm. The name 'Quraysh' is said to have been a nickname for Fihr ibn Mālik ibn Kinānah, one of the remote forebears of the Prophet of Islam, *ṣallā Allāhu 'alayhi wa sallam.* The name itself denotes the fact that Fihr was a successful trader who enjoyed substantial profits from his business.

The descendants of Fihr, the Quraysh, lived in Makkah around the Ka'bah which they sanctified and maintained. As a result of their custodianship of the Ka'bah their honour, stature and prestige grew. They must have mingled freely with Jurhum, the remnants of Hyksos (the Amalekites) and other minor Arab tribes in the surroundings of Makkah. Then a new tribe migrated to Makkah from Yemen, apparently one of several which moved northward on a major wave of migration. The reason for the mass migration appears to have been the bursting of the Ma'rib Dam[6] which resulted in major floods and a great loss of crops. The newcomers from the south were the famous tribe of Khuzā'ah. The Khuzā'ah ruthlessly ousted the Quraysh and established themselves for some time as the paramount occupants of the valley and the new custodians of its valuable and famous sanctuary.

Quṣayy and the Building of Makkah

Custodianship of the Ka'bah was traditionally vested in the chiefs of the Quraysh and was passed on through hereditary succession. Their custodianship lapsed for some time until the coming of one Quṣayy ibn Kilāb (ibn . . . ibn Quraysh). By the time he reached manhood, the custodian of the Ka'bah was a member of the tribe Khuzā'ah, a certain Ḥulayl ibn Ḥabshīyah. Quṣayy (lit. 'the one who is far away') was a promising youth who had been brought up by his step-father far away from Makkah, in the territory of Banī ‘Udhrah in southern Syria. He returned to Makkah after reaching manhood, and he married the daughter of Ḥulayl ibn Ḥabshīyah at the suggestion of Ḥulayl himself. The marriage proved fruitful, and Quṣayy became rich and the father of many sons and daughters. Influence and power were added to his great wealth and large family. He was a Quraysh *par excellence,* and the Quraysh were the original custodians of the Ka‘bah, an honour and privilege which they had inherited from their fathers Ibrāhīm and Ismā‘īl. So Quṣayy felt that he was both entitled and qualified to claim the custodianship of the ancient sanctuary, whose foundations had been laid by his ancestors. Quṣayy came to be known as *Mujammi‘* or ‘accumulator’ because he accumulated so much power in his hands. Neither Islamic nor pre-Islamic Arabs favoured a ‘God-Caesar dichotomy’ with respect to sovereignty over the general affairs of the Makkans. The Arabs insisted upon a total monistic fusion of the two domains – the religious and the political. Political authority was for them both based on and derived from religious authority. As priests and custodians of the *Ḥaram* or ‘Sacred Sanctuary’ the Quraysh attained the highest position of honour, political authority and leadership among all pre-Islamic Arabs.

The Conflict Between the Descendants of Quṣayy

After the death of Quṣayy, his elder son ‘Abd ad-Dār assumed the position of ruler over Makkah but, as custodian of the Ka‘bah, he was neither a strong nor distinguished man. His younger brothers, especially one called ‘Abd Manāf, were far more competent than he was. But Quṣayy preferred ‘Abd ad-Dār, and had drawn up his will in such a way that all his powers and authority were inherited by him. The other brothers felt bitter but open conflict was temporarily avoided. The sons of Quṣayy acknowledged the authority of their elder brother ‘Abd ad-Dār, and managed to retain normal and cordial relationships amongst themselves.

THE QURAYSH

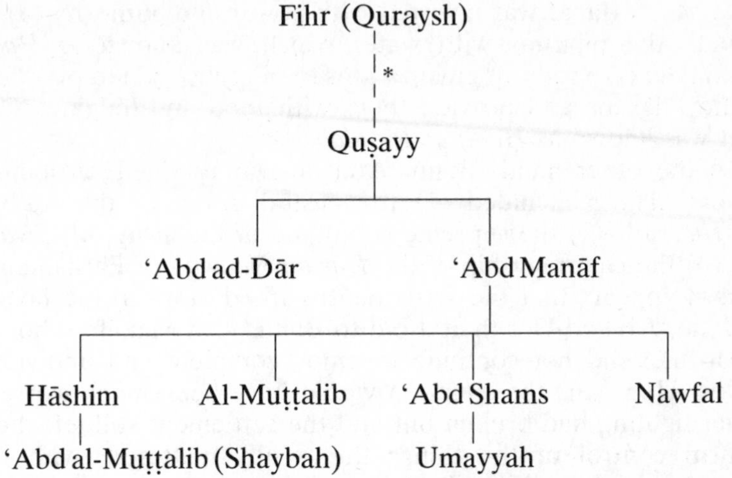

*The broken line indicates that Quṣayy was not the immediate descendant of Fihr and that there were many intermediaries.

But, at length, the jealousy and rivalry which Banū 'Abd Manāf felt against their cousins Banū 'Abd ad-Dār, burst into open conflict. The sons of 'Abd Manāf, led by 'Abd Shams and Hāshim, the celebrated great grandfather of the Prophet, challenged the authority of the sons of 'Abd ad-Dār. They demanded a power-sharing arrangement between the two powerful clans of the Quraysh. The situation deteriorated till it reached the brink of war. When war seemed inevitable, each faction feverishly sought allies and confederates. Two opposing alliances thus came into existence:

The *ḥilf* (or alliance) of *al-Muṭayyabūn*[7] and the *Aḥlāf* (or confederates). Members of these alliances were as follows:

(i) *Al-Muṭayyabūn:* Banū Asad, Banū Zuhrah, Banū Taym, Banū al-Ḥārith ibn Fihr.
(ii) *Al-Aḥlāf:* Makhzūm, Sahm, Jumah, 'Adī.

Group (i) (the *Muṭayyabūn* or the perfumed) were the allies of Banū 'Abd Manāf (i.e. 'Abd Shams, Hāshim and others) while group (ii) were the allies of Banū 'Abd ad-Dār. Actual fighting was, however, averted. A peaceful settlement was reached which stipulated a sharing of powers between the two opposing clans: Banū 'Abd Manāf was invested with power and authority (1) to provide the pilgrims with water which was known as *Ḥaqq as-Siqāyah* (the right of giving water to pilgrims); (2) to play host to the pilgrims and provide them with food and lodging. This right was known as *Ḥaqq ar-Rifādah*.

On the other hand, Banū 'Abd ad-Dār retained substantial powers. These included (1) the custodianship of the Ka'bah *(al-Ḥijābah)*; (2) the supreme command of the army *(al-Liwā')*; and (3) the chairmanship of the *Dār an-Nadwah* or Parliament.[8] Thus it appears that the settlement worked more to the favour of Banū 'Abd ad-Dār than it did to Banū 'Abd Manāf, although the former did not continue to enjoy complete and undivided power. However, the situation would have been much worse if actual fighting had broken out and the settlement still left them in firm control of the things that really mattered, with the exception of the pilgrims' affairs which were more a matter of prestige.[9]

The Feud Between 'Abd Shams and Hāshim

Our sources do not mention the existence of any animosity between the two prominent sons of 'Abd Manāf, Hāshim and 'Abd Shams. But the fact that Umayyah ibn 'Abd Shams actually challenged his uncle, during the lifetime of his father, 'Abd Shams,[10] suggests that the relationship between the two brothers was not cordial.

We do not possess any information about the relative ages of Hāshim and 'Abd Shams. Ibn Sa'd has it that the oldest of the sons of 'Abd Manāf was al-Muṭṭalib; Hāshim is mentioned next to him, and 'Abd Shams is mentioned after that.[11] Ibn Hishām, however, maintains that 'Abd Shams was the eldest of the sons of 'Abd Manāf. Both sources, however, assign more importance and social influence to Hāshim than they do to 'Abd Shams.

Ibn Hishām, although he represents 'Abd Shams as the head of the alliance of *Muṭayyabūn*, portrays Hāshim as having emerged as the strong man of the alliance and as being the chief beneficiary of the peaceful settlement between *al-Muṭayyabūn* (perfumed) and the *Aḥlāf:* Banū ʻAbd Manāf were accorded the rights of *Siqāyah* and *Rifādah* (i.e. providing the pilgrims with water, food and lodging) and it was Hāshim who was installed by his clan to supervise and discharge this traditional responsibility. The election of Hāshim to fulfil this duty was at once both a great honour and privilege for him. The selection of Hāshim rather than ʻAbd Shams for this post must have strained the relationship between the two brothers, especially if Ibn Hishām's report that ʻAbd Shams was older than Hāshim is authentic. Irrespective of age there can be little doubt that Hāshim was better qualified for this post than his brother:

(a) both Ibn Hishām and Ibn Saʻd state that he was a man of considerable means;[12]

(b) both sources agree that he was very generous and took great pleasure in providing the pilgrims with water, food and lodging;

(c) both sources describe him as a man of charisma who was held in some esteem by the Byzantine authorities. Ibn Saʻd credits him with having met Heraclius and successfully negotiated favourable trade terms for the Quraysh in Syria. These included a guarantee of safety to Quraysh merchants during their stay in Syria.

(d) both Ibn Hishām and Ibn Saʻd credit him with initiating and instituting trading journeys for the Quraysh caravans in winter southwards to Abyssinia and Yemen, and in summer northwards to Syria. These trips are mentioned in the Qur'ān in the chapter entitled *'Quraysh'*:

> For the taming of the Quraysh; For their taming (We cause) the caravans to set forth in winter and summer. So let them worship the Lord of this House (the Kaʻbah), Who has fed them against hunger and has made them safe from fear.[13]

Hāshim is thus depicted by our sources as a man of energy and means, one who was greatly honoured and esteemed not only within the confines of Makkah but in the distant Byzantine and Abyssinian courts. By contrast, we are able to collect only scant information about his brother ‘Abd Shams. He was rather poor, had many children and spent most of his life in unsuccessful trading ventures. Although older than Hāshim, according to Ibn Hishām, he was not chosen to assume the important responsibility of looking after the pilgrims. One may contest this portrait of Hāshim, given by the source books, and ascribe it to later additions – seeking to glorify Hāshim because of kinship to the Prophet. But, there is little or no evidence that such additions were fabricated. The Prophet completely dissociated himself from any of his ancestors who were not monotheists.

The Animosity Between Umayyah and Hāshim

The feud between Umayyah and his uncle Hāshim had far-reaching consequences. Perhaps there are a few family quarrels in history which lasted so long, and had such wide repercussions. In the history of Islam, the feud between Banū Hāshim and the Umayyads raged for centuries, initiating and destroying whole dynasties in its wake. Whether or not there was animosity between Hāshim and ‘Abd Shams, there certainly was between Hāshim and his nephew Umayyah.

Ibn Hishām totally ignores the existence of this feud. But the definite animosity between Banū Hāshim and the Umayyads during the birth of Islam in the sixth century C.E. and its continuation long after it, tend to confirm the sources which assert that this animosity did exist. Ibn Sa‘d gives the following account of how this animosity came into being:

> Years of drought befell the Quraysh, and provisions were gone (because of them). Hāshim set out for ash-Shām (Syria). He ordered a great quantity of bread to be baked for him. He loaded it on camels, and when he came to Makkah he broke the bread and put hot soup and sauces on it. The camels were all slaughtered. He ordered cooks to prepare the food, then it was served and the people of Makkah ate until they were satisfied. . . . For this reason he was called Hāshim (‘the one who breaks (bread) to distribute’).
>
> As a result of this deed, the people of Makkah were greatly impressed by him. (Seeing this), Umayyah Ibn ‘Abd Shams ibn ‘Abd Manāf ibn Quṣayy became envious of him. He was

a man of (considerable) wealth. He acted as if he could do the same as Hāshim, but he could not. Some people of the Quraysh (openly) sneered at him. He became angry with Hāshim (or blamed him for the people's reaction). He called upon Hāshim for a contest (or a fight). Hāshim declined due to his advanced age and his (high social) status. But the Quraysh did not concur with (his refusal to accept the challenge) and alienated him. He then said to Umayyah, 'I am ready to bet with you (and whoever loses) is to slaughter in Makkah fifty dark-eyed camels and to go into exile from Makkah for ten years.'

Umayyah accepted the bet (or contest). A priest from the Khuzā'ah drew the lots. Hāshim won and Umayyah took the fifty camels, slaughtered them and offered the food to those present. Umayyah set out for ash-Shām (Syria) and stayed there for ten years. This was the first (instance of) animosity between Hāshim and Umayyah.[14]

The Emergence of 'Abd al-Muṭṭalib

'Abd al-Muṭṭalib was the most prominent son of Hāshim. He was the grandfather of the Prophet Muḥammad, *ṣallā Allāhu 'alayhi wa sallam*. His mother was from Yathrib, four hundred and twenty-five kilometres (approximately) to the north of Makkah. Hāshim saw her in the market place as he was passing through the city on his way to Syria. She was a woman of outstanding beauty and bearing, and she managed her own affairs. Hāshim was attracted to her and proposed to her. She accepted after being told about his high status amongst the Quraysh. She was known to have declined many marriage proposals before and made it publicly known that she was going to reserve to herself the right to divorce in case she found that she did not like whoever she married. Hāshim left her expecting his child and continued on his journey to Syria. When he reached Ghazah (Palestine) he fell ill and died. It was Hāshim's wish that his unborn offspring be under the guardianship of his brother, al-Muṭṭalib.[15] This also tends to confirm our earlier hypothesis that relations between Hāshim and 'Abd Shams were not cordial.[16] A boy was later born, who had a white patch of hair on his head. For this reason he was named Shaybah (grey-haired). The fact that he was better known by the name ‘Abd al-Muṭṭalib (the slave of al-Muṭṭalib) has a story attached to it. When the boy grew up, sturdy, and good-looking, al-Muṭṭalib brought him back to Makkah from Yathrib. As they entered Makkah riding on the same camel people said that al-Muṭṭalib had brought a new *‘abd* or slave. Even though al-Muṭṭalib stated publicly that this was no *‘abd* but the Yathribite son of the celebrated Hāshim, people continued to call the boy ‘Abd al-Muṭṭalib, at first in jest and later out of habit.

The boy ‘Abd al-Muṭṭalib grew up to occupy the eminent position of his forebears, Hāshim and Quṣayy. After the death of al-Muṭṭalib in the Yemen, ‘Abd al-Muṭṭalib assumed the traditional family responsibility of feeding and lodging the pilgrims. Since Jurhum, when they were being banished from Makkah, had covered up the ancient well of Zamzam, he decided to re-dig the well in the courtyard of the sanctuary.

It is narrated that ‘Abd al-Muṭṭalib decided to re-dig the well of Zamzam as a result of a vision which he had as he was sleeping in the courtyard of the Ka‘bah. The vision recurred for three successive nights. In the vision the well was commended as a source of blessing and goodness: it would be the fountain from which the great pilgrim processions would drink ever-flowing water. He was shown exactly where to dig for it. Following his instructions well, and after three days of digging, the water level was reached. He is said to have recognized the wall of the well as that laid down by Ismā‘īl when he first dug the well.[17] During the digging of Zamzam ‘Abd al-Muṭṭalib was aided by his sole son al-Ḥārith. He must have felt the need for more sons because, the sources[18] have it, he passionately prayed for more of them and vowed that if he was blessed with ten sons, and if these sons reached manhood and aided him, he would sacrifice one of them at the Ka‘bah as an offering to God.

The Prophet’s Father

‘Abd al-Muṭṭalib’s wish was granted. Ten handsome and dignified sons were born to him. ‘Abd Allāh was the most remarkable of them and resembled his father in appearance and nobility. ‘Abd al-Muṭṭalib loved the boy dearly and could not bear to part with him. He was his favourite. When they all reached manhood, he called them for a meeting and told them about his vow. They all displayed their willingness to honour their father's vow. Lots were immediately drawn, and the choice fell on 'Abd Allāh. Ibn Sa'd narrates that 'Abd al-Muṭṭalib, despite his great love for 'Abd Allāh took him to the courtyard of the Ka'bah, with a knife in his hand. It was an anxious moment for the people of Makkah. His sisters stood by weeping loudly, and a multitude of people gathered to witness the terrible event. At length, 'Abd al-Muṭṭalib was persuaded that he could without incurring the wrath of God spare the life of his little son, if he would slaughter as many camels as the high priests of Arabia (a soothsayer of Khaybar, according to Ibn Hishām) advised. The suggestion was to draw lots between 'Abd Allāh on the one hand and ten camels on the other. If 'Abd Allāh was chosen the camels would be increased by another ten and the lots drawn again.

When the number of camels reached a hundred, the lots were again drawn. To everyone's relief, the camels were chosen for the first time. But 'Abd al-Muṭṭalib was not satisfied. He repeated the drawing of the lots, but again the camels were chosen. However, 'Abd al-Muṭṭalib insisted on a third drawing so as to make absolutely sure that this was what God wanted. So the lots were drawn for the third time. But again the camels were chosen, and 'Abd Allāh, to everybody's relief and satisfaction, was finally spared. The hundred camels were of course slaughtered and left for the poor people to eat. After this incident 'Abd Allāh's popularity soared. The sources mention that a woman waited outside the Ka'bah and when 'Abd Allāh emerged beaming, handsome and gratified, eagerly proposed to him. He politely declined, giving the lack of his father's approval as an excuse.

The Year of the Prophet's Birth

(i) *The Invasion of Makkah by the Abyssinians*

The campaign against Makkah by the Abyssinian rulers and colonizers of Arabia Felix was primarily aimed at destroying the Ka'bah and eliminating its hold on the people. The commander of the campaign, Abrahah, was reportedly consumed by jealousy at the Arabs' excessive veneration of this House. He was advised that the best way to divert the pilgrims from Makkah was to build a very great church, far excelling the Ka'bah in its grandeur and elaborate decorations. The church was built, Abrahah spending so much money and labour on it that the resources of Yemen were badly depleted. After the building was completed delegations were sent out to publicize it and to attract the expected caravans of pilgrims. However, to the bitter disappointment of Abrahah, no such caravans arrived. Instead, an Arab from the tribe of Kinānah near Makkah heard of Abrahah's mischievous designs and was so enraged that he resolved to journey to Yemen with the sole purpose of contaminating the new Temple. He managed to get inside the building and contaminate the interior. Abrahah was so incensed that he set out at once to invade Makkah and destroy the Ka'bah.

'Abd al-Muṭṭalib, the grandfather of the Prophet, was the ruler of Makkah. 'He was the most handsome among the Quraysh, very tall, most merciful, and generous and exceedingly good and uncorrupt. He never met a ruler who did not hold him in high esteem and respect. He was the leader of the Quraysh, until he died.'[19]

When Abrahah came to the gates of Makkah with his huge army, one of his generals must have been mounted on an elephant. He sent for 'Abd al-Muṭṭalib. Abrahah was so impressed by him that he made him sit at his side. 'Abd al-Muṭṭalib plainly informed Abrahah that the Quraysh could not and would not defend the sanctuary against his mighty army but that the House had an owner Who would adequately defend it.

On returning to Makkah, 'Abd al-Muṭṭalib advised his people to evacuate the city. Abrahah began his attack on the ancient city but his whole army was totally annihilated by mysterious forces of nature. The Qur'ān tells the story of the defeat of the mighty army of Abrahah that sought the destruction of the Ka'bah:

> Have you not seen how your Lord dealt with the owners of the Elephant? Did He not bring their stratagem to naught and sent against them swarms of birds which pelted them with stones of baked clay and made them like green crops devoured (by cattle)?[20]

The attempted invasion of Makkah by Abrahah took place in 571 C.E. That year was called the Year of the Elephant, the year that also witnessed the epoch-making event of the birth of the future Prophet of Islam.

(ii) *The Short-Lived 'Abd Allāh*

We possess only scant information about 'Abd Allāh, the father of the Prophet. We know that he was, like his father, tall and handsome, with a rather prominent nose, that he was the favourite of his father, the celebrated 'Abd al-Muṭṭalib, and that he had a narrow escape from being sacrificed at the Ka'bah in fulfilment of his father's vow. Soon after this rather traumatic experience which must have won him a lot of sympathy and affection,[21] he was married to a noble lady from Banū Zuhrah of the Quraysh. Her name was Āminah bint Wahb. The marriage was extremely short-lived. 'Abd Allāh set out on a trading expedition to Syria, leaving 'Āminah expecting his child. The traveller never returned and an infant destined to change the world for ever was born who would never set eyes on his father. 'Abd Allāh died in Yathrib on his return trip from Syria. When the caravan reached Yathrib, he was already very sick and his maternal uncles from Banū an-Najjār insisted that he stayed behind until he was well. When the news of his death reached Makkah, Banū Hāshim, especially the noble 'Abd al-Muṭṭalib, were grief-stricken. His sisters went into mourning for four days. The future Prophet of Islam was not yet born.[22] 'Abd Allāh had no children except the future Prophet, nor had Āminah any other child. The mourning widow, Āminah, awaited in great expectation the birth of her child. According to Ibn Sa'd, she composed panegyric verses in memory of her late husband in which she described him as excessively generous and affectionate.[23]

The Birth of the Prophet

Ibn Sa'd narrates that Āminah had a very easy pregnancy before giving birth to the future Prophet of Islam. She was reported to have said:

> I did not feel that I was pregnant, nor did I find myself heavy because of it, as is customary for (pregnant) women to find themselves. However, I was puzzled by the absence of my menstruation (and I thought that) it would perhaps return (soon). But I saw a vision as I was between sleep and wakefulness. It said unto me: 'Have you felt that you are

> pregnant?' and I replied that I did not know. But it continued: 'You are pregnant, with (the future) chief and prophet of this nation'. Then it (the vision) left me until I was about to give birth. Then it returned (and commanded me to say): 'I put it (the child) under the protection and refuge of the One, Who is eternally besought by all, from the evil and mischief of every envious person'. (I) used to say these words and respect them.[24]

According to the majority of our sources, the Prophet, *ṣallā Allāhu 'alayhi wa sallam,* was born on the 12th Rabī' al-Awwal, the year of the Elephant (571 C.E.) only fifty-five days after the unsuccessful expedition of Abrahah against Makkah. Āminah describes that historic moment as follows:

> When it (the baby) was separated from me, a flood of light radiated from him which illuminated the entire horizon from the east to the west.[25]

The Prophet himself was reported to have said:

> Just as I was born, my mother saw a light radiating from me which illuminated the palaces of Buṣrā (Syria).[26]

The new baby was conspicuously healthy, good-looking and well-built. Besides his mother, the second person who rejoiced most at his birth was the ageing patriarch, 'Abd al-Muṭṭalib, foremost chief of Makkah and the undisputed leader of Banū Hāshim. He was reportedly so pleased with the new baby that he carried him to the Ka'bah where he voiced, in a passionate manner, an elaborate invocation of thanks and gratitude. When Āminah told him about the strange signs and phenomena that accompanied her pregnancy and the birth of the child, he was even more enchanted and predicted that he would grow up to be a man of 'great rank'. He declared that the infant was to be named Muḥammad.[27]

The Qur'ān asserts that the coming of a Prophet, by the name Aḥmed (which comes from the same linguistic root as Muḥammad and likewise means 'the praised one') had been foretold in previous Scriptures. The matter is unequivocably stated in the following manner:

> And (remember) when Jesus, son of Mary said: 'O children of Israel, verily, I am the messenger of Allah unto you, attesting to what was (revealed) before me in the Torah, and giving good tidings of a messenger who comes after me, whose name is Aḥmad.'[28]

Accordingly, some Muslim scholars have tried to relate certain references in the Bible to the coming of the Prophet Muḥammad, *ṣallā Allāhu 'alayhi wa sallam.* A discussion of this matter is outside the scope of this study.

The exact place in which the future Prophet of Islam was born is said to be either the Shi'b (quarter) of Abū Ṭālib or the quarter of 'Abd al-Muṭṭalib near the mount of Ṣafā by the side of the Ka'bah. The latter possibility seems more credible, since 'Abd al-Muṭṭalib was both the principal of Banū Hāshim and the future guardian of the Prophet. (The house in which he was born is said to have passed into the possession of Muḥammad ibn Yūsuf (brother of the infamous al-Ḥajjāj ibn Yūsuf, the Umayyad governor who killed thousands and attacked the Ka'bah). Then it was purchased by Zubaydah, wife of Hārūn ar-Rashīd. It was subsequently converted into a public library which was in operation until recently.)

It was customary among the aristocrats of the Quraysh to have their babies nursed by the bedouins around Makkah. The idea was that a bedouin foster-mother gave a strong physical constitution to the child as well as the easy manners and the pure characteristics of the desert Arabs. Thus Muḥammad was given to Ḥalīmah as-Sa'diyah of Banū Sa'd, a clan of Hawāzin. Ḥalīmah was rather poor but her limited means were blessed and the coming of the new member into the family brought about a change for the better in her fortunes. Ḥalīmah looked after him with the fondest love and care and her little girl, ash-Shaymā', was devoted to him. She looked after him, played with him during the day and slept beside him at night. At the age of two he was so robust and healthy that he appeared as if he was a child of four. Ḥalīmah thought it was time to return him to his mother. Āminah returned the child to her because she was afraid that he might contract some of the illnesses of the city. Ḥalīmah gladly took him back to the desert.

At the age of four, when Muḥammad was with his foster-sister and brother looking after the sheep, a strange incident happened. Two strangers, both men, approached the unsuspecting children. They took Muḥammad and, laying him on his back, cut open his chest and took something out. Muḥammad's little companions came running to Ḥalīmah and her husband. When the latter reached the scene, the two men had gone and Muḥammad, so our sources narrate,[29] was standing alone, pale and shaken.

Although some recent researchers[30] have doubted the reality of this incident, yet, insofar as it has been affirmed by our most reliable sources, it cannot be categorically dismissed. If there is no conclusive evidence that the incident did take place, likewise there is no conclusive evidence to the contrary. In all matters relating to a Prophet and to the phenomenon of prophethood, we draw very close to the mysterious and the metaphysical.

When he was five years old, the future Prophet, of robust figure and with fine and unaffected manners, was finally reunited with his mother in Makkah. He was for ever to retain the fondest attachment and admiration for the bedouins of Banū Sa'd.

'I am the most pure Arab amongst you', he often repeated in later times. 'My lineage is from the Quraysh, and having been suckled amongst Banū Sa'd, I have acquired their tongue.' In a nation where eloquence was a very great asset, the future Prophet's appreciation of his pure speech is quite understandable. When his foster-mother Ḥalīmah visited him in Makkah in a year of drought, the future Prophet made sure that she got what she needed of food and provisions. He also presented her with a camel and forty sheep. In the battle of Ḥunayn against the Hawāzin (of which Banū Sa'd was a prominent clan) his foster-sister ash-Shaymā' fell captive to the advancing Muslim forces. When told about her capture, the Prophet, *ṣallā Allāhu 'alayhi wa sallam,* acted promptly to restore her to her people with honour and dignity.

The Death of Āminah

The reunion of the orphan Muḥammad with his real mother was destined to be short-lived indeed. When Muḥammad was approximately six years of age, Āminah, a lonely and grief-stricken widow in her early twenties, set out for Yathrib to visit the grave of her beloved husband, ‘Abd Allāh. The journey would give the widowed mother ample time to tell the little boy something about his father, a topic which was very close to her heart. A visit to Yathrib would also provide a good chance for the youthful Muḥammad to become acquainted with his maternal relatives of Banū an-Najjār (Khazraj). These, it must be remembered, were the relatives of Salmah, mother of the Banū Hāshim patriarch ‘Abd al-Muṭṭalib. It was on their way back from Yathrib that Āminah became ill and died.[31]

The youthful Muḥammad, already an orphan and now more than ever conscious of memories of his father because of his visit to Yathrib, must have been almost crushed by the loss of his mother. He became more and more withdrawn and sad, and of a mild and sensitive disposition. Much later in his life, when he was honoured and blessed with Divine revelation, Muḥammad whilst assured of continued Divine help and favour was reminded of the mercies of his Lord with respect to these early days of disorientation and poverty.

> And verily, your Lord will give unto you until you are satisfied.
> Did He not find you an orphan, and furnished you with a refuge?
> Did He not find you astray and guided you?
> Did He not find you destitute and enriched (you)?[32]

Even in later days, whenever the Prophet recalled the loss of his mother emotion would overcome him and he would weep passionately.

The lonely orphan now passed into the guardianship of his grandfather, the ageing patriarch of Banū Hāshim, the noble ‘Abd al-Muṭṭalib. The patriarch was fond of his lonely grandson and their intimate relationship grew even stronger as time passed. Muḥammad could gain access to the renowned patriarch anywhere and at any time. He would sit nearer to him than anyone else, including his own sons. But, alas, him too Muḥammad was destined to lose very soon. Umm Ayman (the Prophet’s long-time governess) reported that she had seen the youthful Muḥammad weeping as he quickened his pace to keep up with the bier of his last guardian and protector. The princely patriarch died at the age of eighty-two, according to the most reliable source. Other sources put his age at over a hundred years when he died. ‘Abd al-Muṭṭalib delegated the guardianship of his beloved grandson to his son Abū Ṭālib. He was neither the oldest nor the more resourceful of the family. But, like his father, he was dignified, honoured and greatly respected by his people. But owing to lack of means he was unable to succeed to the position of ‘Abd al-Muṭṭalib, as Makkah's foremost chief. More influential than him was the wicked Abū Lahab. Rich and imposing, Abū Lahab was destined later on to be among the arch-enemies of the Prophet. Abū Ṭālib, unable to fulfil the family's traditional role of providing for the pilgrims due to his poverty, passed this responsibility to his younger brother al-‘Abbās.

Al-‘Abbās was a skilful financier and trader. He was rich and the new post providing the pilgrims with water from Zamzam which he now controlled, gave him power and prestige. But he was never able to attain to his father's position. The eminent position of ‘Abd al-Muṭṭalib was destined to remain vacant for a long time to come. Makkah never had an effective and undisputed ruler after him, until the rise of Islam more than thirty years later. In fact, the dominance and prestige of Banū Hāshim was considerably diminished after his death. The rival faction of the Umayyads gained in power and influence, but the overall authority over Makkah was not exercised by anyone, a circumstance which substantially contributed to the inability of Makkah later on, to match the skill and energy of the Prophet's leadership located in al-Madīnah, four hundred and twenty-five kilometres to the north.

So, youthful Muḥammad, sensitive and unusually thoughtful, was thus destined, for the second time within a short while, to suffer the pain and sorrow of the death of someone dear and intimate. To this pain and sorrow was now added the hardship of poverty, as Abū Ṭālib was a man of modest means. But Muḥammad was by no means unhappy at this time. Abū Ṭālib's unlimited love for him and the deep interest which he sustained in him and his welfare must have touched his tender heart deeply. He soon developed a lasting attachment to his noble uncle. For his part, Abū Ṭālib spared no effort or means to gladden the heart of his orphaned nephew. He would make him eat with him, take him wherever he went, and during the night he would have him sleep beside his bed. As we shall see later, this mutual attachment between uncle and nephew was to play a decisive role in the momentous events which were about to shake the ancient valley as it had never been shaken before.

Notes and References

1. Qur'ān, 3 (*Āl 'Imrān*): 96–7.
2. Qur'ān, 2 (*Al-Baqarah*): 127.
3. *'Atīq* also means 'liberated' and 'protected'.
4. See Ibn Hishām, Part I (Arabic), p. 111.
5. *Ibid.*, pp. 112ff.
6. The Ma'rib dam was built by the powerful Banū Ḥimyar of the Yemen. See Haykal, *Ḥayāt Muḥammad,* Ch. I, Arabia before Islam.
7. They were called 'Muṭayyabūn' because of the 'Tīb' or perfume which they put on their hands as they made their vow of alliance.
8. Ibn Hishām, p. 130.
9. Cf. *Muḥammad at Mecca,* Oxford University Press, p. 5. Prof. Montgomery Watt maintains that 'Abd Manāf acquired the substance of power while 'Abd ad-Dār retained certain privileges, largely nominal.
10. Ibn Hishām, p. 138, maintains that of the four prominent sons of 'Abd Manāf, Hāshim was the first to die. Like all his brothers, with the exception of 'Abd Shams, Hāshim died outside Makkah, in the town of Ghazzah (Gaza) where he was buried.
11. Ibn Sa'd, *Aṭ-Ṭabaqāt al-Kubrā,* Vol. I, p. 75.
12. Ibn Hishām, p. 135f; Ibn Sa'd, pp. 75ff.
13. Qur'ān, 106 (*Quraysh*): 1–5.
14. Ibn Sa'd, p. 76.
15. *Ibid.*, p. 79.
16. Ibn Sa'd, p. 81, postulates a permanent schism among the sons of 'Abd Manāf – Hāshim and 'Abd al-Muṭṭalib on the one hand and 'Abd ash-Shams and Nawfal on the other.
17. Ibn Hishām, p. 142f and Ibn Sa'd, p. 83. The former gives the story in much greater detail.
18. Ibn Hishām, p. 151; Ibn Sa'd, p. 88f.
19. Ibn Hishām, p. 49.
20. Qur'ān, 105 (*Al-Fīl*): 1–5.
21. The sources mention two ladies who were enamoured of him. See Ibn Hishām, pp. 155–7.
22. This is the most reliable information according to both Ibn Hishām (p. 158) and Ibn Sa'd (p. 94).
23. Ibn Sa'd, p. 100.
24. *Ibid.*, p. 98.
25. *Ibid.*, p. 102.
26. *Ibid.*
27. *Ibid.*
28. Qur'ān, 61 (*Aṣ-Ṣaff*): 6.

29. See Ibn Hishām (p. 165f) where Ibn Isḥāq asserts that the Prophet himself later (after he had attained prophethood) confirmed this incident. Ibn Sa‘d (p. 112) restates the incident in rather emphatic terms.
30. See, for example, Sir William Muir, *The Life of Muhammad,* p. 6.
31. The spot where she died and was buried is called al-Abwā’, halfway between Yathrib and Makkah.
32. Qur’ān, 92 (*Aḍ-Ḍuḥā*): 5–8.

CHAPTER 3

The Search for God

The major events in the life of Muḥammad, *ṣallā Allāhu ʻalayhi wa sallam,* from the tender age of eight to the time immediately preceding his momentous call to prophethood just over thirty years later is the theme of this chapter. This period saw the noble, sensitive soul profoundly agitated by spiritual unrest and greatly troubled by the quality of life and the trend of events in pre-Islamic Arabia. Such a soul could not be diverted from undertaking a thorough and relentless search for Reality and for the meaning and purpose of life. Muḥammad's life was totally devoted to and wholly consumed by this search.

The Trip to Syria with Abū Ṭālib

After the death of ʻAbd al-Muṭṭalib his gentle, but rather poor son Abū Ṭālib, acting on the wish of his late father, assumed the guardianship of the orphan Muḥammad. At the age of about eight years, he was apparently grown up enough to withstand the pain and sorrow of the death of his grandfather. He soon recovered his usual tranquillity and his sweet disposition. Yet these tragedies left their permanent mark on the personality of the sensitive youth. His capacity to endure suffering and hardship led him to acquire that great quality of never failing to sympathize with the distressed and the deprived. Also, the child's awareness of life, of its rising and falling fortunes must have been greatly heightened as a result of those early agonizing experiences. His mind was furnished with an ever-expanding panorama of the realities of the human condition. We have already noted the strong sentimental attachment which speedily developed between the affectionate child and his new guardian. Muḥammad soon took to the life of his new home. It was a rather humble and unpretentious household. Nonetheless, it was blessed, and by no means unhappy. If Abū Ṭālib did not possess the munificent means to fulfil the functions so ably performed by his father, ʻAbd al-Muṭṭalib, and Hāshim, he was, however, extremely sympathetic and affectionate. Allusion has already been made to the kind of love and care with which he tended his nephew. No wonder, then, that the sensitive child should have developed a strong attachment to him, and be overcome with emotion when his uncle got ready to depart to Syria on a trading venture. The prospect of a long absence of the one person to whom he could justifiably look for love, affection and protection was just a little more than the already afflicted child could bear without loss of composure. He broke into passionate sobs and obstinately clung to his uncle. It was a very moving scene and Abū Ṭālib was deeply touched. He promptly assured the child that he could go with him to Syria.

The trip to Syria, at the age of twelve, was no doubt a major event in the life of the future Prophet. During the trip his world was greatly expanded and his understanding of its phenomena was considerably enhanced. His versatile but young and inexperienced mind was fed by hundreds of new experiences and impressions. For the first time, he saw the bustling commercial centres of Syria. The land and the scenery too provided a fresh and absorbing contrast to the monotonous aridity of the vast deserts of Arabia. It was green and abounded with orchards and fields, lakes and rivers. The fauna was rich and varied. Flocks of beautiful birds hovered in the clear summer skies, filling the air with the sound of their wings. These varied experiences provided material for the ponderings of his nature-loving heart and musings for his active mind. The child's natural disposition for elegance and harmony and his keen taste for natural beauty were greatly enhanced. The trip also brought him into contact with a society which differed considerably from the one in which he had grown up.

He also saw Yathrib for the second time. Whatever feelings for the city he harboured during his first trip there, in the company of his late mother when he was six, must have greatly deepened due to his mother's premature death during that trip. But Yathrib also contained the grave of his father, whom he had never seen, but whom he learned to love and cherish through the stories which his widowed mother used to tell about him, during many a long and lonely night. The first trip by the mother and child was meant as a tribute to the memory of ‘Abdullāh who died at the early age of twenty-five.

An incident during this Syrian trip which was reported by almost all the authoritative sources[1] has gained wide circulation in most of the popular hagiographies of the Prophet. It is the story of a meeting that is alleged to have taken place between Abū Ṭālib and his nephew, and a Nestorian monk. The language in which both Ibn Hishām and Ibn Sa‘d have chosen to narrate the incident indicates that they perhaps did not possess independent means to check its authenticity. Ibn Hishām[2] used such expressions as ‘they claimed’ or ‘as the story goes’, and Ibn Sa‘d[3] gives the story a very cursory treatment, paraphrasing it in a few lines. As to the perfectionist scholar, Ibn Hishām,[4] the story must have possessed such a measure of reality and significance as to justify its inclusion in his *tahdhīb* or refinement of the Prophet’s biography. At this time, we are no better off with regard to its verification than were our scholarly predecessors. Lacking any *a priori* reason for dismissing it as a fabrication dictated by fond imagination, we find the anecdote of sufficient interest as to justify its inclusion in the present study. Here is Watt’s translation[5] of the story as it occurs in Ibn Hishām:

> Ibn Isḥāq said: Later Abū Ṭālib set out with a party to trade in Syria. When the preparations were completed and the party assembled, the Messenger of God (God bless and preserve him) showed his affection for him, so they say, and Abū Ṭālib was moved to pity and said, By God, I shall take him with me, and we shall never leave one another, or something like that. So he took him with him. (At last) the party camped at Buṣrā in Syria. There was a monk there in his cell called Baḥīrā, who was versed in the lore of the Christians. From time immemorial there had been in that cell a monk well versed in their lore from a book that was there, so the story goes; as one grew old he handed it on to another. So they camped near Baḥīrā that year. Now many times previously they had passed, and he had not spoken to them nor even showed himself to them; but this year when

they camped near his cell, he got ready abundant food for them, because of something he had seen in his cell, they say; for, so the story goes, while in his cell he had seen the Messenger of God (God bless and preserve him) among the party as they drew near, and a white cloud shading him alone among the people; then they came up and alighted in the shade of a tree near him and he observed the cloud overshadowing the tree, and the branches of it bending together over the Messenger of God (God bless and preserve him) so that he found shelter under them. When Baḥīrā saw that, he went down from his cell having already given orders for that food. When it was ready, he sent to them saying, I have made ready food for you, O tribe of Quraysh, and I would like all of you to come small and great, slave and free. One of them said to him, By God, O Baḥīrā, what is the matter with you today? You have never at any time treated us thus, although we have passed by you many times. What is the matter with you today? Baḥīrā said to him, True, it is as you say: but you are guests and it has pleased me to honour you and prepare food for you that you may all eat of it. So they went together to him. Because of his youthful years, however, the Messenger of God (God bless and preserve him) was not with the party but stayed behind among their stuff beneath the tree. When Baḥīrā looked among the party, he did not see the mark he was familiar with and had found in his (book), so he said, O tribe of Quraysh, none of you is to stay away from my food. They said to him, O Baḥīrā, none of us has stayed away from you whom it befits to come to you, except a lad, the youngest of the party in years; he has stayed behind among the stuff. That is not right, he said; call him and let him join in this feast with you. Then a man of the Quraysh in the party said, By al-Lāt and al-'Uzzā, it is shameful that the son of 'Abdullāh b. 'Abd al-Muṭṭalib should not be with us but should stay away from the feast. So he went to him and embraced him and set him among the party. When Baḥīrā saw him he began to eye him keenly and to observe features of his body which he had already found present. Then when the party had finished eating and had broken up, Baḥīrā went up to him and said, Young man, I adjure you by al-Lāt and al-'Uzzā to answer my questions. Baḥīrā said

> that to him only because he had heard his people swearing by these two. They say that the Messenger of God (God bless and preserve him) said to him, Don't ask me by al-Lāt and al-'Uzzā, for by God, there is absolutely nothing I detest so much as these two. So Baḥīrā said to him, Then, in God's name, answer what I ask you. Ask what seems good to you, he said. So Baḥīrā began to ask him about certain particulars of his condition in sleep, his outward appearance and his affairs. Then the Messenger of God (God bless and preserve him) set about answering him; and what he said agreed with the description of him in Baḥīrā's (book). Then Baḥīrā looked at his back and saw the seal of prophethood between his shoulders in the place where it was described as being in his (book). Ibn Hishām said: It was like the imprint of a cupping glass. Ibn Isḥāq continued: when he was finished, he went up to his uncle, Abū Ṭālib, and said, how is this youth related to you? He said, he is my son. Baḥīrā said to him, he is not your son, this young man's father cannot be alive. He said, indeed, he is my brother's son. What did his father do? he said. He died, he said, while his mother was pregnant with him. True, he said; return to your own country with your nephew, and take care of him against the Jews, for by God if they see him and know what I know about him they will desire evil; for great importance is in store for this young nephew. So hurry to your country with him. So his uncle Abū Ṭālib set out with him quickly, and soon reached Makkah, on the completion of their trade with Syria.[6]

The leading Orientalists have denied the authenticity of the incident in question. They have noted that the anecdote did not figure in the later statements of the Prophet himself.[7] They reject the story as a fable prompted by the demands of the debates between Muslims and the followers of other faiths especially the Christians. Some Muslim scholars (e.g. Muḥammad 'Abduh in his commentary on the Qur'ān)[8] have also denied its validity. But denial by these Muslim authorities seems to be motivated by their desire to refute the statement, made by some Christian sceptics, that Baḥīrā taught the future Prophet some doctrines which he later incorporated in his religion. On the other hand, some Orientalists who wrote on the life of the Prophet with a confessed

Christian bias,[9] and who had no scruples in denying the Divine nature of his mission, would no doubt want to reject this and similar anecdotes which, if true, would assuredly imply that Muḥammad, *ṣallā Allāhu 'alayhi wa sallam,* was a vehicle of Divine election, and an object of that unfailing loving care and kindness with which all true Prophets are blessed.

If Muḥammad, *ṣallā Allāhu 'alayhi wa sallam,* is a true Prophet and messenger, with a Divinely ordained mission as indeed millions of Muslims believe him to be, then there is no *a priori* reason for suggesting he could not be, in fact, a vehicle of Divine election and all that it entails. One of the characteristics of Divine election is the Divine care and protection which is bestowed on all would-be Prophets even in their early childhood. The belief that Muḥammad, *ṣallā Allāhu 'alayhi wa sallam,* was Divinely elected, and that his education and character was fashioned under direct Divine supervision is a logical corollary of the belief in the divinely-inspired nature of his apostolic mission. If one's religious or philosophic presuppositions or bias tend to reject Muḥammad's claims to Divine guidance and to having received Divine revelations, then *a fortiori,* they would tend to resist any anecdotes to the effect that he was blessed with Divine care in his childhood, or that his prophetic life and career was attested to by supernatural phenomena. It would not help, in justifying this trend, to claim that since Muḥammad, *ṣallā Allāhu 'alayhi wa sallam,* himself never claimed any supernatural miracles as proofs for the validity of his Divine mission there is no point in sustaining these strange anecdotes. It may well be the case that miracles do not play any major role in Islam, a religion which is characterized by social pragmatism and common sense rationality. But this last consideration ought not to lead us uncritically to reject all that pertains to the transcendental domain in the life of Muḥammad, *ṣallā Allāhu 'alayhi wa sallam.* If there is a likelihood, no matter how small, that some of these events that do pertain to this domain did actually take place, then the tendency to reject them *a priori* would be sheer prejudice.

No matter how Western scholars may judge the issue of the encounter between Muḥammad, *ṣallā Allāhu 'alayhi wa sallam,* and the Nestorian, Muslims believe that Muḥammad, *ṣallā Allāhu 'alayhi wa sallam,* was brought up under the loving 'eye' of Providence and that the perfection and excellence which he displayed from his early childhood was not only human excellence and perfection but rather human perfection and excellence taken to greater heights by Providential care and guidance.

The Fijār War

Another major event in the life of Muḥammad, *ṣallā Allāhu 'alayhi wa sallam,* and one which must have had a great impact on the moulding of his character was the Fijār or Sacrilegious war which took place during his later teens. Being the first armed conflict which he witnessed, he could not have escaped its martial influences on his mild and peace-loving temperament. It is very likely that it was at that time that the future Prophet gained that military experience so vital to any person destined to be a leader of people through a major socio-religious revolution. Although of a temperament which was profoundly peace-loving and characterized by utter aversion to the unjustifiable taking of human life, nonetheless Muḥammad, *ṣallā Allāhu 'alayhi wa sallam,* was known to possess physical courage and fortitude in battle of the highest order. Both at Uḥud and later at Ḥunayn, during the Madinan period, he firmly and bravely held his ground when his soldiers were fleeing by the hundreds in panic and disorder. The brave 'Alī ibn Abī Ṭālib narrated that when the fighting intensified, they used to find protection and refuge behind the Prophet and he would be in the forefront of the struggle against the advancing enemy.

The Fijār War which the Prophet witnessed was not the first war during which the sanctity of the sacred months[10] and the sacred territory of Makkah was violated. In fact it was the fourth occasion. But this latest Fijār War is of interest to us because of the Prophet's participation in it. Our sources do not agree on the precise age of the Prophet when this war broke out. It is maintained by some that he was fourteen and by others fifteen. But Ibn Isḥāq[11] asserts that he was twenty years old when he actually took part in the fighting which resumed the same month each year. We may assert that these reports about his age do not necessarily conflict with one another. But if we accept Ibn Isḥāq's version, and take the other reports into serious consideration, we would be inclined to assume that the actual fighting which the Prophet witnessed might be either the last engagement or the penultimate one. Given that he was twenty years old during this engagement, then the first battle of this war must have been fought when he was only sixteen, the war having lasted for four years.

The war was fought between the Quraysh and their confederates of Banū Kinānah on the one side and the Hawāzin on the other. The direct cause of the hostilities was typically quite trivial; a spirit of jealousy and animosity was ignited between two men, one belonging to the Kinānah and the other to the Qays-'Aylān (an important clan of the Hawāzin). The reason for the animosity was that both men were competing to win the stewardship of the important commercial caravan which the prince of Ḥīrah used to send to the famous annual fair of 'Ukāẓ. The man of the Hawāzin succeeded in getting the stewardship and the man of the Kinānah, who was known for his spitefulness to the extent that even his own tribe criticized him, secretly resolved to kill his rival. He followed him around, until an opportunity presented itself while the man of the Hawāzin was off his guard at the fair. The men of the Kinānah and the Quraysh immediately left the fair and set out for Makkah. News of the incident then reached the Hawāzin and at once the mysterious and sudden disappearance of the Quraysh and the Kinānah from the fair became fully comprehensible. They hotly pursued them and some fighting took place between them and the Quraysh, before the latter entered their sacred territory. The Hawāzin did not pursue them beyond that, but neither did they depart until they had exacted an undertaking from the Quraysh that the war would be continued the following year at the same time. The general command of the Quraysh and the Kinānah was in the hands of the chivalrous 'Abdullāh ibn Jud'ān and Ḥarb ibn Umayyah ibn 'Abd Shams; Banū Hāshim were represented by their leader, az-Zubayr ibn 'Abd al-Muṭṭalib, who was not a distinguished man of arms though he played a respectable role in the diplomatic arrangements following the war. So it was Banū 'Abd Shams, rather than Banū Hāshim that were the champions of this meaningless conflict. Despite the good fight that the Quraysh and the Kinānah put up their efforts fell short of a decisive and clear victory. Because of the rather long duration of the war, the traditionally high reputation of the Quraysh among the other tribes of Arabia did not fare very well. In fact, it suffered a terrible blow, and this was a major consideration which prompted az-Zubayr and 'Abdullāh ibn Jud'ān to form the Fuḍūl league or alliance against injustice and lawlessness.

The sources do not give us a clear picture of the role of the future Prophet in this major war. Some authorities assign to him the rather minor task of helping his uncle gather up the arrows discharged by the enemy. Others, however, mention that he himself discharged arrows against the enemy and was quite proud, in later times, of this active role. He is reported to have said: 'I remember being present with my uncles in the Fijār War; I discharged arrows at the enemy and I do not regret it.'[12] But irrespective of the extent of his role in the actual fighting, the important point is that he was emotionally deeply involved in the course of the war. On the negative side, his impressions were most probably concerned with the agonizing and tragic consequences of war; the meaningless bloodshed, the unnecessary human suffering, the wanton cruelty and the ugly glimpses of the selfish and unjust sides of human nature which become glaringly manifest in every war. The sensitive and peaceful temperament of the Prophet must have developed a strong, and lasting abhorrence for war. War, judicially justifiable war, may be resorted to only as a last extreme and after exhausting all other means to avert it and to solve the conflict peacefully. As we know, though the Prophet never banned war as a means of solving conflicts, he never, not even once, allowed its use for vain or foolish aims. What wars he launched against the enemies of the Divine will, as was revealed to him in the Qur'ān, were always well calculated and carefully organized.

The Fijār War, in addition to doing a great deal of harm to the prestige of the Quraysh, gave a demonstration of the lack of leadership in Makkah after the death of 'Abd al-Muṭṭalib. The doubts, unrest and the gradual breakdown of the traditional trust in the Quraysh and its leadership which followed as an aftermath of the Fijār, became a permanent social fact of Makkan society on the eve of the emergence of Islam. Furthermore, it must have provided a vigorous impetus to those kindred souls who were restlessly searching for the truth, an alternative to the life of *Jāhiliyyah* (ignorance) that prevailed in pre-Islamic Arabia. Muḥammad, *ṣallā Allāhu 'alayhi wa sallam,* himself had been very preoccupied with this search since an early stage of his life. The Fijār must have further stimulated and kindled his passionate search for truth and for human dignity.

Ḥilf al-Fuḍūl (Alliance of the Virtuous)

Ḥilf al-Fuḍūl was a kind of league against injustice. It was sponsored mainly by Banū Hāshim and Banū al-Muṭṭalib, having been proposed specifically by az-Zubayr ibn 'Abd al-Muṭṭalib ibn Hāshim. Muḥammad, *ṣallā Allāhu 'alayhi wa sallam,* must have been about twenty years old when he witnessed the formation of this noble alliance. The immediate reason for forming this alliance was an injustice suffered by a merchant from the southern tribe of Zubayd in the Yemen. The Qurayshite al-'Āṣ ibn Wā'il received goods from him but refused to pay him. The Yemeni in vain sought the help of the *Aḥlāf.* When Banū Hāshim heard this they called a meeting which resulted in the formation of *Ḥilf al-Fuḍūl* (the alliance of the virtuous), and of course the return of the money to the Yemeni merchant. The clans that participated in this alliance were:

(i) Banū Hāshim, represented by az-Zubayr ibn 'Abd al-Muṭṭalib and others. The would-be Prophet, Muḥammad, *ṣallā Allāhu 'alayhi wa sallam,* was also present.[13] It is rather puzzling that our sources mention nothing about 'Abd al-Muṭṭalib (who was virtually the ruler of Makkah) in this respect. But perhaps he was absent from Makkah on one of his trading journeys. However, there can be no doubt that Banū Hāshim were the initiators of this alliance.

(ii) Banū al-Muṭṭalib, who were the usual allies of Banū Hāshim. It should be remembered that Hāshim himself was not on good terms with his other brothers, 'Abd Shams and Nawfal. In this misunderstanding al-Muṭṭalib sided with Hāshim and Nawfal with 'Abd Shams.

The rift between Hāshim and al-Muṭṭalib on the one hand and 'Abd Shams and Nawfal on the other must have been further aggravated by a fresh quarrel between 'Abd al-Muṭṭalib and Ḥarb ibn Umayyah. According to Ibn Sa'd, this quarrel was so vicious and complicated that the two parties sought the ruling of the Negus of Abyssinia.[14] But the Negus, finding the dispute difficult to solve, finally declined to make any ruling. The very fact that the Arabs, with their customary genius for striking compromises between disputants, had felt the need to refer this dispute to a third party, outside Arabia, is indeed a measure of how deep the animosity between Banū Hāshim and the Umayyads had grown.

(iii) Asad ibn ‘Abd al-‘Uzzā, Zuhrah ibn Kilāb and Taym ibn Murrah which were less significant.

Thus neither ‘Abd Shams nor Nawfal were parties to this alliance, although they were both members of the former *Ḥilf of al-Muṭayyabūn* (the perfumed). It is not unlikely that ‘Abd Shams and Nawfal stayed aloof from the *Ḥilf al-Fuḍūl* because of their animosity to Banū Hāshim. The meeting took place in the house of ‘Abdullāh ibn Jud‘ān who was a wise and respected man. An oath was taken by the members of this assembly that whenever they found someone in Makkah whether he be a citizen of it or a stranger visiting it to whom injustice had been done they would stand by him against his oppressor until the wrong had been redressed. Muḥammad, *ṣallā Allāhu ‘alayhi wa sallam,* was among those who attended this meeting and was so impressed by its noble objectives that he remained loyal to it. Long after he would say, ‘I attended at the house of ‘Abdullāh ibn Jud‘ān the conclusion of an agreement which I would not exchange for the best of material gains, and if someone appeals to it in Islam I would respond.’

Khadījah al-Kubrā

Khadījah al-Kubrā, or Khadījah the Grand, was the first wife of Muḥammad, *ṣallā Allāhu ‘alayhi wa sallam,* whom he loved as he never loved any other woman in his life, and who, during his early days of doubt and spiritual anguish was an oasis of rest, assurance and comfort. Her sweet countenance, affection and unfailing sympathy and understanding was his sole sustenance during the agonizing period (approximately six months) in which Gabriel (Jibrīl), the messenger of Divine revelation, ceased to come to him, after the first visit in which he was commanded to ‘recite’ and told that he was the chosen Messenger of God. The story of how she stood by his side, supporting and encouraging him, how she assured him that the charitable, benevolent Deity would not abandon him, being the good man he was, represents one of the most fascinating and moving episodes in human history. Khadījah’s role in the great events attending the beginning of the call will be reviewed and assessed in a later section. Our present concern is to introduce this noble lady to the reader, and in so doing say something about her position in the esteem and affection of the Prophet and about her image as it has come down to millions of present-day Muslims. Of the Prophet's affection for her we need only point out that 'Ā'ishah, the attractive young woman who was the Prophet's favourite wife after the death of Khadījah (although she never saw Khadījah) was by her own admission very jealous of the Prophet's lingering love for her. Concerning her popular standing, she is widely known as Khadījah al-Kubrā, an epithet indicating the deep sense of affection and veneration with which she is regarded by the community of the faithful. The epithet also refers to her position as the first wife of the Prophet and the mother of his surviving offspring. The wives of the Prophet are also called 'the mothers of the faithful', but Khadījah is the first (al-Kubrā) mother, and Ibn Isḥāq narrates that when Divine revelation resumed its flow after its abrupt cessation following the first visit of Gabriel, Khadījah received a Divine tribute and a salutation of peace *(salām)* from God. The Message was communicated to Muḥammad, *ṣallā Allāhu 'alayhi wa sallam,* by Gabriel, and when he conveyed it to Khadījah, she promptly replied: 'God is peace *(as-Salām),* and from Him is all peace, and may peace be on Gabriel.'[15]

Khadījah was of the Quraysh. The lineage of the Prophet meets with hers in the celebrated Quṣayy, the great founder of Makkah and famous patriarch of the Quraysh. Khadījah's lineage connects with Quṣayy through his not so famous son, 'Abd al-'Uzzā. She is Khadījah bint (daughter of) Khuwaylid ibn Asad ibn 'Abd al-'Uzzā ibn Quṣayy.

The future Prophet and Khadījah became known to each other when he undertook a journey to Syria in charge of a huge commercial caravan that belonged to her. At that time, she was a widow at the rather advanced age of about forty.[16] Very wealthy and with a strong and independent will, she repeatedly declined marriage offers made by some of the most prominent men of the Quraysh. She obviously preferred the quietness and independence of widowhood to the male domination and cares inherent in married life of those days. The easy and comfortable life which her great wealth made possible enabled her to maintain a pleasant and radiant countenance, despite her comparatively advanced age. Her house in Makkah consisted of several storeys and she was attended by a number of maids. Her main concern was to expand her trade and, no doubt, play some role in the general policy-making of the government of the city. Despite her wealth and prestige, she was neither lacking in sympathy nor arrogant in bearing. She was discreet, affectionate and of noble character. Muḥammad, *ṣallā Allāhu 'alayhi wa sallam,* succeeded very well in his business mission. The profits were unusually high and his mild manners and agreeable temperament won him the hearts of men whom he employed in the course of the journey. In particular one of Khadījah's men, by the name of Maysarah, was so impressed by the personal qualities of Muḥammad, *ṣallā Allāhu 'alayhi wa sallam,* that, on his return, he could not help singing the praises of his new manager, the sweetness of his manners, his kindness and his unusually impressive character. Our sources also record various observations which Maysarah had made during the course of the trip, and which deeply imprinted in his consciousness that Muḥammad, *ṣallā Allāhu 'alayhi wa sallam,* was somehow attended by mysterious phenomena.[17]

On returning to Makkah, after coming home from Khadījah's house, Muḥammad, *ṣallā Allāhu 'alayhi wa sallam,* was contacted by an agent of Khadījah.[18]

'What is it, O Muḥammad', said Khadījah's agent in a tactful, persuading voice, 'that prevents you from marrying?' 'But I do not have in my hands what I can marry with', replied Muḥammad, *ṣallā Allāhu 'alayhi wa sallam,* promptly. 'What if that difficulty was removed and you were invited to marry someone of beauty, wealth, noble birth and discretion, would you not accept?' 'Who is she?' Muḥammad, *ṣallā Allāhu 'alayhi wa sallam,* asked with obvious interest. 'Khadījah', she said. 'But how can I attain unto her?' 'Let me take care of that', replied the agent of Khadījah. 'I will accept', was the decisive reply which sent the agent hurrying to Khadījah with the happy news.

Both Ibn Sa'd and Ibn Hishām assert that Khadījah arranged to address Muḥammad, *ṣallā Allāhu 'alayhi wa sallam,* in person and make the marriage proposal directly to him. We may suppose that this meeting took place after the initial contact made by the woman agent. The future Prophet of Islam was approximately twenty-five years old. He was in the prime of his youth, with a well-built physique but of average size and middle height, broad shoulders, his eyes dark and pensive and remarkably wide. There was unusual charm in his noble eyes, with heavy eyelashes of a reddish tint. A thick black beard that reached to his chest reflected a natural and thoughtful temperament. It added to his noble and conspicuous presence. This presence inspired awe and fear at the first encounter,[19] but thereafter, the awe and fear would give way to lasting love and loyalty. A measure of this loyalty can be seen when the Quraysh emissary to Muḥammad, *ṣallā Allāhu 'alayhi wa sallam,* when he was at the gates of Makkah, during the expedition of Ḥudaybiyyah came back to them with the disquieting report:

'O tribe of Quraysh, I have been to Chosroes, Caesar and the Negus, each in his own realm, but, by God, I have never seen a king (loved and held in such awe) as Muḥammad (is held) among his people.'

To complete the description of the personal appearance of the future Prophet, as he faced Khadījah sitting in the upper storey of her spacious, stately mansion, surrounded by her domestic attendants, we must add some more details about his appearance and general bearing. His complexion was ruddy, rendered clear and radiant by the deep inner peace and serenity which were some of the natural gifts with which he was blessed. His steps were decisive, full of energy and solemnity. When he moved, he did so promptly and energetically. He walked as if descending from a hill, and when called from behind, he never turned partially but turned his whole body. When anyone shook hands with him, he would never be the first to withdraw his hand. Nor would he be the first to discontinue the conversation, unless he had some urgent business to attend to. So sensitive was he to human feelings and so mindful never to injure the feelings of anybody without necessity, that, even during the hard and busy days, in which the Qur'ān was constantly being revealed to him, he would always be willing to stop reciting the holy book in order to attend to a casual visitor, no matter how unimportant he might be. Later on, when he was the busy ruler of the Muslim state at al-Madīnah, whenever he could afford to he would give his hand to a slave or a little girl to take him to wherever he or she wanted to go. He would also participate in the childish games of his young relatives.

As Muḥammad, *ṣallā Allāhu 'alayhi wa sallam,* and Khadījah met on the balcony in her mansion she must have glimpsed in him some aspects of the vast human and (later) proven prophetic greatness. So great was her attraction to him and so passionate was the desire of her noble heart to be united with him in marriage that she dropped her usual reserve and cautious approach and proceeded, without delay, to make a direct and frank proposal to him to marry her.

'O cousin, I have desired to marry you because of your relation (of kith and kin), and because of your noble birth and honour among your people, and because of your honesty, your fine manners and the truthfulness of your discourse.'

And fine indeed and sweet was the discourse of Muḥammad, *ṣallā Allāhu 'alayhi wa sallam,* and pure and uncorrupted was the bedouin accent of his language. His delivery was clear and audible, yet he would never raise his voice more than was necessary to make himself heard. With a fine mouth, rather wide, his Arab eloquence was a rare gift. His teeth were fine and snowy white; he was known to have strong abhorrence for yellow teeth and bad breath. The marriage ceremony soon took place. A little party of Banū Hāshim and Banū Asad gathered at the stately house of Khadījah. Banū Asad were headed by Khuwaylid, Khadījah's ageing father, and Banū Hāshim were headed by the noble Abū Ṭālib. Our sources report that Khuwaylid was rather reluctant to give his consent to the conclusion of the marriage, an episode which gave a sad opening to one of the noblest unions ever concluded between man and woman.

The marriage proved to be one of affection and happiness; and despite Khadījah's comparatively advanced age, it was the most fruitful the Prophet ever had. All his sons and daughters, with the exception of Ibrāhīm who died as a little boy, were the fruit of this marriage. Khadījah bore the Prophet two sons, al-Qāsim and 'Abdullāh (aṭ-Ṭāhir) who died at a very early age.

Muḥammad's marriage to this powerful and highly regarded lady of the Quraysh was an early indication of his tremendous potential and promise. It was an acknowledgement of those great personal traits which manifested themselves in later years and enabled him to win the obedience and loyalty of the many thousands of men who loved and followed him: these were the qualities of humility, deference and sympathy, and that inexhaustible readiness to provide service and help to others. It was from the desert life that he had gained his simple tastes, his aversion to luxuries of all sorts, and a general conduct characterized by austerity and purity. Our sources inform us that twice he thought of engaging himself in the gross and unchaste night life of the city of Makkah, and on both occasions he was saved by the grace of Providence. On the first occasion he was absorbed in watching a wedding reception on the outskirts of the city; at length he fell asleep and only awoke next morning. On the second occasion, he was arrested by a divinely sweet melody, and he slept, wholesome and peaceful, until the next day. 'After that', reported Muḥammad, *ṣallā Allāhu 'alayhi wa sallam,* in later days, 'I never sought after vice.'

Thus Providence had reared the future Prophet and he grew up among his people easily distinguished by rare moral qualities, modesty and mild manners and an extraordinary purity of nature and temperament.

A quality that gained him the love and respect of his people was his deep sensitivity concerning the feelings of others irrespective of their age or social standing. He would take care not to injure the feelings of anyone unnecessarily and was under all circumstances deeply interested in the welfare and well-being of others. He would easily become engaged in conversation with anyone although he normally preferred to listen. When he was spoken to by his Companions, he would not only listen intently but would turn his face and his whole body towards them. He is never known to have interrupted anyone who was talking to him. Always faithful and truthful, people used to deposit their valuables with him for safe keeping. For all these great personal qualities and for the services he rendered to his community, he was designated *al-Amīn* (the Trustworthy) by common consent.

The Quraysh Rebuild the Ka'bah

The rebuilding of the Ka'bah was perhaps the first major event in which the future Prophet appeared in public after his much-talked-about marriage to the famous lady of the Quraysh. Being situated in perhaps the lowest part of the valley of Makkah, the ancient House was constantly flooded by torrents of water coming down from the surrounding high ground and hills. Gradually the condition of the building deteriorated; and as it was roofless, its valuables were sometimes stolen. Eventually, some Quraysh leaders decided to pull down the edifice and build it anew. With such reverence was the Ka'bah regarded by them, that they hesitated to start the demolition, lest the wrath of God would be heaped upon them. It was the daring of al-Walīd ibn al-Mughīrah that put an end to their doubts and fears. He started the demolition by pulling down a portion of the southern wall. They waited till the next morning to see what evil would befall him. When nothing happened, they all joined in the demolition.

As they were thus engaged in pulling down the old building, a great ship was wrecked by bad weather and stranded in the port of Jeddah, some seventy kilometres west of Makkah. Al-Walīd and others managed to buy the wreck and to persuade the captain, by the name of Bāqūm, who was said to be also an architect, to come to Makkah and help in the project of rebuilding the ancient sanctuary. Four major clans of the Quraysh worked together harmoniously, each clan building one wall of the four-walled sacred structure. When the building was as high as an average man's height, it was time to place the sacred Black Stone in place, in the eastern corner. The act of putting the Black Stone in place was considered to be the highest honour, and each of the clans was determined to claim it. A dispute arose which could have broken out into serious conflict. But thanks to the wisdom of an ageing chief of Banū Makhzūm, whose name was Abū Umayyah ibn al-Mughīrah, bloodshed was averted and a peaceful plan was agreed upon. The wise chief suggested to the Quraysh that the first man to enter through the door of aṣ-Ṣafā be entrusted with the task of placing the sacred, mysterious stone in place. The plan was arbitrary, but it worked. As the Quraysh assembled for the ceremony, expectantly waiting with their eyes fixed on the door of aṣ-Ṣafā, Muḥammad, *ṣallā Allāhu ʿalayhi wa sallam,* entered. He was given a warm welcome, and they cried with satisfaction and excitement, 'Here comes Muḥammad, here comes ibn ʿAbd al-Muṭṭalib, and here comes *al-Amīn* (the Trustworthy).'

Muḥammad, *ṣallā Allāhu ʿalayhi wa sallam,* undertook his commission with wisdom, firmness and promptness. He threw down his mantle and spread it on the ground. Then he ordered the Black Stone be placed in the middle. This done, he invited the four major clans of the Quraysh that were involved in the reconstruction of the Kaʿbah to each take one corner of the cloth. At his direction, the mantle with the Black Stone was raised until it was level with the spot in which it was to be placed. At this point, the future Prophet of Islam took the Stone and placed it firmly in position. It was an ingenious plan and provided yet another proof of his gift for decision-making and leadership.

The incident of Muḥammad's arbitration in this important matter also effectively demonstrates the absence of paramount authority in Makkah. Since that authority was traditionally invested with Banū Hāshim ever since the celebrated Quṣayy, we can legitimately infer that their worldly fortunes since the death of 'Abd al-Muṭṭalib had suffered major setbacks. This inference is further reinforced by the absence of their representatives in the ceremony of placing the Black Stone in position. It was the rival clan of the Umayyads that represented Banū 'Abd Manāf.

Ibn Isḥāq narrates some of the things which were found during the course of reconstructing the ancient edifice. The most important among these were the *green* foundation which resisted any further demolition and Syriac writings about the history of the House and Makkah. One of the manuscripts found is reported to have read as follows:

> I am the lord of Bakkah (i.e. Makkah). I have created it the same day I created the heaven and the earth. And I have surrounded it with seven righteous angels; it does not pass out of existence, until its two Akhshbis (two mountain peaks overlooking Makkah) are destroyed. Its water and milk are blessed for its people . . .[20]

While these anecdotes might possibly be the creation of sentimental reverence for the sacred sanctuary, yet we do not have at our disposal any justification for dismissing them as such. However, they are of interest because they do reflect the Quraysh's firm belief in the antiquity and sanctity of this much venerated and adored sanctuary, a belief which may be well-founded and which has been shared by adherents of the Muslim faith throughout the ages.

Social Disorder in Makkah

The Fijār War, the event that led to the conclusion of the *Fuḍūl* Alliance and the notorious conflict over the Black Stone affair are events which must have aroused the most profound anxieties in the reflective mind of the future Prophet of Islam. His trips to

Syria opened his mind to the possibility of a different type of social organization. His early career as a shepherd helped in fostering his natural predilection towards repose and meditation. His recent marriage to the affectionate, beautiful and wealthy Khadījah provided just the type of quiet, easy life he needed in order to continue his musings and philosophic ponderings. As he reflected upon the tenor of life in Makkah particularly and in Arabia generally, he became more and more convinced that it was degradingly low. Most of all he was disgusted at the prevalence of gross idolatry and vulgar fetishism. He thought it to be far below the dignity of an intelligent human being to subjugate himself and enslave his mind and soul to inanimate objects. For him, idolatry was the most serious of all evils because it effectively quelled the voice of reason and thus deprived people of their human worth. It bred nothing but falsehood and vice. Makkan society abounded with vice and social evils. Despite the existence of some great Arab personalities, and perhaps partly because of such people, the major cities of Arabia, especially Makkah and Yathrib, were fast moving towards anarchy and social strife. In both cities, a state of lawlessness and disorder prevailed, in the wake of the absence of any temporal authority and the gradual loosening of the grip of idolatry. In Makkah, after the collapse of Banū Hāshim control, there was no other government to succeed it, and in Yathrib the pretensions of 'Abdullāh ibn Ubayy (who later on assumed the leadership of the Hypocrites) to the governorship of the city went unheeded by the warring tribes of the Aws and Khazraj. And in both cities there was evident tension between monotheistic and idolatrous elements, partly induced by the existence of Jewish and Christian influences. In Yathrib, the Jews represented an advanced and comparatively progressive enclave. But their inability to mix easily with others, and the characteristically traditional disdain with which they viewed other ethnic and sociological groups, coupled with their pride in things Jewish and their belief in the supremacy of Jewish 'nationality' rendered them an additional factor of instability in a society already badly shaken.

In Makkah, the existence of several power centres (witness the conflict over the Black Stone), the absence of a paramount authority and the existence of several highly energetic and capable individuals created an atmosphere of unrest and strife. There was neither peace nor security nor truth nor fidelity in Makkah. A pensive and truth-loving man such as Muḥammad, *ṣallā Allāhu ʻalayhi wa sallam,* both by disposition and by upbringing, could not find either peace or repose in such a society. The longing of his heart for peace and truth made it impossible for him to accept or to reconcile himself with such a situation.

Meditation at Mount Ḥirā'

Suffering spiritual unrest, intellectual discomfort, and unable to harmonize with the degrading social conditions in Makkah, Muḥammad, *ṣallā Allāhu ʻalayhi wa sallam,* found temporary peace in solitude and isolation. Since his marriage with Khadījah, it became his habit to withdraw to a cave on the neighbouring Mount Ḥirā'. There, he would remain plunged in deep thought and reflection. His dissatisfaction with the religious and social conditions in Makkah only served to stimulate his mind to begin a passionate and thorough search into the mysteries of the ultimate realities. A radical mind such as Muḥammad, *ṣallā Allāhu ʻalayhi wa sallam,* possessed could not be prevented from undertaking a searching inquiry into the mysteries of the unseen, of life and death, of power and disaster and of good and evil. This tender, truth-loving soul was almost shattered with the passion and the desire to communicate with the master Will of the universe, the Ultimate Cause of all order and harmony and the infinite Source of beauty, peace and love.

When he rose from his beautiful, peace-imparting meditations and cast his eyes upon the barren slopes of Mount Ḥirā' towards the direction of Makkah, his noble vision could perceive nothing but dreariness and emptiness. The wild, rugged valley, shadowless and flowerless, reflected the urban wilderness and lack of beauty and harmony in the city of Makkah beyond. The ancient city was no exception to the world-wide instability and strife. The two major powers, the Byzantine and Persian empires, were just recovering from a protracted and savage war that had almost destroyed both of them. We can only say that the Byzantines emerged theoretically as the victors and the Persians as the vanquished, for perhaps the most significant outcome of this conflict was the total collapse of the civic and military defences of both these 'great' powers, rendering them vulnerable to imminent incursion from the Arabian desert.

When such thoughts crowded upon the serene mind of Muḥammad, *ṣallā Allāhu 'alayhi wa sallam,* he would again steep himself in prayer and meditation. The quest of his soul was for explanation and truth and the longing of his heart was for communion with the true God, the nature of whom he knew not. In his solitary retreat in the cave of Ḥirā', Muḥammad, *ṣallā Allāhu 'alayhi wa sallam,* would be quite alone most of the time. Khadījah's employees provided him with food and drink and other basic needs. She herself would visit him from time to time, and would sometimes bring along his little daughters. His male children had all died in early infancy, bringing him again the sadness and suffering he had experienced earlier with the death of his parents. The favourite time of the year for his retreat at Mount Ḥirā' was the month of Ramaḍān. He would spend the whole month there in acts of piety and purification. Whoever happened to pass by or visit him in his retreat would be treated with liberality and hospitality. Khadījah, with her loyal and generous character made available to him whatever he needed for these purposes. She understood with love and sympathy her husband's strenuous spiritual search and did her utmost to make his retreats comfortable and agreeable for him. Such retreats were not unknown among the Quraysh but Muḥammad, *ṣallā Allāhu 'alayhi wa sallam,* continued his search for God in the silent and barren mountains of Makkah long after his marriage and until he received Divine revelations at the age of forty.

Our sources[21] tell us that some years before he achieved his prophethood, Muḥammad, *ṣallā Allāhu 'alayhi wa sallam,* received signs of impending communion with the Transcendental mystery of the universe. He began to see in his dreams at night that which was later realized and confirmed by actual reality in vivid and minute detail. Objects of nature, trees, bushes and stones, were said to have greeted him as he passed by in the Makkan desert. Muḥammad, *ṣallā Allāhu 'alayhi wa sallam,* startled, would turn around but, seeing that no one was there, would continue on his way, greatly puzzled.

Notes and References

1. The story is reported by Ibn Hishām, Ibn Sa'd and aṭ-Ṭabarī.
2. Ibn Hishām, p. 180.
3. Ibn Sa'd, p. 120.
4. Ibn Hishām maintained that he subjected Ibn Isḥāq's original manuscript of the *Sīrah* (biography of the Prophet) to rigorous verification, omitting such anecdotes as he deemed unauthentic.
5. Ibn Hishām, pp. 180–3.
6. W. Montgomery Watt, *Muhammad at Mecca,* p. 36f.
7. The story of Baḥīrā actually figures in some sayings of the Prophet but the authenticity of these has been questioned. At-Tirmidhī, a learned jurist and an authority on *Ḥadīth,* mentions the story but does not mention the name of Baḥīrā.
8. Muḥammad 'Abduh, *Tafsīr al-Manār,* Vol. II, pp. 169–70.
9. See for example, Tor Andrae, *Mohammed the Man and His Faith.*
10. The sacred months are four, including Dhu'l-Qa'dah, Dhu'l-Ḥijjah and Muḥarram.
11. Ibn Hishām, p. 184f; see also Ibn Sa'd, p.126f.
12. Ibn Sa'd, p. 128.
13. Ibn Sa'd, p. 128f; Ibn Hishām, p. 134.
14. Ibn Sa'd, p. 87.
15. Ibn Hishām, p. 241.
16. Our sources give Khadījah's age at the time of her marriage to Muḥammad as forty years. But since she bore the Prophet six children with about a two years' interval between them, we may suppose that she was a few years less than forty.
17. Ibn Isḥāq narrates that Maysarah was told by a Christian monk who had seen Muḥammad, *ṣallā Allāhu 'alayhi wa sallam,* and enquired about him that Muḥammad, *ṣallā Allāhu 'alayhi wa sallam,* would be a Prophet. Moreover, he noticed that Muḥammad, *ṣallā Allāhu 'alayhi wa sallam,* alone among the travellers was shadowed by two angels who flew over his camel during the intense heat of the day. This is reported to have been a major motive for Khadījah's subsequent desire to marry the Prophet.
18. The agent's name was Nafīsah bint Munyah, according to Ibn Sa'd, p. 131.
19. It is reported in the *Sīrah* that a bedouin was so struck by awe and fear on seeing the Prophet (after he had received Divine revelation) that he stood shaking like a leaf, unable to utter a word. The Prophet went to him in warm assurance.
20. Ibn Hishām, p. 196.
21. *Ibid.,* p. 234.

CHAPTER 4

Prophethood

At the close of the last chapter we left the future Prophet of Islam in his lonely retreat amongst the arid, desolate hills of Makkah. He was in his fortieth year. As had been his habit for the past three years during Ramaḍān, he had withdrawn from the bustling city of Makkah to a cave on the top of Mount Ḥirā', not far from the city. The ancient city of Makkah is situated in a valley, and is surrounded by rugged mountains on all sides. That year, Muḥammad, *ṣallā Allāhu 'alayhi wa sallam,* was deeply absorbed in his meditation amongst the silent hills. There he somehow felt at ease. He seemed to appreciate and even enjoy the silence and the solitude. From what we have said in the previous chapter, it is perhaps not very difficult to guess some of the thoughts that were engaging his mind at this crucial juncture of his life. Being strongly averse to vice, ignorance and the crude self-indulgence characteristic of Makkah, he felt utterly alienated from its society. His abhorrence of heathenism and idolatry, universally practised in Makkah and other towns of Arabia, was complete. His aversion to the social institutions of Makkah was equally strong. The arrogance and haughtiness of the Makkan aristocracy, the lack of authority, and the prevalence of lawlessness and disorder must have deeply saddened his sensitive and justice-loving heart. Other evils of Makkan society, such as slavery, harshness and cruelty towards women and children, could not have escaped his critical eyes. These must have been among the causes of his profound detestation of the pre-Islamic society of Makkah, endearing him to retreat and isolation with his inmost meditation.

Divine Election and Education

In these retreats Muḥammad, *ṣallā Allāhu 'alayhi wa sallam,* sought the peace and tranquillity which he did not find in city life. Whether he was consciously searching for an explanation of the ultimate Reality, we shall never know for certain. Nevertheless, we may assume that he pondered questions to which he could find no answers, wonders which he could not explain and mysteries to which there were no solutions. Deep in his heart, he knew that the ideas and beliefs of Makkan life were both false and degrading. Unconsciously at least, he was looking for truth and guidance elsewhere. The quest of his mind, at this stage, was for explanations that would illumine the darkness that filled his world, and the desire of his perplexed heart was for practical guidance which could bring peace and serenity to his troubled life. He experienced a profound sense of dissatisfaction and acute discomfort as he yearned for guidance and illumination. And so great and persistent was this yearning of his noble heart, that he felt himself being pushed to the verge of self-destruction. Such was the state of his mind and the nature of his temperament when he experienced the first revelations of the Archangel Gabriel in the cave on Mount Ḥirā', in the arid and remote outskirts of Makkah. This was indeed his dominant mood when Gabriel after the first visitation on Ḥirā' did not soon come again. However, it would be a serious mistake to believe that Muḥammad, *ṣallā Allāhu 'alayhi wa sallam,* in the cave on Ḥirā' resembled a philosopher engaged in working out a system of thought, philosophy or religion. He did not at that time expound any of the teachings which he so enthusiastically advocated after the commencement of his prophetic call. Then, as we shall presently recount, he was utterly shaken by the first appearance of the Angel Gabriel on Mount Ḥirā'. Long after the disappearance of the Angel, he had serious misgivings about the genuineness of his extraordinary experiences. It was the wisdom and discretion of Khadījah that was instrumental in bringing calm and reassurance to his greatly disturbed mind. Had Muḥammad, *ṣallā Allāhu 'alayhi wa sallam,* actually thought, or even embellished his teachings, he would, in the very nature of things, have claimed credit for the fruits of his intellectual labours. But we know that he never made any such claim. In fact he spared no effort to demonstrate that he was the passive instrument of Divine revelation and Divine will.

The Qur'ān is the word of God, which he only received, as Divine revelation:

> And thus have We inspired in you (Muḥammad) a spirit of Our command. You know not (before) what the Scripture was, nor what the Faith. But We have made it a light whereby We guide whom We will of our servants and assuredly you guide unto a right path.[1]

We have seen that Muḥammad, *ṣallā Allāhu 'alayhi wa sallam,* was designated *al-Amīn,* an epithet meaning both the truthful and trustworthy. He is not known to have ever told a lie either in earnest or in jest. It is totally inconceivable that he could have pretended that he was the instrument of Divine inspiration, and that the Qur'ān was the word of God, which he merely received from Him and which he was both destined and ordered to communicate to all mankind.

'It is strongly corroborative of Muḥammad's sincerity', writes Sir William Muir, 'that the earliest converts to Islam were not only of upright character, but his own bosom friends and people of his household who, intimately acquainted with his private life, could not fail otherwise to have detected those discrepancies which ever more or less exist between the professions of the hypocritical deceiver abroad and his actions at home. The faithful Khadījah is already known to the reader as a sharer in her husband's searchings of heart and probably[2] the first convert to his creed.'[3]

The true explanation of Muḥammad's preparedness and aptitude for prophethood and to receive Divine inspiration can only be resolved in terms of Divine Election and Divine Education with which he is believed to have been blessed.

> The proof of the condition of Muḥammad, *ṣallā Allāhu 'alayhi wa sallam,* since early childhood and of God's preparation of him for His prophethood and His message is that He created him with a nature of rational humanity so as to send him forth with the religion that was for the original (rational) nature of man. And He created him with a rational mind and a consummate intellectual ability to send him forth with

> the religion of reason and scientific method. He perfected him with rare virtues so as to send him forth to expound the virtues of noble manners and behaviour. He fashioned him from early youth in such a manner as to detest idolatry and superstition and the vices of those who practised them. He caused him to love solitude so that his soul would desire neither the material pleasures for which men so avidly strive nor the bloodthirsty savagery of those who inflicted injustice and violence upon others, nor even the envy of other people's wealth. Thus He fashioned him the supreme Human Example so that he was able to establish the supreme law with which He would inspire him.[4]

Muslim sociologists and philosophers have constructed sophisticated theories of Prophethood concerning the life of Muḥammad, *ṣallā Allāhu 'alayhi wa sallam.* Let us consider very briefly the theory developed by Ibn Khaldūn.

Ibn Khaldūn's Theory of Prophecy

In his *Muqaddimah,* Ibn Khaldūn gives both a diagnosis and criteria for prophecy. The diagnosis consists of an ingenious description of the phenomenon of prophecy. In remarkably elegant style, he discusses the nature of the *prophetic experience,* giving a metaphysical exposition of its various signs and symptoms. The criteria, on the other hand, consist of traits and properties which are alleged to be useful in distinguishing between genuine and spurious Prophets. As the leading Muslim sociologist, Ibn Khaldūn believes that prophets are both chosen and prepared for their *prophetic role* by Providence, the essence of this role being to communicate *Divine guidance* to their respective peoples. The essence of Divine guidance is to acquaint man with his Creator and Lord and help him attain salvation, lasting happiness and bliss in the Hereafter. But first, let us see how Ibn Khaldūn characterizes the *prophetic experience*.

The Nature of Prophetic Experience

(i) For Ibn Khaldūn, prophetic experience is essentially a kind of trance, a sudden leap, from the human level of consciousness to that of the Divine order. In this trance or leap the ordinary human cognitive powers are drastically transformed so that the subject undergoing the experience becomes able to partake of the perception and understanding of the Divine order.

(ii) This transformation is described by him as a momentary exchange of the human consciousness with pure angelic consciousness, uninhibited by the mediation of the human body. As a result of this exchange or transformation, the subject becomes totally *immersed* in the *spiritual* medium of the realm of the angels. The subject becomes, momentarily that is, part and parcel of that higher realm, and thus becomes able to partake in its activities, its perception and experience.

(iii) At the termination of the prophetic experience, which normally takes the form of a trance, the subject returns to the ordinary human condition. However, he does not lose or forget the experiences and the perception which he attained whilst in that higher realm. He retains them in an exceptionally vivid manner as if engraved on his heart. This ability to memorize things perceived in visionary trances, is achieved by the subject during the training which he receives in preparation for his imminent prophetic role.

(iv) By a process rather similar to translation but whose precise nature is unknown, the mystical content of the experience is rendered comprehensible in ordinary human discourse.

(v) The prophetic role consists in communicating the content of the prophetic experience to the people, rationally and completely unchanged. This material provides Divine guidance to the people and the conveying of this guidance is the very essence of the prophetic role.

(vi) The actual transformation which makes the prophetic experience possible is quite painful and exhausting to the subject who shows visible signs of fatigue and hardship.

Criteria for Recognizing a Genuine Prophetic Experience

(i) True Prophets experience a trance which can be described as follows:

It is not a state of unconsciousness, nor is it a failure of physical or mental powers. The agent does not exhibit any signs of suffering mental or physical illness. And quite definitely it is not any form of epileptic unconsciousness. The agent experiencing this trance *becomes unaware of his surroundings,* like someone asleep.

Like a sleeping person who is experiencing some kind of unusual dream, the agent exhibits visible signs of fatigue and hardship. These include (i) heavy breathing, (ii) sweating heavily, and (iii) loud snoring. According to Ibn Khaldūn, the fatigue and hardship is due to 'an immersion in (and) encounter with the spiritual kingdom, the result of perception congenial to them but entirely foreign to the (ordinary) perception of men.'[5]

(ii) Even before receiving Divine Revelation the would-be Prophets are recognizable as good and innocent persons, naturally averse to any reprehensible or sinful actions. That is to say they are immune from sin and vice. This is the well-known doctrine of *'Iṣmah* (or infallibility) with which all true Prophets are endowed. Prophets, that is truly inspired Prophets, are by nature disposed to avoid and shun blameworthy actions, as if such actions are the negation of their very nature.

(iii) True Prophets are also recognizable by the honest and sincere means which they employ to spread their messages. They use Divine worship and prayer, observe chastity and practise alms-giving. They are kind and sympathetic to the depressed and the underprivileged and dispense justice and equity to all people and under all circumstances. They are neither wealthy nor status seekers. Nor are they possessed by any craving for power or influence. Above all they desire and seek to impart Divine guidance at any cost to all members of their respective peoples.

(iv) They must enjoy the support of some powerful group. This support is necessary, because it serves as a buffer that protects them against their antagonists and gives them a measure of security which enables them to carry out their Divine mission.

(v) All true Prophets produce miracles, accompanied by some advance challenge of some sort. The challenge is in many cases made by their antagonists who seek to deny, belie and upset their prophetic claims. The Prophets then produce the miracles as answers to these challenges, and furthermore, as attestations to the truth and sincerity of their claims. The miracle of Muḥammad, *ṣallā Allāhu 'alayhi wa sallam,* was the Qur'ān. In the case of previous Prophets their miracles were meant to be proofs and confirmations of the Divine nature of their inspiration. But the Qur'ān was both the Divine Revelation and the miraculous proof of that Revelation. If it is the wondrous miracle it is, it requires no proof outside itself. If the Qur'ān is to be shown to be a product of human endeavours, then something comparable to its charm, nobility and the elegance and gloriousness of its style, must be produced or shown to have existed before.

Although it is not our concern, at this juncture, to demonstrate the miraculous nature of the Qur'ān, it may be useful, nevertheless, to give the uninitiated reader one or two glimpses of the supernatural beauty and profundity of this book, in confirmation of Ibn Khaldūn's thesis.

On the Development of the Human Foetus:

> Indeed, We have created Man from a stock of clay. Then We made him a drop (of sperm placed) in a deep-seated lodge. Then We created the drop of sperm into a clot of congealed blood. Then We created of the clot a little lump (of foetus). Then We created the lump into bones, then We clothed the bones with flesh, then We fashioned him (i.e. man) into another creation. So blessed be Allah, the Best of all creators.[6]

On the Resurrection:

> Does Man think that We shall not assemble his bones (on the day of resurrection)?
> Nay, We are able to remake his very finger-tips.[7]

The beauty of these verses is that they single out the finger-tips as being among perhaps the most subtle parts of the human body. By asserting God's ability to remake and recreate them after death, the Qur'ān is, *a fortiori,* asserting His ability to recreate the entire human body. That the finger-tips are in fact quite subtle and complicated is attested by (i) the fineness and subtlety of the bones of the fingers; (ii) the finger-tips of each human being are unique, as is shown by the fact that each person has unique finger-prints; (iii) the human hand by virtue of these fingers is among the most sophisticated instruments there are. It can perform more functions than any human-made machine is ever capable of performing. Early commentators of the Qur'ān were quite oblivious to some of these peculiarities of the human fingers, in particular they had no idea of the recent notion of finger-prints and the tremendous use they are put to in detecting crimes.

The same chapter contains verses that rebut the misgivings of the unbelievers that the notion of bodily resurrection is absurd. The verse simply points out that He who created man out of nothing is surely capable of recreating him after his death:

> Does man think that he will be left aimless?
> Was he not a drop of sperm being emitted?
> Then he became a lump (of foetus), then (He) created and fashioned (it).
> Then He made of him the two sexes, the male and female.
> Is not He (who does so) able to bring the dead to life?[8]

On the Byzantine Victory:

Shortly before the *Hijrah* (620 C.E.) the Persians defeated the Byzantines and drove them out of Palestine. The Muslims at Makkah grieved at the defeat of the Christians (people with scripture) while the pagan Arabs for their part rejoiced openly at the victory of the Persians. At this point the following verses were revealed, both predicting the imminent victory of the Byzantines *(ar-Rūm)* over their foes and giving good tidings to the Muslims at Makkah:

> *Alif Lām Mīm*
> The Byzantines have been defeated
> In the nearer land; and they, after their defeat, will be victorious
> Within a few years, with Allah's command (both) before (the incident) and after (it); and in that day shall the believers rejoice
> In Allah's victory (imparted unto them). He makes victorious whom He wills, and He is Exalted in Might, the most Merciful.
> (It is) the promise of Allah. Never does Allah fail in His

> promise but most people do not know.
> They know only the outer appearance of things in this life,
> but of the Hereafter they are heedless.[9]

The prophecy in these verses was fulfilled in less than ten years when Heraclius defeated the Persians in 627 C.E.

On Some Natural Phenomena:

The first set of verses quoted below deal with the psychological condition of the unbelievers. It compares this condition with a deep ocean, and the layers of darkness in its remote depths. The second set mentions rain and clouds, describing the latter as mountains – a miraculously novel description which can only be realistically appreciated by one who has travelled by air. It must be borne in mind that Muḥammad, *ṣallā Allāhu 'alayhi wa sallam,* never saw either the sea or the ocean.

> Or (the state of unbelievers) is like the layers of darkness in a vast deep ocean. Overwhelmed by waves on top, of which are (dark) clouds. Depths of darkness, some of which are over the others. If he (the unbeliever) put out his hand, he can hardly see it. For he whom Allah has not given any light, has no light.[10]

What is interesting in the above Qur'ānic verse is the possible allusion to the fact, discovered quite recently, that there are actually internal waves in the depth of the ocean. The Qur'ānic text at issue refers to the ocean as consisting of layers of waves. The unbelievers are groping, lost – overwhelmed by these layers of darkness.

> Do you not see that Allah disperses clouds, then joins them together, then makes them into a heap, (so that) you see rain coming forth from their midst. And He sends down from the sky mountain masses (of clouds) wherein is hail. He strikes with it whom He pleases, and turns it away from whom He pleases. The vivid flash of His lightning well-nigh blinds the sight.[11]

More Natural Phenomena:

The following verses actually compel the mind to think in terms of the relatively novel notion of the roundness of the Earth:

> He created the heavens and the earth in truth. He makes the night follow the day (in a revolutionary movement); and the day follow the night (in a revolutionary movement) and He has constrained the sun and the moon (to obey His law) each running on (in a prescribed course) for a term appointed; surely He is the Exalted in Might, the oft-Forgiving.[12]

From the brief quotations and remarks above, we may note that (i) these ideas contained in the foregoing Qur'ānic verses could not possibly have been imparted to Muḥammad, *ṣallā Allāhu 'alayhi wa sallam,* by his social environment, since the people of Arabia at the turn of the sixth century C.E. were in general unlettered; (ii) Muḥammad, *ṣallā Allāhu 'alayhi wa sallam,* himself was a complete unlettered who could neither read nor write. This is attested both by the unchallenged account of the Qur'ān and the universal agreement of all the sources; (iii) the validity and authenticity of the Qur'ān do not depend on the confirmation of modern science or any of its human exponents. What is human is, *ipso facto,* fallible while the Qur'ān is infallible and eternal. Thus even if the foregoing remarks are invalidated, that does not detract from the beauty and rare force of this Divine Book. A reader of the original text in Arabic immediately experiences this beauty, power and grandeur without resorting to the use of rational analysis. Nevertheless, the novel information imparted by the foregoing sample of the Qur'ānic texts which, incidentally, could be multiplied indefinitely, compel the modern reader to understand them in terms of modern notions which they seem to express so naturally and with such perfect ease. The content and rare stylistic beauty of this Book combine to produce in a thoughtful reader an overwhelming sense of wonder and adoration.

The foregoing is the crux of Ibn Khaldūn's ideas on the question of prophecy and revelation. His criteria for genuine Prophets set a rather high standard, which may not be achieved by some of the acknowledged Prophets of ancient cultures and nations. After impartial study of the circumstances in which Muḥammad, *ṣallā*

Allāhu 'alayhi wa sallam, proclaimed his mission it will have to be admitted that he easily and clearly satisfies these conditions. In other words, his mission could only be the fulfilment of the Divine will and purpose insofar as they have been revealed to him by God Himself.

We shall now proceed to give a precise, factual description of the circumstances in which Muḥammad, *ṣallā Allāhu 'alayhi wa sallam,* was told that he was the chosen Prophet of God and that his task consisted in reading and reciting the praises of his Lord, fulfilling His will and commandments and in calling the Arabs and mankind as a whole to acknowledge and recognize God's will and design, accepting and complying with that will and thereby achieving peace and prosperity both in this world and in the Hereafter.

The First Revelation

It was a night of Ramaḍān, in the year 610 C.E. The future Prophet of Islam was keeping his vigil and meditation among the peaks of Mount Ḥirā'. Ramaḍān was drawing to its close, and that night was one of the last ten nights of the month. Muḥammad, *ṣallā Allāhu 'alayhi wa sallam,* must have dozed off after a prolonged period of meditation and prayer, when suddenly an event of immeasurable magnitude and significance took place. The doors of heaven were flung wide open and in that instant contact between the Earth and its humble contents and the Heavens and its mighty Lord was established. Every single object of nature must have been mysteriously influenced; and every atom of those remote and silent peaks and declivities of Mount Ḥirā' must have been animated and irradiated by the sudden illumination. The hills of the valley of Makkah became suddenly alive with the sounds of the heavenly coming, and the Divine presence. The light was focused forcefully and intensely on that cave of Destiny. The nodding, fatigued and exhausted Muḥammad, *ṣallā Allāhu 'alayhi wa sallam,* was seized by the luminous focus of power and light. His human nature was momentarily transformed into a new prophetic nature that could be integrated with the spiritual medium of the Mover, and thus would be able to receive the new supernatural perceptions and revelations. The seizure was so powerful that his noble person showed signs of utter exhaustion. No better description can be given of what actually happened on that 'Night of Power and Destiny'[13] than Muḥammad's own account of what he experienced.

'The Prophet, *ṣallā Allāhu 'alayhi wa sallam,* went out to Mount Ḥirā',' relates Ibn Isḥāq, 'until it was the night in which God honoured him by (investing him with) His Message, and therewith bestowed His mercy on His servant. Gabriel, peace be upon him, came to him with the command of God, highly exalted is He. Said the Prophet, *ṣallā Allāhu 'alayhi wa sallam*:

> The Angel Gabriel came to me, as I was sleeping, with a sheet of cloth in which there was a book.
> "Read," he said.
> "I do not read," I replied.
> He forcefully squeezed me with it (i.e. the cloth) till I thought it was death. He then released me and said,
> "Read!"
> "I do not read," I said (again). He again took and squeezed me vehemently with it (i.e. the cloth) until I thought it was death, and said,
> "Read!"
> "What shall I read?" I said.
> He squeezed me with it (i.e. the cloth) until I thought it was death, then he released me, and said,
> "Read!"
> "What shall I read?" I said. I did not say that except to spare myself lest he repeated what he had done to me.
> But he said:
> "Read in the name of your Lord who created – created man out of a clot (of congealed blood).
> Read and your Lord is the Most Bounteous,
> Who taught by the pen,
> Taught man what he knew not".'[14]

The experience of Ḥirā' was also reported by Az-Zuhrī, on the authority of 'Urwah ibn az-Zubair who was reporting the words of 'Ā'ishah. This version is recorded in Imām Aḥmad's *Musnad* and is also found in *aṣ-Ṣaḥīḥayn* of Muslim and al-Bukhārī. This particular version of az-Zuhrī differs from that of Ibn Hishām quoted above in that instead of the ambiguous phrase *Mā aqra'* which could either mean (i) 'I am not a reader' (i.e. do not know how to read), or (ii) 'What shall I read?', we find the phrase *mā ana biqāri'* which means straightforwardly, 'I do not know how to read' or 'I am not a reader'. Az-Zuhrī's version also differs from that of Ibn Hishām by omitting the phrase *Mādhā aqra'?* which means *'What shall I read?'* The Prophet Muḥammad, *ṣallā Allāhu 'alayhi wa sallam,* was indeed a complete unlettered – as all our sources testify.

Our sources unanimously agree that the five verses of *Sūrah al-'Alaq* were the very first Divine revelation ever received by the Prophet. The rest of the *sūrah* was clearly revealed at a later stage, since it consists of verses that refer to such topics as Prayer *(aṣ-Ṣalāh)* which was prescribed much later and the existence of opposition to the new religion.

The Prophet Muḥammad, *ṣallā Allāhu 'alayhi wa sallam,* narrates that he repeated these five verses after the Angel Gabriel who then left him and disappeared. The Prophet then immediately woke from his slumber but the words of his visitant were as vivid in his memory as if they were engraved thereon. He hurried from the cave towards his home. When he was among the hilltops he heard a voice in the sky calling, 'O Muḥammad, you are the Messenger of Allah, and I am Gabriel.' Muḥammad, *ṣallā Allāhu 'alayhi wa sallam,* lifted his eyes to the direction of the voice; it was Gabriel in the image of a man. The Prophet narrates that he became transfixed in his position, moving neither forward nor backward. And wherever he directed his vision, there was Gabriel. He stood there for a considerable time while Khadījah's messengers searched for him everywhere without success. The heavenly visitant then left him and he hurried to Khadījah. Sitting close by her side and leaning against her, he breathlessly told her the unusual experience which he had just undergone and poured out his agonizing fears and doubts which he felt as a result: was it possible that he was possessed by *jinn* (demons) or was he a wretched victim of illusions and hallucinations? Or was he perhaps having his first experiments with soothsaying? Or was he perhaps becoming a visionary poet? – but there was nothing that he detested or abhorred more than soothsaying and poetry. Such were the terrible fears and misgivings which engulfed him after his first experience of Divine inspiration. Khadījah however assured and comforted him, saying:

> Nay, son of my uncle, do not say that. For Allah will surely not let such a thing happen to you, for you keep good relations with your relatives, speak the truth, keep trusts for their owners and your manners are noble.[15]

Having uttered those comforting words, Khadījah hurried to the house of a Christian cousin of hers called Waraqah ibn Nawfal. He was recognized as a scholar, well-versed in the lores of Christianity. Waraqah eagerly questioned her about Muḥammad's physical condition during the moments in which he claimed to have received the Divine visitant. When she described them, he shouted with excitement: '*Quddūsun! Quddūsun*! (Holy! Holy!) and by Him, in whose hands is the life of Waraqah, if you have told me the truth, O Khadījah, he (Muḥammad, *ṣallā Allāhu 'alayhi wa sallam*) has been visited by *an-Nāmūs al-Akbar* (the Archangel Gabriel) who used to visit Moses, and verily he is the Prophet of this people. Say to him: Be brave and resolute.'[16]

Khadījah hurried back with the reassuring message and the glad tidings of Waraqah which Muḥammad, *ṣallā Allāhu 'alayhi wa sallam,* received with great relief. Soon afterwards, after the exhausting and extraordinary experience in Ḥirā', he allowed himself a long and much-needed slumber.

Thus was Muḥammad, *ṣallā Allāhu 'alayhi wa sallam* – who had suffered the loss of both parents, had endured the hardships of poverty throughout his childhood and early youth, and who was denied any formal education, growing up as an unlettered – chosen and ordained as the Messenger of God. The Qur'ān in language that shines with extraordinary beauty and elegance, recounts these favours that God bestowed on him:

> Did He not find you an orphan and gave you refuge?
> Did He not find you astray, and guided you aright?
> Did He not find you poor and enriched you?[17]

Deceit, Sincere Illusion, or Authentic Inspiration?

Let us now consider, in a rather critical manner, the nature of the unusual experience which Muḥammad, *ṣallā Allāhu 'alayhi wa sallam,* went through and which he proclaimed was nothing less than the commencement, in his person, of Divine inspiration.

Two possibilities suggest themselves:

(a) either he was merely simulating the role of an inspired Prophet for some reason or other, or (b) he was sincerely convinced that he had been the agent and recipient of Divine inspiration. Of the second possibility, we can further choose between two alternatives: (i) that he was sincerely convinced but that this conviction, notwithstanding its sincerity, was the result of a grand and subtle illusion to which Muḥammad, *ṣallā Allāhu ʻalayhi wa sallam,* was both victim and captive; (ii) that not only was he profoundly convinced of being a subject of Divine Inspiration but, furthermore, that this conviction was objectively true and in no way illusory.

If possibility (a) is to be tenable, we must be able without ignoring or doing violence to the specific factual details of the experience which Muḥammad, *ṣallā Allāhu ʻalayhi wa sallam,* went through, to pronounce it a fabrication invented as part of a dangerous game of deceit. Furthermore, we must be able to spell out what the aims and objects of that deceit were since no such deception could be conceived, let alone practised, without some prior objectives. What could these objectives possibly be? They could only be: (1) wealth, (2) honour and social status, or (3) political power. Conclusive evidence is not hard to find in the behaviour and career of Muḥammad, *ṣallā Allāhu ʻalayhi wa sallam,* both before and after his call to prophethood which easily refutes the alleged existence of any of those three objectives. As for money, it was shunned by him at the peak of his power. He definitely preferred simple, austere living to luxury and extravagance. When he died, he left no money or property to his heirs. As for personal honour and social status, the facts of his life and family background even before prophethood show that he was not wanting in these. He was a prominent member of the Banū Hāshim family which enjoyed political power and social prestige for generations before him. He led an honest and distinguished life which earned him the title *al-Amīn* (the Trustworthy) by common consent. The wealthy and prestigious Khadījah regarded him as more than an equal, as is attested by her eager efforts to win his heart. His acceptance as an arbiter in the dispute over the placing of the Black Stone in the newly-constructed Kaʻbah, was a decisive indication of the high esteem with which he was regarded by his fellow tribesmen. Thus Muḥammad, *ṣallā Allāhu 'alayhi wa sallam,* was lacking neither in honour and noble birth, nor was he lacking in social standing and prestige. True, he was rather poor before he was married to Khadījah. But this too was altered by his marriage to this rich and generous lady. Immediately after their marriage Khadījah gave the future Prophet of Islam a free hand in managing and developing her wealth. To the high trust which he earned by demonstrating complete honesty and competence on the commercial journey to Syria was now added the strongest ties of love and marriage. Moreover, it must be remembered that poverty was not a permanent feature of Banū Hashim. Rather, it was an interlude brought about by the excessive generosity of Hāshim himself and his celebrated son, 'Abd al-Muṭṭalib, the grandfather of Muḥammad, *ṣallā Allāhu 'alayhi wa sallam.* These two were particularly noted for their lavish spending to ensure the comfort and well-being of the pilgrims to the Ka'bah.

More telling proof of the disinterestedness of Muḥammad, *ṣallā Allāhu 'alayhi wa sallam,* is provided by an authentic incident in which the leaders of the Quraysh sought, in vain, to buy his silence by worldly inducements. They offered him money, political leadership and social prestige. But he firmly and promptly declined, reiterating anew in the strongest of terms, the aims and objectives of his Divine mission. He could take no course except the one ordained for him by his Lord – to warn and to give good tidings. The Quraysh leaders said to him:

> O Muḥammad, we have been delegated to talk to you, for by Allah, we know not of any Arab before you who has caused more distress and mishap amongst his people such as you have caused. You have reviled our forefathers, criticized our religion and gods, undermined our judgements and caused dissent in our community. So if you have innovated this new talk because you want money, we will collect money for you until you become the richest amongst us all. If you desire honour amongst us, we will make you a master over us. And if you want royal authority, we will make you a king over us.[18]

Muḥammad's reply to these offers, made by the deputies of the Quraysh chiefs, was both frank and straightforward:

> I do not have any of the things you have accused me of. And I have not brought what I have brought to you desiring your money or honour amongst you, or royal authority over you. But God has sent me to you as a Messenger, and revealed to me a Book, and commanded me to be an announcer of good tidings (to you in case you believe) and a warner (to you in case you disbelieve).[19]

Having demonstrated the absence of any of the alleged objectives, whose existence is necessary in order to sustain the belief that Muḥammad, *ṣallā Allāhu 'alayhi wa sallam,* played a game of deception in connection with his experience on Ḥirā', we have *a fortiori* established the impossibility of such a game. For, it is irrational to postulate a game of deception with no objectives whatsoever. Thus we ought, with good justification, to uphold a strong belief in the sincerity of Muḥammad, *ṣallā Allāhu 'alayhi wa sallam,* concerning his claims about his experience on Ḥirā'. We have already quoted Sir William Muir's remark that 'it is strongly corroborative of Muḥammad's sincerity that the earliest converts to Islam were not only of upright character but his own bosom friends and people of his household.' Sir William's remark represents a sound insight into human relations, because even if someone could deceive outsiders concerning his aims and character, it is very difficult, indeed next to impossible, for him to do so with respect to his intimates and members of his family for an unlimited time.

Having refuted the possibility of deceit, and established a good case for the sincerity of Muḥammad, *ṣallā Allāhu 'alayhi wa sallam,* in his statement of what happened to him on Ḥirā', we must proceed to the next step; for our task would not be complete until we further demonstrate that Muḥammad's sincerity was in fact genuine and not a product of illusions and hallucinations. This is not a simple undertaking, because it amounts to the verification and substantiation of the entire body of doctrines, rites and practices of Islam. However, we can make the following statement in this connection: the strongest proof of the sincerity of Muḥammad's belief in the Divine nature of his mission is the Qur'ān itself. Its noble language and teachings, its lofty moral directives, the exciting and revealing accounts which it conveys of former nations, their Prophets and anti-Prophets, their fates and their fortunes, the information which it contains about things to come and the fore-knowledge which it conveys about a diversity of subjects – these are some of the considerations which make it extremely unrealistic to pronounce it a product and an outcome of a hallucinatory and illusory vision. The purity, sweetness, rare force and beauty which characterize the Qur'ānic language and literary style, render any suggestion to the effect that it is human-made untenable. Moreover, the world-view which the Qur'ān incorporates, its elaborateness and internal consistency and cohesion, and the broad vision of life and human possibilities which it envisages compel reason and common sense to reject the suggestion that it is the mutterings and utterances of a visionary caught in the spell of hallucinatory dreams. Irrespective of whether he would eventually adopt the Qur'ānic interpretation of Reality or reject it, an intelligent, unbiased reader cannot but admit that this interpretation, with its pure monotheism and its consummate integration of all aspects of life and reality is the result of a superior, authentic spiritual experience of the highest order.

The Significance of the Ḥirā' Experience

The events that took place on Ḥirā' and their effect on the historical development of Arabia and the entire world, represent the focal point of the eternal message of Islam, and constitute the cornerstone of the conceptual framework of the Muslim's world-view. We therefore ask the question: What is the real significance of this experience from the Muslim's point of view? Following are given the thoughtful reflections of the well-known Muslim thinker and scholar, Sayyid Quṭb, who wrote an eight-volume commentary on the Qur'ān. He writes:

> What is the real significance of the incident that took place at that moment?
>
> Its real significance is that God, the Mighty, Omnipotent, Obliging and Magnificent God, Possessor of every sovereignty and authority, graciously decided to concern Himself with this humble creature called Man, lodged in a small, remote corner of the Universe, only faintly visible, called Earth. He honoured and exalted this (humble) species

of creature by choosing one of them as the recipient of His wisdom, the depository of His words and the agent of His Destiny which He, Highly Exalted, wills for this creature.

This (the foregoing remark) represents an enormous reality, enormous beyond any estimation. Aspects of this reality will be uncovered if man strives to conceive, as much as he can, the reality and essence of the Absolute, Eternal, Everlasting God. Against the background of this (Divine) reality, man ought to conceive of the reality of his servitude, its limited, temporary and destructible nature. Having done this, he would feel and experience the impact of this Divine care upon this human creature. He would taste the sweetness of this feeling, and his response (to his Lord) would be one of obedience, gratitude, pleasure and rejoicing, as he conceives of the words of God being echoed by all parts of the Cosmos. Those words find their descending way to Man, in his little out-of-the-way corner (the earth), little in relation to the vast and glorious dimensions of this Universe.

What is the significance of this Incident (on Ḥirā')?

Its significance on the part of Allah, may He be Exalted, is that He is manifested as possessor of the most wide Munificence, and the most far-reaching Mercy – the most Generous, the most Loving and the most Compassionate One. He overflows with His bounty and mercy without cause or reason except that overflowing with munificence and liberality are some of His Essential, Divine properties.

Its significance for Man, is that Allah, Exalted be He, has honoured him to a degree which he could neither (properly) conceive, nor duly offer thanks for. He could not adequately thank (Allah) for it, even if he spent his entire life prostrating – for what a great blessing it is that Allah was aware of him, has turned to him, has linked him unto Himself, and has chosen of his (human) genus a Messenger unto whom He reveals His words. He has chosen his habitat, the Earth, to become the descending place of those words, which have been echoed by the entire reaches of the wide cosmos, in the most humble and pious manner.

As to the consequences of this stupendous incident, they began to take effect from the very first moment. They began to change the course of history, by re-directing the course of the human conscience. The direction in which Man would look for obtaining his concepts, values and measures has now been defined. It is *not* the earth, nor is it man's desires. But it is heaven and Divine Revelation.

And since that moment, the inhabitants of this Earth who have grasped its real significance, have lived in the direct care and protection of Allah. They lived, looking up directly to Allah for (guidance) in all their affairs, small and big, feeling and moving under the seeing eye of Allah. They lived expecting the hand of Allah to be extended to them, to guide them on the path (of life) step by step (in His way). It keeps them back from wrong-doing and guides them towards goodness and righteousness . . . Every night they sleep with the expectation that God would talk to them about what is in their souls and minds, that He would reveal to them a ruling in their (daily) problems, saying do this and do not do that.

Therefore, it was really a strange and wonderful period, the period of the twenty-three years that followed (the incident on Ḥirā' and until the death of the Prophet), and in which this direct link between heaven and mankind was continued – a period whose true conception cannot be grasped except by those who actually lived through it, experienced it and witnessed its beginning and end. For those who actually tasted the sweetness of this noble link and who felt the hand of God actually guiding their footsteps . . . when they compare where they had been (before the Revelation on Ḥirā') and where they had been transferred (after Ḥirā') it was really a great distance, a distance immeasurable by any earthly standards. It was the distance that existed between the *Jāhiliyyah* (the pre-Islamic age of Ignorance) and Islam, the distance between heathenism and belief in and worship of the One, True God.

On the authority of Anas (may God be pleased with him), Abū Bakr (the first Caliph of the Prophet) said to 'Umar (the second Caliph): 'Let us go to Umm Ayman (the Prophet's childhood nurse) to visit her as the Prophet used to do'. When they came to her, she cried. They asked, 'What makes you cry, Umm Ayman? Don't you know that what God has prepared in the Hereafter for the Messenger of Allah (may God bless and preserve him) is better for him? She replied, 'O yes, I do know that what is with God for the Messenger of Allah (may God bless and preserve him) is better; but I cry because the *Wahy* (the Divine Inspiration) from Heaven has ceased'. That (remark of Umm Ayman) moved them to passionate sobs, and they started to cry with her . . .[20]

The Second Coming of the Archangel Gabriel

In the preceding pages we have discussed at length the question of the genuineness of the prophetic mission and the nature and significance of the Ḥirā' experience from the Muslim point of view. But the torrent of great events which had been released by the new dynamic call to 'Read' soon engulfed the Makkan valley and eventually the entire Arabian peninsula. Now we resume our narrative of the chequered career of the Prophet. The reader will remember that we left Muḥammad, *ṣallā Allāhu 'alayhi wa sallam,* in a deep and restful sleep, after being assured and encouraged by the noble Khadījah.

When he woke up, Khadījah told him more about her visit to Waraqah, the learned Christian scholar of the Scriptures. Eventually, Muḥammad, *ṣallā Allāhu 'alayhi wa sallam,* went to meet him. Although Waraqah's words to him further confirmed and strengthened Khadījah's assurance that his visitant on Ḥirā' was Divine, and not diabolical, yet they stirred in his mind and soul an anxiety, depression and sadness of a new type. Waraqah said to him:

> 'It is the *nāmūs* which God sent down to Moses. Would that I were a young man during your prophetic career! Would that I might be alive when your people expel you!' God's messenger asked, 'Will they expel me?' and he replied, 'Yes, no man has ever brought anything like what you have brought, without meeting hostility. If I see your day, I shall give you strong help.'[21]

Both Bukhārī and Muslim[22] narrate that Waraqah died soon

afterwards, and an Intermission or *Fatrah* in revelation followed. In the above tradition, the impression is conveyed that this Intermission followed closely the revelation of *Sūrah al-'Alaq* on Ḥirā', the very commencement of Divine inspiration. Al-Maqrīzī (Taqiuddīn Aḥmad ibn 'Alī) concurs with this version of Bukhārī and Muslim:

> The verified (statement on the question of the chronological order of Qur'ānic revelation) is that when Gabriel (may peace be upon him) came to him (the Prophet) in the cave on Ḥirā', and bid him 'Read! in the name of thy Lord, who created', and he (the Prophet) returned to Khadījah, he remained for some time seeing nothing (i.e. seeing no visions). Inspiration discontinued with respect to him. He grieved because of this, and repeatedly went out to the peaks of the hills (of Makkah) seeking to throw himself down (and thus commit suicide) in longing for what he had experienced the first time (on Ḥirā') of the sweetness of visualizing the agent of Divine Revelation to him. It is said that the duration of the intermission of Revelation was nearly two years, and it is (also) said that it was two years and a half. In the commentary of 'Abdullāh Ibn 'Abbās (on the Qur'ān), the period is maintained to be forty days. In al-Zaqqāq's book on the Meanings of the Qur'ān, it is said to be fifteen days; and in the Commentary of Muqātil, it is given as three days. This (last version) was favoured by some (commentators) who said it is more fitting to his (Muḥammad's) status in (the esteem) of his Lord.[23]

There is no unanimity existing with respect to the duration of the intermission. Also no unanimity exists with respect to the date of its occurrence whether it was immediately after Ḥirā' or whether it took place a good while after it. Also, consensus is lacking on the religious significance of the *Fatrah* or intermission: does it perhaps mark the transition from *Nubuwwah* (Prophethood) to *Risālah* (Apostleship), or was it merely an important stage in the psychic preparation of Muḥammad, *ṣallā Allāhu 'alayhi wa sallam,* for the difficult task which lay ahead, and of which he received early warning from Waraqah. A fourth consideration, which is related to the intermission in Divine revelation, and with respect to which there is also a great deal of uncertainty, is the question concerning the identity of the verses or *sūrahs* of the Qur'ān which were revealed to Muḥammad, *ṣallā Allāhu ʻalayhi wa sallam,* after *Sūrah al-ʻAlaq* on Ḥirā'. This last question will be considered below.

Concerning the duration of the intermission it may be reasonable to maintain that it was in fact short, lasting only a matter of days or a few months, not exceeding six at the most. The traditions reported by Muslim and Bukhārī quoted above and the account by al-Maqrīzī tend to suggest a short intermission and this is also supported by Ibn Saʻd who estimates it to be a matter of days as is implicit in the following account:

> After revelation came to him (Muḥammad) at Ḥirā', he waited for some days in which he did not see Gabriel. He then grieved tremendously, and so great was his grief that he frequented Thubayr and Ḥirā' (two mountains overlooking Makkah) with the intention of throwing himself down from their peaks. One day, as he was wandering amongst these mountains, he heard a voice from heaven. The Messenger of God stopped, greatly shaken by the voice. Then he looked up, and it was Gabriel sitting on a throne between the ground and the sky. 'O Muḥammad! Thou art the Messenger of God, and I am Gabriel.'[24]

With regard to the date at which the intermission took place, Bukhārī and Muslim, Ibn Saʻd and al-Maqrīzi all seem to support the view that it actually took place not long after the first Divine revelation at Ḥirā'. Ibn Hishām, however, implies a different view by stating that after the first five verses of *Sūrah al-ʻAlaq,* Divine revelation continued for some time. The inference is that a number of *sūrahs* were actually revealed before the intermission.

Concerning the religious significance of the intermission it is reasonable, as far as the textual evidence goes, to suppose that the intermission did perhaps mark a transition from *Nubuwwah* (Prophethood), which does not incorporate an obligation to convey any message to others, and *Risālah* (Apostleship) which does incorporate such an obligation. The initial verses of *Sūrah al-ʻAlaq* (or *Iqra'*) does not in fact entail any command or obligation to preach publicly. However, according to the sources quoted above, the second appearance of Gabriel carried the assurance to Muḥammad, *ṣallā Allāhu 'alayhi wa sallam,* that he was the 'Messenger of God'. As we shall see presently, this line of interpretation also maintains that the second set of verses revealed to Muḥammad, *ṣallā Allāhu 'alayhi wa sallam,* was the opening verses of *Sūrah al-Muddaththir* as follows:

> O thou wrapped up (in a mantle).
> Arise and warn!
> And thy Lord, do thou magnify!
> And thy raiment do thou purify!
> And abomination shun!
> Give not, thinking to gain greater.
> And be patient unto thy Lord.[25]

The second verse ('Arise and Warn') does indeed clearly entail some kind of *Risālah* (Message or Apostleship). Whether this *Risālah* was, in fact, a private or public ministry, and the distinction needs to be made, is not our concern at this stage.

Chronological Order of the First Qur'ānic Revelations

Let us now examine the evidence concerning the verses to be revealed after *Sūrah al-'Alaq.* It is related in *Ṣaḥīḥ Muslim* that the Messenger of Allah was heard talking about the intermission in the Divine inspiration as follows:

> As I walked (amongst the hills of Makkah)[26] I heard a voice coming from heaven. I turned my eyes towards the sky to find that it was the angel who came to me on Ḥirā', sitting on a throne between the earth and the sky. I fell to the ground (out of apprehension and fear). Then I went home and I said to my family '*Zammilūnī*' (cover me) and *Dath-thirūnī* (and wrap me up).

Shortly afterwards God revealed to him (the verses of *Sūrah al-Muddaththir* quoted above).

Al-Bukhārī narrates this same *ḥadīth* of Jābir Ibn 'Abdullāh al-Anṣārī, but from a different chain of narrators. The interesting thing about al-Bukhārī's version is the insistence of Jābir himself that *Sūrah al-Muddaththir* (not *Sūrah al-'Alaq*) was the first Qur'ānic revelation ever. We must take Jābir's insistence on the chronological priority of *al-Muddaththir* as referring to the fact that it was indeed the first verses to be revealed after the intermission. This is the only meaningful sense in which this insistence can be understood, in the face of the overwhelming evidence to the effect that *al-'Alaq* was actually the very first Divine revelation.

According to the compilers of *Muṣḥaf al-'Uthmānī* (the Transcription of the Qur'ān sanctioned by 'Uthmān the third Caliph) it is *Sūrah al-Qalam* (the Pen) and not *Sūrah al-Muddaththir* (the Wrapped One) that was second in the order of the Qur'ānic Revelation. According to this transcription *Sūrah al-Muzzammil* also preceded *Sūrah al-Muddaththir*. As a matter of fact, there are independent traditions which support the view that *Sūrah al-Muzzammil* was in fact revealed before *al-Muddaththir*. It must be borne in mind that when we talk about the chronological order of these verses, we are only referring to their opening verses, and not to the *sūrahs* in their entirety. The opening verses (1–9) of *Sūrah al-Muzzammil* read as follows:

> O thou folded in garments.
> Keep vigil the nightlong, save a little.
> A half thereof or abate a little thereof.
> Or add (a little) thereto – and recite the Qur'ān in measured tones.
> For soon We shall send down to thee a weighty Message.
> Truly, the rising by night is more exhausting (to the body), but more suitable for speech (of recitation and prayer).
> For truly, there is for thee by day prolonged occupation.
> So remember the name of thy Lord and devote thyself with a complete devotion.
> Lord of the East and the West; there is no God save Him; so choose thou Him alone for thy defender.[27]

That *Sūrah al-Muzzammil* (the Covered) might have been revealed before that of *al-Muddaththir* does seem a valid hypothesis. As a matter of fact, its contents which emphasize (a) night vigil, the exhausting of the body to make way for the domination of the soul, (b) the clear and unambiguous reference to the impending 'weighty Message' which was soon to be revealed, and (c) the appellation of Muḥammad, *ṣallā Allāhu 'alayhi wa sallam,* in the opening verse, as wrapped, enveloped or covered, indicate its proximity to *Sūrah al-Muddaththir.* In view of the existence of two separate Traditions, one of which asserts that it is *Sūrah al-Muddaththir* (verses 1–5) which was revealed immediately after the intermission, while the other says it is *Sūrah al-Muzzammil* (verses 1–9), I find it difficult to dismiss a belief to the effect that it is likely that both *al-Muzzammil* and *al-Muddaththir* were revealed in one and the same visit of Gabriel, namely the one that marked the end of the intermission, and in so doing marked the end of the un-apostolic prophethood and the beginning of the Messenger-Prophet stage of his career. And in view of the different nature of the contents of the opening verses of the two *sūrahs,* the fact that those of *Sūrah al-Muddaththir* consist of a direct commandment to 'Rise and Warn' while those of *Sūrah al-Muzzammil* only commend night vigil and merely refer to the impending weighty Message in anticipation of which Muḥammad, *ṣallā Allāhu 'alayhi wa sallam,* was being alerted and directed to undertake strenuous spiritual training and preparation, I am rather inclined to think that the compilers of the 'Uthmānī Transcription of the Qur'ān were right in their view that the opening verses of *Sūrah al-Muzzammil,* in fact, preceded those of *Sūrah al-Muddaththir.*

However, I beg, with utter humility, to differ with the learned compilers of the 'Uthmānī Transcriptions in their view that *Sūrah al-Qalam* (the Pen) had preceded both *al-Muzzammil* and *al-Muddaththir,* and that it came second only to *Sūrah al-'Alaq.* As Sayyid Quṭb has pointed out,[28] *Sūrah al-Qalam* could not have been revealed before the order to 'Rise and Warn' of *Sūrah al-Muddaththir. Sūrah al-Qalam* contains verses that clearly refer to a period which belongs to the later stage of public ministry in the career of Muḥammad, *ṣallā Allāhu 'alayhi wa sallam,* namely:

> Therefore obey not thou the rejectors. Who desire that thou would compromise, that they may compromise.
> Neither obey thou any insignificant Oath-monger;
> Slanderer, going out with calumnies;
> (Habitual) hinderer of the good; transgressor, deeply steeped in sin;
> Coarse (and thick) therewithal, ignoble.
> It is because he is possessed of wealth and children,

That, when Our revelations are recited unto him,
Saith: mere fables of the men of old.
We shall brand him on the nose.[29]

Verses (10–16) above are said to be a reference to and a condemnation of the meanness of al-Walīd Ibn al-Mughīrah (al-Mukhzūmī), one of the chief opponents of the Prophet after he staged the public period of his mission. As such, they clearly refer to a much later period in his Prophetic career. Even the opening verses of *Sūrah al-Qalam,* with decidedly polemical overtones, deal with incidents that must belong to the public period of the mission.

A noble and moving *sūrah* that was revealed to Muḥammad, *ṣallā Allāhu 'alayhi wa sallam,* immediately after the end of the Intermission of Divine Revelation is *Sūrah aḍ-Ḍuḥā* (The Morning Hours) part of which we have already quoted.

By the morning hours,
And by the night when it becomes still.
Your Lord has not forsaken you, nor is He displeased with you.
And surely, the Hereafter will be better for you than the Former.
And soon will your Lord give you that you may be well-pleased.
Did He not find you an orphan, and sheltered (you)?
And found you astray, and guided (you aright)?
And found you poor, and enriched (you)?
Therefore, the orphan oppress not,
And the beggar repulse not,
And the bounty of your Lord, proclaim![30]

This *sūrah* is said to have been revealed in answer to the doubts and anguish of Muḥammad, *ṣallā Allāhu 'alayhi wa sallam,* when Gabriel, agent of Divine Revelation, ceased to visit him abruptly after the opening visit on Ḥirā'. Khadījah, too, worried a great deal and in her anguish gave vent at one time to her doubts and said to Muḥammad, *ṣallā Allāhu 'alayhi wa sallam,* that perhaps his Lord was 'displeased with him' and therefore saw fit to abandon him. These doubts were silenced by this noble *sūrah* and the Prophet's family were duly solaced and comforted. This *sūrah* is an early Makkan one, and it could not have been revealed much later than the opening verses of *al-Muzzammil* and *al-Muddaththir.* The clear reference in it to the Intermission, firmly place it in close chronological proximity to these two great *sūrahs.*

Thus we may venture to put the chronological order of the early *sūrahs* as follows:

CHRONOLOGICAL ORDER OF QUR'ĀNIC REVELATION

According to the 'Uthmānī Transcription	*No.*	*According to our reading here*
Al-'Alaq	1	*Al-'Alaq*
Al-Qalam	2	*Al-Muzzammil* and *Al-Muddaththir*
Al-Muzzammil	3	*Al-Muzzammil* and *Al-Muddaththir*
Al-Muddaththir	4	*Aḍ-Ḍuḥā* (perhaps)

One final remark on the question of the chronological order of the Qur'ānic Revelation is that, according to many traditions, *Sūrah al-Muddaththir* is believed to be the second *sūrah* to be revealed after *Al-'Alaq*. Thus neither our arrangement nor that of the 'Uthmānī Transcription receives any consensus.

However we may order those early *sūrahs,* it is virtually certain that the great *sūrahs* of *al-Muzzammil* and *al-Muddaththir* were revealed very early after the Intermission in the Divine Revelation. And the clear, decisive message they convey to the Prophet, *ṣallā Allāhu 'alayhi wa sallam,* is remarkable. He was firmly commanded to 'Rise' not only during the day, which, he was informed, he would have to spend in prolonged endeavours and striving, but was also commanded to rise at night and observe vigil and devotion. He was ordered to 'Rise' and prepare himself for the 'weighty Message' that he was about to receive. And 'Rise' he indeed did – in all its possible aspects and dimensions, until he met his Lord, twenty-three years later. These twenty-three years he spent vigorously and relentlessly striving to comply with the noble and weighty order to 'Rise and Warn'. Sitting at the side of his bed as he was getting ready to depart from this life, Fāṭimah, the daughter whom he loved dearly, wept passionately and said, 'O what suffering my father is going through!' The Prophet Muḥammad, *ṣallā Allāhu 'alayhi wa sallam,* turned his tender, smiling eyes to her and said cheerfully, 'No suffering shall befall your father after this day!'

Now, we must undertake the task of keeping pace with Muḥammad, *ṣallā Allāhu 'alayhi wa sallam,* as he strove to comply with his Lord's order. His actions and sayings, movements and encounters and the chain of great events which profoundly shook the valley of Makkah were soon to be echoed throughout the entire Arabian peninsula and eventually the world at large. It was Divine revelation that both set the pace and guided Muḥammad's endeavours to comply with the noble Divine commandment. It assured him when he doubted, strengthened him when he stood alone against a hostile, rebellious Quraysh, and solaced and comforted him when he was disbelieved, vilified and even physically harmed. His was on the whole a truly chequered career, at Makkah and eventually at al-Madīnah, full of struggle, sorrow and suffering. But at the same time it was the fullest life a human being was capable of living through, with a great deal of personal enjoyment and satisfaction, for he was satisfied with his Lord and He with him – as is indeed attested to by *Sūrah aḍ-Ḍuḥā* quoted above.

Muḥammad's preparation to comply with the Divine command to 'Rise and Warn' started exactly where he was directed by the Qur'ān *(Sūrah al-Muzzammil)* to start: he started to keep vigil, worship, devotion and prayer, all night long, for the duration of a whole year. For this was the year in which night vigil was made obligatory for Muḥammad, *ṣallā Allāhu 'alayhi wa sallam,* and his Companions by the Qur'ān. Later on this obligation was waived and night vigil remained merely commendable. So, it must have been during the period in which night vigil was obligatory that the Prophet used to stand in prayer for such prolonged periods that his feet became swollen. 'Ā'ishah later asked the Prophet why he urged himself to such lengths in devotional exercises when God had forgiven all his sins, both earlier and later ones. To this the Prophet firmly answered, 'Should I not be a grateful servant?'

The reservoir of endurance, fortitude and psychical powers which he managed to store up during those preparatory, devotional exercises were to be put to good use in later times. Those were times of sustained effort, of prolonged struggle against the evil in society and striving to transform a primitive, illiterate and idolatrous human environment into one which was both willing to accept and ready to comply with the Divine design and purpose for Man.

Notes and References

1. Qur'ān, 42 *(Ash-Shūrā)*: 52.
2. Khadījah was actually the first to become a Muslim, according to the most widely accepted accounts.
3. Sir William Muir, *The Life of Muhammad,* p. 55.
4. Muḥammad 'Abduh, *Tafsīr al-Manār* (Arabic), Vol. II, p. 151.
5. *The Muqaddimah,* trans. by F. Rosenthal, Vol. I, pp. 184ff.
6. Qur'ān, 23 *(Al-Mu'minūn)*: 12–14.
7. Qur'ān, 75 *(Al-Qiyāmah)*: 3–4.
8. *Ibid.,* 36–40.
9. Qur'ān, 30 *(Ar-Rūm)*: 1–7. The prophecy in these verses was fulfilled in less than ten years when Heraclius defeated the Persians in 627 C.E.
10. Qur'ān, 24 *(An-Nūr)*: 40.
11. *Ibid.,* 43.
12. Qur'ān, 39 *(Az-Zumar)*: 5.
13. This is *Laylatu'l-Qadr* (the Night of Power and Destiny) referred to in the Qur'ān as that in which the first Revelations came. See the Qur'ān, Chapter 97.
14. Qur'ān, 96 *(Al-'Alaq)*: 1–5.
15. This last quotation is from Ibn Sa'd, p. 195. However, I have drawn mainly from Ibn Hishām for the general information on this period.
16. Ibn Hishām, p. 238.
17. Qur'ān, 93 *(Aḍ-Ḍuḥā)*: 6–7.
18. Ibn Hishām, Part I, p. 295.
19. *Ibid.,* p. 296.
20. Sayyid Quṭb, *Fī Ẓilāl al-Qur'ān,* Vol. 8, p. 198. (Quotation translated by author of the present study.)
21. This is narrated by both al-Bukhārī and Muslim in *Mishkāt al-Maṣābīḥ,* trans. by J. Robson, Ashraf, Lahore, Vol. IV, p. 1253.
22. *Ibid.*
23. Al-Maqrīzī, *Imtā' al-Asmā',* Vol. I, p. 14.
24. Ibn Sa'd, p. 196.
25. Qur'ān, 74 *(Al-Muddaththir)*: 1–6.
26. Parentheses added.
27. Qur'ān, 73 *(Al-Muzzammil)*: 1–9.
28. Sayyid Quṭb, *Fī Ẓilāl al-Qur'ān.*
29. Qur'ān, 68 *(Al-Qalam)*: 10–16.
30. Qur'ān, 93 *(Aḍ-Ḍuḥā)*: 1–11.

CHAPTER 5

The Call to Islam in Makkah – The Private Stage

When Muḥammad, *ṣallā Allāhu 'alayhi wa sallam,* received his Lord's command to 'Rise and Warn', he complied with unique vigour, energy and dedication. His endeavours in this respect fall into two major stages: a private stage lasting approximately for the first three years of his mission and a public stage which lasted until he finally left Makkah on his famous *Hijrah* (or migration) to Yathrib.

The private stage was characterized by secrecy in conveying the new message, care and caution in selecting certain individuals to be approached and invited to Islam, and a general absence of harsh or direct polemics against the idolaters and the heathenistic ways of their *Jāhiliyyah*. At first, the Prophet only conveyed the Divine stirrings of his heart and soul to members of his household and to Abū Bakr who was a loyal and life-long companion. With the help of Abū Bakr, he set out to contact secretly such men and women as he deemed likely to champion the cause of Islam.

The public stage was inaugurated by the revelation of the Qur'ānic verses:

> And warn your nearest kinsmen.
> And lower your wing (in kindness) to whoever follow you from the believers.
> And if they disobey you, say:
> I am free (of responsibility) of what you do.[1]

These verses were revealed roughly three years after the initial revelation at Ḥirā'. A second revelation which is also associated with the transition from private to public stage is as follows:

> Therefore proclaim (openly) that which you are commanded, and turn away from the polytheists.
> Verily, We are sufficient unto you against the scoffers,
> Who take with Allah another God but they will come to know.[2]

On the authority of al-Bukhārī,[3] Ibn 'Abbās narrates that when 'And warn your nearest kinsmen' was revealed to the Prophet he ascended the hill of aṣ-Ṣafā, near the Ka'bah, and proclaimed loudly: 'O Banī Fihr, O Banī 'Adī,' calling the clans of the Quraysh till they all gathered. Those who could not come themselves sent agents. Among those present was Abū Lahab,[4] an uncle of the Prophet. The Prophet then addressed them:

'Tell me, if I were to inform you that some cavalry in the valley were about to attack you, would you believe me?' They said, 'Yes, we have not experienced anything except truthfulness from you.' He then said, 'I am a warner to you before a severe chastisement.' Abū Lahab shouted angrily, *'Tabban Lak'* – Damn you – the rest of the day. 'Is it for this that you have gathered us?'

The Prophet was dismayed by the disappointing response. But his Lord comforted him. Abū Lahab was strongly condemned, together with his wife,[5] in terms that eloquently underlined the futility of their design against the grand purpose of God for the Muslims:

> Damned be the efforts (lit. hands) of Abū Lahab and may he be damned.
> His wealth and his gain will not avail him.
> He will be burnt in a fire of blazing flame.
> And his wife, the wood-carrier[6] (will suffer the same fate).
> Upon her neck (will be) a rope of palm-fibre.[7]

The foregoing tradition from al-Bukhārī clearly underlines the beginning of the public stage in which the Prophet openly invited the Quraysh to acknowledge and worship no god(s) beside Allah, the Omnipotent, Omniscient and the One True God.

Although the response of the Quraysh was not warm and was even hostile in the case of Abū Lahab, nevertheless they did not show bitterness or hatred towards the Prophet. However, open enmity was shown towards him as soon as he began to criticize and condemn their heathen ways. It was particularly hard for them to bear his condemnation of their much-venerated ancestors who died in unbelief before the advent of Islam. He bluntly declared that since they had not heeded God's guidance as it had been revealed in the previous scriptures, they would be consigned to the fire of hell. This confrontation did not take place until some time after the first public address at aṣ-Ṣafā. Before that, when he used to pass by, they would point at him and say, 'There goes the child of 'Abd al-Muṭṭalib who is spoken to from Heaven,' or 'The child of 'Abd al-Muṭṭalib is spoken to from Heaven.' But then his open and firm criticism of their traditional legacy displeased them and deeply offended their strong 'national' pride. Moreover his call to the belief in One God threatened to undermine their privileged status in pre-Islamic Arabia. There were other considerations that promoted their hostility to him which will be dealt with later. For the time being, let us look more closely into the great moments and the decisive events that were slowly, yet inexorably, taking place in the ancient valley of Makkah. Those events were to change the course of human history and leave their permanent stamp on posterity.

The Early Doctrines of Islam

We begin by attempting an outline of the essentials of the Prophet's call to his people. It was in reaction to this call that the great events at issue took shape.

The Call to Monotheism
Lā ilāha illā Allāh (There is no god but Allah)

This is the famous Muslim call to pure monotheism addressed in the first instance to the idolaters of the Quraysh in Makkah. It may appear strange that such innocent words should evoke the hatred, enmity and the bloody violence of the Quraysh against the Prophet of Islam, *ṣallā Allāhu 'alayhi wa sallam,* and the small, peaceful band of dedicated people who followed him. But the reflective mind can readily perceive the tremendous threat that these four words constitute for any society, today no less than fourteen centuries ago, that does not acknowledge the total and absolute dominion of Allah, and His complete sovereignty over all things natural as well as human. To the idolaters of Makkah, conscious of their privileged status as custodians of the grand sanctuary of heathen Arabia, the revolutionary import of this doctrine could not have been more direct. It did not merely offend and undermine their pride in the heathenistic legacy of their ancestors but also struck at the very foundation of their economic, political and social institutions. Vested interests were naturally among the first to be awakened to the new threat. In particular, the aristocrats of the Quraysh felt that their economic and social eminence was gravely imperilled by the general egalitarian orientation of the new religion. This orientation is actually implicit in the cardinal monotheistic doctrine *'Lā ilāha illā Allāh'*.

'Lā ilāha illā Allāh' is perhaps the most oft-repeated sentence in any language that has ever been spoken. Not only is it called out, proclaimed and chanted through loudspeakers from the tens of thousands of minarets throughout the Muslim world five times a day, being repeated three times in each call, but it is the formula that is never absent from the utterances of a pious Muslim. Hardly do a couple of hours pass by without his uttering it. He utters it when praying, and when he is wondering or exclaiming. If he is excited, or if his sense of beauty is greatly stimulated, then these words readily find their way to his lips. If he is in great fear or if his anger and disapproval is being greatly aroused these words will be the spontaneous utterance in which he seeks refuge and comfort.

The dictum consists of two phrases – one a negation, the other an affirmation – that fit together in perfect harmony.

The phrase *'Lā ilāha'* (i.e. there is no other god) negates the existence of any false gods and condemns false worship. The word *Ilāh* could refer to any matter, person or concept which is undeservedly taken or adopted as an object of adoration or worship, irrespective of whether this is done out of excessive love or excessive fear. The heathen Arabs had a great variety of such *ilāhs* (gods), from idols of various shapes, sizes and locations to demons, divines and soothsayers. Ancestors were also given quasi-divine status. They were greatly venerated and their legacy was much esteemed and cherished. The enjoyment of women, wine, poetry and horses held sway over their minds and tastes. Inasmuch as they clung to them and persisted in satisfying them at any cost, they constituted values that approached the status of adored and worshipped objects. Thus we can talk of these hedonistic desires and pleasures as some sort of quasi-gods. Their material wealth and their social status were also highly valued as were their chivalrous war heroes, their clanish or tribal chiefs and their distinguished 'national' poets. The tribal *'Aṣabiyyah* (or solidarity) was something that was much cherished and adhered to. Fear of poverty and of shame due to permissive, licentious sexual behaviour of female members of the family plunged them into the murderous, genocidal practice of burying their little girls alive. It is true that this practice was not widespread amongst the Quraysh, but nevertheless it was one of the most outrageous evils of Makkan society.

The idolatrous Makkans were thus labouring under a gross intellectual and spiritual bondage due to their wilful subjugation to a whole host of false and superstitious gods. Those gods consisted of real or imaginary personalities or personified objects or things. In worshipping them the idolaters forfeited their dignity and liberty. And what is more humiliating, degrading and enslaving to the human intellect and dignity than to subjugate oneself to another human being, no matter how powerful, or to worship and adore a finite, perishable and inanimate object?

Those false gods had to be exposed for what they were, and their worship discouraged and condemned. This was accomplished in one decisive stroke by the negative thesis – *lā ilāha* – of the great and powerful monotheistic formulation – *lā ilāha illā Allāh*.

The Affirmation

The two words *illā Allāh* assert the necessary existence of the One, True Deity who is the Ultimate source of all power and all efficacy. He is Allah, 'the Lord and creator of all that there is'. The whole dictum *Lā ilāha illā Allāh* (There is no god except Allah) is an elegant statement of the pure and radiant doctrine of monotheism which today only Islam can offer to a rebellious, sacrilegious and indulgent humanity. The old Scriptures before Islam as revealed to Muhammad, *ṣallā Allāhu 'alayhi wa sallam,* scriptures in which monotheism was also decreed and expounded, were subjected in the course of time to processes by which they were confounded, interpolated or utterly distorted. Adherents of those Scriptures whom the Prophet encountered in Arabia were no longer worshippers of the One, True God.

'As the Muslims saw it, the Prophets of Israel were all right, and Jesus was God's last and a great prophet before His final messenger Muḥammad, *ṣallā Allāhu 'alayhi wa sallam.* The Muslim's quarrel was not with the Prophet Jesus but with the Christian Church, which had captivated *Rūm*[8] by capitulating to pagan Greek polytheism and idolatry. From this shameful betrayal of the revelation of the One True God, Islam had retrieved the pure religion of Abraham. Between the Christian polytheists on the one side and the Hindu polytheists on the other there again shone the light of monotheism.'[9]

In one of the very early chapters *(sūrahs)* of the Qur'ān, the positive thesis of our monotheistic dictum is propounded as follows:

> Say: He is Allāh, the One (and Only).
> Allah, the eternally Besought of all!
> He begotteth not, nor is He begotten
> And there is none comparable unto Him.[10]

Al-Wāḥidī gives two versions concerning the circumstances in which the above *sūrah* was revealed:

(a) A group of Jews of Yathrib came to the Prophet and requested him to describe his God to them. They wanted to compare this description with that given in the Torah. In particular, they wanted to know: Of what substance is He made? Of what genus? Does He eat or drink? From whom did He inherit the Universe, and to whom was He going to bequeath it? Then, God revealed *Sūrah al-Ikhlāṣ* (Purity of Faith) emphasizing the absolute purity and incomparability of Allah's being.

(b) The second version asserts that it was a group of Quraysh idolators who enquired about Allah's alleged lineage.

They said to him, 'State your Lord's lineage to us.' Then Allah revealed *Sūrah al-Ikhlāṣ* unto the Prophet.

I am more inclined to adopt the second version, for the

following reasons: (i) The Quraysh, and the Arabs for that matter, are famous for their obsession with questions of lineage; (ii) *Sūrah al-Ikhlāṣ* is one of the very early Makkan *sūrahs,* and it is unlikely that the Prophet had such contacts with the Jews of Yathrib at that early stage; (iii) I am not aware that the Jews of Yathrib entertained such silly beliefs about God, for they are generally believed to have been monotheistic in one sense or other. However, if the first version is the true one, then we must either revise our information concerning the contents of those Jews' religious beliefs or we must suppose that the group who put those questions to the Prophet if they were sincere, belonged to a fringe sect among them that was not representative of their mainstream. Be that as it may, the *sūrah* establishes the absolute unity and uniqueness of God, and that He is the Living, Caring, Ever-Lasting God who is alone worthy of being worshipped. He alone is capable of causing ill or good to befall man; and whatever He wills to be his fate and destiny, nothing can prevent it. True, these notions will strike awe and fear in the heart of man and incline him towards the worship of the One, True God, totally liberating his mind and soul from the worship of a multitude of false, impotent and perishable gods. It will free him from the false and oppressing values of accumulating wealth, seeking social status at any cost and by any means, and prevent him from becoming enslaved to lowly, earth-bound, animal instincts. Even death itself becomes of little consequence since it represents, according to the Qur'ān, no more than the passing away from the temporary life of trouble, strife and imperfections to the everlasting Hereafter which is either one of torment or eternal bliss. The liberating influences of these concepts upon those who believe in them is unmistakable. The Muslim emissary of Caliph 'Umar, al-Muthannā ibn al-Ḥārith, to the Persian Emperor could not contain himself when he saw the elaborate lavishness of the Persian court, the manifestations of the might and tyranny of Chosroes, contrasted with the humiliation and servitude of his subjects and courtiers. In the famous reply to the Emperor's enquiry about the nature of his mission in Persia, al-Muthannā, in addition to giving a precise indication of that mission, condemned those manifestations in the strongest terms:

'We have come (to Persia) to transform people from the state of worshipping other human beings, to that of worshipping God, the One and Mighty' – a brief, yet eloquent statement. Besides giving a concise and pristine statement of the liberating content of the essential mission of Islam, it scored a direct hit on the tyrannical ways of the Persian monarch. Tyranny and dictatorial rule had been rampant among the Persians for many decades. The Persian people themselves evidently venerated this kind of rule, perhaps due to their tendency to exhibit excessive esteem and veneration of their rulers; having been a sedentary, civilized nation for many centuries, when emerging Islam made its rapid advances in their direction, the citizens of Persia had already been reduced to a status of semi-slavery, losing almost all their fundamental liberties and human rights. Citizens of nations that have been sedentarized for long epochs tend to lose their liberties much more readily than do members of bedouin tribes and nations. We have already quoted Ibn Khaldūn's insights on this issue. Al-Muthannā ibn al-Ḥārith was therefore not only stating his religious convictions, but perhaps also exhibiting the bedouin's characteristic disdain for oppressive domination and tyrannical rule.

The negative and positive theses of the Islamic dictum of monotheism – *lā ilāha illā Allāh* – are beautifully synthesized, giving rise to a unique blend of freedom and resignation. Firm conviction in it produces complete freedom from degrading servitude to all types of false deities on the one hand, and on the other hand, absolute resignation and submission to the One, True Deity – Allah. The name of the religion itself reflects the unique blend here referred to.

Islam means 'peace through submission to God'. The roots from which the word 'Islam' is derived means both 'submission' and 'peace and security'. The word 'Islam' thus connotes 'the religion in which peace, security and reconciliation are attained through total submission and resignation to the commandments of God'. It is the shortest and only way to the attainment of these ideals both in this life and the Hereafter. The Muslim's characteristic refusal to worship any false deities stems from a total submission to Allah, Who is Reality, Truth, Beauty, Justice, Mercy and Munificence. The earliest Qur'ānic revelations in Makkah are redolent of such virtues and concepts. Let us examine some of these early revelations to see how these concepts were conveyed and how they were applicable to the human environment they were to transform. The short *sūrah al-'Aṣr* (Time) will illustrate this:

> Consider Time!
> Verily man is in loss,
> Except those who believe and do righteous deeds, and exhort one another to truth and exhort one another to patience and endurance.[11]

This pithy but profound statement declares, in clear and unequivocal language, that all norms, values and endeavours are in vain and amount to naught in the Qur'ānic scale of values, excepting only those decreed by the (Qur'ānic) Faith such as righteous deeds, acts of enjoining Truth, patience and endurance. The connection between upholding religious Faith, enjoining Truth and the injunction to the Believers to exhort each other to patience and endurance is of course quite plain: whoever upholds Faith sincerely and sticks to Truth and righteousness is sure to incur the wrath and enmity of evil and unscrupulous powers. Conflict with these powers and ruthless struggle against them is inevitable and inescapable. Moreover, the emphasis which this noble revelation places upon spiritual and benevolent values is an indirect condemnation of all non-Qur'ānic polytheistic values. Our use of the term 'polytheism' is a very broad one in the present context, for we count among the false gods such behaviour and practices as excessive adoration of persons, chiefs and ancestors, of money, power, social status. Whoever gives any of these things an absolute value even if he intellectually believes in the One, True God, is a polytheist in this sense.

Social and Economic Implications

A more direct condemnation of the capitalistic values of the money-conscious mercantile society of Makkah is couched in the following, beautiful Qur'ānic verses which were also among the earliest to be revealed:

> Woe unto every slanderer, traducer.
> Who accumulates wealth and counts it.
> He thinks that his wealth will render him immortal.
> Nay, he will indeed be flung into the Destroyer.
> And what will convey to you what the Destroyer is?

(It is) the Fire of Allah, kindled.
That which mounts up to the hearts (of men),
Verily it is closed in on them.
In columns outstretched.[12]

The callousness and the hypocrisy of the Quraysh aristocracy towards the socially and economically deprived received the following stern denunciation:

Have you seen him who gives the lie to religion?
That is he who repels the orphan,
And urges not the feeding of the needy.
So woe to those who pray,
Those who are heedless of their prayer,
Those who pretend (by praying),
And refuse to supply (even) a food utensil.[13]

Al-Wāḥidī[14] maintains that those noble verses were revealed in connection with Abū Sufyān ibn Ḥarb. He was giving a big feast and he slaughtered two sheep. An orphan came into the house and asked for some food. Abū Sufyān was greatly annoyed by the intrusion, swore at the orphan and hit him on the head with a stick.

The aristocratic values of the high finance society of Makkah, similarly, received strong denunciation:

Rivalry in worldly increase has distracted you.
Until you visit the graves (as dead bodies).
But nay, you soon shall know (the dire consequence of this practice).
And indeed again, you soon shall know (them),
Nay, were you to know with certainty,
(You will know that) you shall certainly behold the Hell-fire.
Again, you shall behold it with certainty of vision.
Then you shall be questioned on that day concerning the luxury.[15]

Eschatological Reckoning

The foregoing Qur'ānic doctrines propounded in these early *sūrahs* are projected against the backdrop of the cardinal notion of all revealed religion. This is the notion of eschatological reckoning. Whoever belies the Prophet and turns away from the worship of the One, True God, ignoring his commandments, shall be held to account on the day of Resurrection. On the other hand, the obedient worshippers shall be rewarded with the eternal bliss of Paradise. This eschatological reckoning shall take place before Allah, the Master of that awful day of Judgement:

> In the Name of Allah, Most Gracious, Most Merciful:
> Praise be to Allah, the Lord of the Worlds.
> The Most Gracious, Most Merciful.
> Master of the day of Judgement.
> You (alone) we worship, and You (alone) we ask for help.
> Show us the Straight Path.
> The Path of those whom You have favoured.
> Not (the path) of those who receive Your anger nor those who have gone astray.[16]

The foregoing Divine Revelation is the oft-repeated opening *sūrah* of the Qur'ān. It is called *al-Fātiḥah* (the Opening) or *'Fātiḥat al-Kitāb'* (the Opening 'Chapter' of the Book). It is also called *'Ummu'l-Qur'ān'* (the Essence of the Qur'ān). A practising Muslim recites these verses at least twenty times a day, making them the most oft-repeated expressions of any language. It is solemnly recited in concluding business transactions, in marriage ceremonies and in making pledges or concluding alliances. Although it is an early Makkan *sūrah,* the exact date of its revelation is uncertain. But since no prayer is complete or correct without its recitation, it must have been revealed quite early as prayers were held secretly by the early Muslims in Makkah. We know that after the conversion of 'Umar in the fifth year of Muḥammad's mission, these prayers were held in public, much to the anger and resentment of the Quraysh. So *al-Fātiḥah* must have been revealed some time before the fifth year of the Prophetic mission, probably even before the launching of the public phase of the call to Islam in Makkah. Three years after the beginning of his mission, Muḥammad, *ṣallā Allāhu 'alayhi wa sallam,* was 'caught' by his uncle Abū Ṭālib offering prayer with 'Alī – his youthful cousin – on a slope of the Makkan valley, long before the injunction to preach publicly was revealed. Thus *al-Fātiḥah* is probably a very early Makkan *sūrah.*

Chronological Order of the Early *Sūrahs*

For the benefit of the reader who seeks a more comprehensive survey of the religious and intellectual drive of the new monotheistic movement which Muḥammad, *ṣallā Allāhu ʻalayhi wa sallam,* had so vigorously launched, given below is a provisional list of the early Makkan *sūrahs* arranged in chronological order. By early Makkan *sūrahs* is meant those *sūrahs* which were revealed in Makkah mainly in the first three years of the inception of Islam, i.e. during the private stage and the earliest portions of the public stage of Muḥammad's, *ṣallā Allāhu ʻalayhi wa sallam,* mission. They range over the period which extends from the event on Ḥirā' and the beginning of Divine revelation to the banishment of Banū Hāshim and Banū al-Muṭṭalib into the Shiʻb of Abū Ṭālib (see pp. 177–9). By that time, Islam had taken a fairly recognizable shape, and a considerable portion of its fundamental doctrines were revealed. The following list of those *sūrahs* in chronological order is based, entirely, on the order found in ʻUthmānic transcript of the Qur'ān. While the position of some *sūrahs* in this list can be questioned mainly on account of evidence about the dating of events which allegedly attended the revelation of the *sūrahs,* the ordering of the ʻUthmānic transcription is the most complete ordering of the *sūrahs* of the Qur'ān that we possess.

CHRONOLOGICAL ORDER OF THE EARLY *SŪRAHS*

Group I

No. of Sūrah	*Name*	*Remarks*
111	*al-Masad* (Palm Fibre)	EM (Early Makkan). It marks the beginning of the public stage.
81	*at-Takwīr* (The Folding Up)	EM. After the public stage.
87	*al-Aʻlā* (The Most High)	EM. The contents of this *sūrah* seem more suitable for the private stage.
92	*al-Layl* (The Night)	EM. Possibly even VEM (Very Early Makkan).

89	*al-Fajr* (The Dawn)	EM. Possibly quite early VEM.
93	*aḍ-Ḍuḥā* (The Early Morning)	EM, most likely VEM, since it followed the *Fatrah* (or gap) in Revelation.
94	*al-Inshirāḥ* (Comfort *or* Solace)	EM. Probably revealed following the resumption of Divine revelations after the *Fatrah*, and thus it is VEM.
103	*al-'Aṣr* (Time)	VEM.

Group II

108	*al-Kawthar* (Abundance)	EM, 'al-Kauthar' is taken by some commentators as naming a river in Paradise. For others it signifies '*Abundance* of the heavenly Fountain of unbounded grace and knowledge, mercy and goodness, truth and wisdom.'
102	*at-Takāthur* (Rivalry in Worldly Increase)	VEM.
107	*al-Mā'ūn* (Food Utensil)	EM.
109	*al-Kāfirūn* (The Disbelievers)	EM. The idolaters were pressing the Prophet for a compromise.
105	*al-Fīl* (The Elephant)	EM, probably VEM.

Group III

112	*al-Ikhlāṣ* (Purity (of Faith))	EM, but definitely after the beginning of the public stage.
53	*an-Najm* (The Star)	EM, definitely after the beginning of the public stage;

		actually, many commentators think it was revealed in the fifth or sixth year of the mission, i.e. after the first *Hijrah* to Abyssinia.
80	*'Abasa* (He Frowned)	EM, but definitely after the public stage, since it had been revealed at a meeting between the Prophet and a deputation of the Quraysh Chiefs.
97	*al-Qadr* (Power *or* Destiny)	EM.
91	*ash-Shams* (The Sun)	EM, probably VEM; it contains some fundamental concepts.
85	*al-Burūj* (The Star Mansion)	EM, the *sūrah* refers to the persecution of Christians of Yemen (Najrān) by a Jewish ruler.
95	*at-Tīn* (Fig)	EM, probably VEM; it contains fundamental concepts.
106	*Quraysh*	EM, probably VEM.
101	*al-Qāri'ah* (The Striker *or* The Calamity)	EM.
75	*al-Qiyāmah* (The Rising of the Dead)	EM.
104	*al-Humazah* (The Slanderers)	EM, probably belongs to the public stage since it contains a reference to the enemy of Islam, al-Walīd ibn al-Mughīrah.

The First Converts to Islam

According to Ibn Isḥāq,[17] Khadījah was the first convert to the new religion. ʻAlī ibn Abī Ṭālib, merely ten years of age, a cousin of the Prophet and a member of his household, was the next convert. The Prophet undertook to support ʻAlī because of the limited resources of Abū Ṭālib and the large size of his family. The third convert was Zayd ibn Ḥārithah, a Syrian Arab who was formerly a slave of Khadījah who placed him at the service of Muḥammad after their marriage. A very strong affection developed between the Prophet and his attendant. Zayd's father, who spent years searching for him, finally came to the house of the Prophet. He offered a large sum of money as ransom for Zayd. The Prophet who became attached to Zayd, as a father is attached to his son, found it extremely hard to part with him. He told Zayd's father that if Zayd wanted to leave him, he could so without a ransom; but if he decided to stay, then he could. Zayd preferred to stay. Realizing that he was being derided by his father for having preferred slavery to freedom, the Prophet declared him a free man and adopted him as a son. For some time thereafter he used to be known in Makkah as Zayd ibn Muḥammad.

Next, Abū Bakr[18] (from Taym of the Quraysh) who was Muḥammad's close friend and confidant for many years was converted to Islam. Concerning the conversion of Abū Bakr, the Prophet is reported to have said, 'I have not invited anyone to Islam who did not exhibit some hesitation except Abū Bakr. He alone did not tarry when I mentioned it to him, nor did he hesitate.' His conversion was both a source of succour to and a victory for the new faith. He was the first convert outside the immediate household of the Prophet. Only two years younger than the Prophet who was forty years old, he was thus the first male adult to become a Muslim. Being a successful merchant, he possessed considerable wealth and was very popular in Makkah owing to his fine and easy manners, and his thorough knowledge of the lineage of the Quraysh. Ibn Isḥāq mentions that people regularly sought his advice because of his knowledge, his experience and his good counsel. He was the first of the important personalities of Makkah to become a Muslim.

Stories which designate Abū Bakr as the first male convert to Islam do not necessarily conflict with Ibn Isḥāq's version stated above. Whereas 'Alī was a mere child of ten, Zayd's social status as a former slave and a servant may account for the hesitancy of some authorities to accord to him the rank of the second 'freeman' to become a Muslim – thus leaving the status of the first 'freeman' to be fulfilled by Abū Bakr.

Although a number of the first converts were former slaves and persons with a lowly social status, a fuller survey of their number and social conditions leaves no doubt that the Quraysh among them were a clear majority. The assumption that the early converts consisted primarily of slaves, social outcasts and downtrodden persons is both erroneous and biased. It is biased in that it is based on one of the verbal attacks of the idolaters on the Prophet that *'he was only followed by the meanest'*. While this charge does contain a grain of truth – some of the Prophet's early followers were of modest social standing – it constituted part of the heathenistic propaganda against the new, revolutionary religion. The terms used in the denunciation of the Prophet reflected the fear and uneasiness of the Makkan vested interests as they viewed the anti-capitalistic doctrine of the new religion. They felt that their entrenched aristocratic privileges and interests were genuinely threatened by the Qur'ānic exhortations against their practice of hoarding, the pride they took in such practices and their reluctance to permit any degree of 'sharing' of resources with the poor, the needy and the underprivileged.

Let us now attempt a more comprehensive survey of the very first converts to the new, monotheistic religion of Islam. The significance of including the clan and the tribe from which they came may become apparent in the discussion which follows the table.

THE FIRST CONVERTS[19]

No.	*Name*	*Tribe*	*Clan*	*Remarks*
1	Khadījah bint Khuwaylid	Quraysh	Asad	The Prophet's wife.
2	'Alī b. Abī Ṭālib	Quraysh	Hāshim	The Prophet's cousin.
3	Zayd b. Ḥārithah	Confed. of Quraysh	Hāshim	The Prophet's attendant.

4	Abū Bakr b. Abī Quḥāfah	Quraysh	Taym	The first grown-up convert. The first Caliph after the Prophet.
5	‘Uthmān b. ‘Affān	Quraysh	‘Abd Shams	The Prophet’s son-in-law and the third Caliph.
6	Az-Zubayr b. al-‘Awwām	Asad		When converted az-Zubayr was only twelve years old.
7	‘Abd ar-Raḥmān b. ‘Awf	Quraysh	Zuhrah	Migrated both to Abyssinia and to Yathrib, witnessed all the major wars of Islam, and was one of the ten persons assured of entering Paradise.
8	Sa‘d b. Abī Waqqāṣ	Quraysh	Zuhrah	One of the ten persons assured of entering Paradise by the Prophet; a staunch fighter in the cause of Islam; the first Muslim to shed blood in that cause; successfully defended the Prophet when he was badly wounded at Uḥud. He was very young when converted – about seventeen years old. He was the commander of the famous campaigns against the Persians.

9	Ṭalḥah b. 'Ubaydullāh	Quraysh	Taym	Ṭalḥah was also quite young; when converted he conducted trade with Syria.

The last five converts became Muslims through the endeavours of Abū Bakr. Ṭalḥah belonged to the same clan as Abū Bakr (Taym).

10	Abū 'Ubaydah b. al-Jarrāḥ	Quraysh	Fihr	The philosopher-general who commanded campaigns against the Byzantines of Syria and Palestine. One of the ten assured of a place in Paradise. Designated 'The Custodian of the Nation' by the Prophet.
11	Abū Salamah 'Abdullāh b. 'Abd al-Asad	Quraysh	Makhzūm also Banū Hāshim from maternal side	He took part in the two *Hijrahs* to Abyssinia and Yathrib. Died of a wound which he received at Badr.
12	al-Arqam b. al-Arqam	Quraysh	Makhzūm	This was the owner of the celebrated 'House of al-Arqam ibn al-Arqam', in which the Prophet and his early followers used to meet secretly in Makkah, throughout the private stage of his mission.

13	‘Uthmān b. Maẓ‘ūn	Quraysh	Jumaḥ	‘Uthmān is famous for his asceticism in pre-Islamic days. Most of all he disliked wine, the drinking of which he condemned categorically.[20]
14	Qudāmah b. Maẓ‘ūn	Quraysh	Jumaḥ	
15	‘Abdullāh b. Maz‘ūn	Quraysh	Jumaḥ	
16	‘Ubaydah b. al-Ḥārith	Quraysh	Muṭṭalib	Probably, he was the oldest Muslim, being ten years senior to the Prophet, who used to hold him in special esteem no doubt due to his age and his kinship to him. He was converted before the Prophet entered the House of al-Arqam
17	Sa‘īd b. Zayd	Quraysh	‘Adī	Husband of Fāṭimah bint al-Khaṭṭāb, sister of ‘Umar the second Caliph. It was inside the house of Sa‘īd and Fāṭimah that ‘Umar became converted to the new religion.
18	Fāṭimah bint al-Khaṭṭāb	Quraysh		Brave and steadfast sister of ‘Umar, whose confrontation with him caused the

				Truth to shine in his consciousness.
19	Asmā' bint Abī Bakr	Quraysh	Taym	The celebrated daughter of Abū Bakr who helped the Prophet escape the pursuing Quraysh during his *Hijrah* to Yathrib. Also mother of the famous 'Abdullāh b. az-Zubayr.
20	'Ā'ishah bint Abī Bakr	Quraysh	Taym	She was a mere child when she professed Islam with the rest of her family.
21	Khabbāb b. al-Aratt	Quraysh	Confederate of Zuhrah	But his actual clan was either Tamīm or Khuzā'ah.
22	'Umayr b. Abī Waqqāṣ	Quraysh		Brothers of Sa'd b. Abī Waqqāṣ, champion of the Battle of Qādisiyyah (Persia); 'Umayr died a martyr at Badr, at the age of sixteen. The Prophet sought to stop him going to the battle but he sobbed and the Prophet yielded to his desire.
23	'Amir b. Abī Waqqāṣ	Quraysh	Zuhrah	
24	'Abdullāh b. Mas'ūd	Hudhayl	Zuhrah	The Prophet assured him of Paradise; a confederate of 'Uqbah b. Abī

			Mu'ayṭ (Makhzūm); witnessed Badr, killed and beheaded the already wounded Abū Jahl – arch-enemy of Islam. He also witnessed al-Ḥudaybiyyah.

We omit the names of six converts, who were not associated with any significant public events in the subsequent history of Islam. All six were from the Quraysh.

25	'Abdullāh b. Jaḥsh	Khuzaymah	Confederates of 'Abd Shams. From their maternal side, they are Banū Hāshim; their mother was Umaymah bint 'Abd al-Muṭṭalib, the Prophet's aunt. They took part in the migrations to Abyssinia and Yathrib. Their brother 'Ubaydullāh was one of the seekers after the religion of Ibrāhīm. First he became a Muslim and migrated to Abyssinia, but later on, he became a Christian and died in Abyssinia. The Prophet married his widow, Umm Ḥabībah bint Abī
26	Abū Aḥmad b. Jaḥsh	Khuzaymah	

				Sufyān. ‘Abdullāh fought at Badr, and died a martyr at Uḥud.
27	Ja‘far b. Abī Ṭālib	Quraysh	Hāshim	Ja‘far was ten years the senior of ‘Alī; he was most similar to the Prophet both in manners and appearance. His return from Abyssinia coincided with the conquest of Khaybar on which occasion the Prophet said, ‘I do not know whether I am more delighted with the return of Ja‘far or with the conquest of Khaybar.’
28	Asmā’ bint ‘Umays (Ja‘far’s wife)	Khath‘am		Ja‘far commanded an army to Mu’tah at the southern confines of Syria, and there he fell a martyr.
29	Ḥāṭib b. al-Ḥārith	Quraysh	Jumaḥ	He migrated to Abyssinia and died there.
30	Fāṭimah bint al-Mujallal	Quraysh	Jumaḥ	Ḥāṭib’s wife, whilst in Abyssinia; two children were born to them.
31	Ḥaṭṭāb b. al-Ḥārith	Quraysh	Jumaḥ	He migrated to Abyssinia and died there or on the way back.

32	Fukayhah bint Yasār	Quraysh	Jumaḥ	Ḥaṭṭāb's wife.
33	Ma'mar b. al-Ḥārith	Quraysh	Jumaḥ	Ḥāṭib's and Ḥaṭṭāb's brother, migrated with them to Abyssinia, was converted before the Prophet's use of the House of Arqam b. al-Arqam, witnessed Badr and Uḥud, and died during the rule of Caliph 'Umar.
34	al-Sā'ib b. 'Uthmān b. Maẓ'ūn	Quraysh	Jumaḥ	Son of 'Uthmān b. Maẓ'ūn; migrated with his father and two uncles to Abyssinia, fell a martyr at Yamāmah fighting against the apostates during the rule of Abū Bakr, the first Caliph.
35	al-Muṭṭalib b. Azhar	Quraysh	Zuhrah	Migrated with his two brothers 'Abdur Raḥmān and Ṭulayb to Abyssinia, accompanied by his wife Ramlah. She bore him a child there, whom they called 'Abdullāh.
36	Ramlah bint Abī 'Awf	Quraysh	Sahm	Wife of al-Muṭṭalib b. Azhar.
37	An-Naḥḥām	Quraysh	'Adī	His full name is Nu'aym b.

'Abdullāh, nicknamed an-Naḥḥām by the Prophet who assured him of Paradise; was converted just prior to the conversion of 'Umar (only ten persons were converted between his conversion and that of 'Umar). He was one of the foremost chiefs of 'Adī (the clan of 'Umar) famous for his charitable practice of looking after widows and orphans. His clan, for this reason delayed his migration, apparently by persuasion. Finally, he fell a martyr on the battlefield during the administration of Abū Bakr, in the Battle of Ajnādayn, according to some, whilst others maintain that he died in the Battle of Yarmūk.

The foregoing converts are almost exclusively from the Quraysh. True, the majority did not belong to the leading clans of 'Abd Shams and Makhzūm, though of course the Prophet and his family were from Banū Hāshim, the traditional house of leadership in the Quraysh.

38	‘Āmir b. Fuhayrah	Non-Arab		‘Āmir was a bondman of Abū Bakr, formerly he was a bondman of Asad. He became a Muslim before the entry of the Prophet to the House of al-Arqam. He was killed at Bi’r Ma‘ūnah by the traitor ‘Āmir b. aṭ-Ṭufayl. He was selected by the Prophet as a scholar and a teacher of the Qur’ān to the tribe of ‘Āmir. ‘Āmir b. Fuhayrah was black and probably so was his mother, Fuhayrah.
39	Khālid b. Sa‘īd b. al-‘Aṣ	Quraysh	‘Abd Shams	Khālid b. Sa‘īd was probably one of the earliest to adopt Islam; some even maintain that he was next only to Abū Bakr in embracing the new religion. He migrated with his wife Āminah to Abyssinia. Their son Sa‘īd and daughter Umm Khālid were born there. His brother ‘Umar b. Sa‘īd was also an immigrant with him.

				Khālid's family was powerful and so was his clan 'Abd Shams.
40	Umaynah bint Khalaf	Khuzā'ah		Khālid b. Sa'īd's wife.
41	Ḥāṭib b. 'Amr	Quraysh	'Āmir	The first to arrive in Abyssinia, took part in both migrations to it, and was converted before the Prophet's entry into the House of al-Arqam.
42	Abū Ḥudhayfah	Quraysh	'Abd Shams	Ibn Hishām mentions that Abū Ḥudhayfah's name was Mahsham, but as-Suhaylī maintains that his real name was Qays.
43	Wāqid b. 'Abdullāh	Con-federate	'Adī	An early convert, became a Muslim before the Prophet's entry into the House of al-Arqam. Witnessed Badr, Uḥud, and took part in most campaigns. He died in the Caliphate of 'Umar.
44	Khālid b. al-Bukayr			He witnessed Badr, and fell a martyr in ar-Rajī' engagement at the age of thirty-five.

45	ʻĀmir b. al-Bukayr		He also witnessed Badr, and fell a martyr in the Battle of al-Yamāmah.
46	ʻĀqil b. Bukayr	Confederates of ʻAdī	He died a martyr at Badr at the age of thirty-four. He was the first convert at Dār al-Arqam. Before his conversion, he was called Ghāfil (unaware); when he became a Muslim the Prophet renamed him ʻĀqil (mature or rational).
47	Iyās b. Bukayr		He witnessed Badr, Uḥud, al-Khandaq and most of the other campaigns.
48	ʻAmmār b. Yāsir	Confederate of Makhzūm	ʻAmmār's father Yāsir was an Arab from Yemen. But he married a bondwoman of Makhzūm, so ʻAmmār was born in bondage, according to the social rules regulating this affair, but he was later made a freeman by his master Abū Ḥudhayfah b. al-Mughīrah.

49	Ṣuhayb b. Sinān	Non-Arab Con- federate of Taym		Persian by birth, but grew up among the Byzantines; was converted to Islam the same day as 'Ammār b. Yāsir. He died at al-Madīnah at the age of seventy-three; some maintain that he died at the age of ninety. He was commended by the Prophet and described as 'Preceding ar-Rūm' (the Byzantines) (to Islam).
50	Yāsir al-'Ansī	(Yemen)	Muzhij	'Ammār's father; came from Yemen to Makkah with his two brothers, al-Ḥārith and Mālik, in search of a lost brother of theirs; al-Ḥārith and Mālik returned, whilst Yāsir settled in Makkah and married Sumayyah bint al-Khayyāṭ.
51	Sumayyah bint al-Khayyāṭ	Non-Arab		'Ammār's mother. First to die in the cause of Islam. She and her son were tortured in an attempt to make them recant their

			faith. ‘Ammār did verbally recant his faith, but internally he was serene.
52	Bilāl b. Rabāḥ	Non-Arab	The particular version of Ibn Hishām (Cairo) consulted does not mention Bilāl among the earliest converts. However, Ibn Sa‘d, Vol. 11, mentions his name. The idolatrous persecutors were not able to obtain a recantation from Bilāl, not even a verbal one.

Observations Concerning the First Muslim Converts

Some facts stand out clearly from the information contained in the above table:

(i) It is clear that the vast majority of those early Muslims were Quraysh freemen and were not slaves or bondmen. True, not many of them belonged to Banū Hāshim, ‘Abd Shams or Makhzūm, the three leading clans of the Quraysh, yet the clans from which they came were purely Quraysh clans that wielded reasonable influence in the affairs of Makkah. Moreover, from the lesser Quraysh clans such as the ‘Adī, Zuhrah, Taym, Jumaḥ, ‘Āmir, Fihr and others, came men of considerable integrity, and extraordinary personal qualities, people like Abū Bakr, ‘Umar ‘Abū ‘Ubaydah ibn al-Jarrāḥ, Sa‘d ibn Abī Waqqāṣ, ‘Abd ar-Raḥmān ibn ‘Awf, az-Zubayr ibn al-‘Awwām and Khadījah bint Khuwaylid. Thus, clearly, the assertion that the Prophet was initially mainly followed by slaves and outcasts is plainly unfounded, despite the fact that some of those followers were actually such men.

(ii) The small number of those early converts belonging to the powerful clans of Banū Hāshim, ʻAbd Shams and Makhzūm may be explained by the fact that:

(a) those clans had enormous vested interests in the status quo at that time;
(b) the rise and success of the new movement of Islam clearly entailed the destruction of those interests – the new order could only be constructed on the ruins of the old one;
(c) owing to the traditional rivalry between Banū Hāshim and ʻAbd Shams on the one hand, and between those two clans and Makhzūm on the other, both ʻAbd Shams and Makhzūm resented the fact that Muḥammad belonged to Banū Hāshim. But, alas, Banū Hāshim themselves did not accept his egalitarian message though of course they consistently protected his person against the offences of the idolaters because of the obvious implications it had for their aristocratic dominance in Makkah. Clearly, Abū Lahab, the wealthiest of Banū Hāshim, felt those implications much more keenly than the others – hence his strong resistance and enmity to the Prophet, *ṣallā Allāhu ʻalayhi wa sallam*.

(iii) The description 'was converted before the Prophet's entry into the House of al-Arqam' merely indicates that those whom it fitted were among the very early Muslims. Ibn Hishām[21] maintains that al-Arqam b. Abī al-Arqam was the tenth person to be converted. So probably the Prophet entered his house during the first year of his mission. If this is so then those who were 'converted before the Prophet entered the House of al-Arqam' were actually converted in the first year of the mission. Those early Muslims included:

1. Khadījah
2. ʻAlī b. Abī Ṭālib
3. Zayd b. al-Ḥārithah
4. Abū Bakr aṣ-Ṣiddīq

5. ʻUthmān b. ʻAffān
6. az-Zubayr b. al-ʻAwwām
7. ʻAbd ar-Raḥmān b. ʻAwf
8. Saʻd b. Abī Waqqāṣ
9. ʻUbaydullāh b. al-Ḥārith
10. Maʻmar b. al-Ḥārith

However, Ibn Hishām maintains that al-Arqam b. Abī al-Arqam was the tenth person to adopt Islam.[22] Be that as it may, there can be little doubt that this fine man of Makhzūm, whose dedication of life and property to the new religion played a major role in its subsequent spread and victory, was one of the very early Muslims.

(iv) It is to be noted that many of those early Muslims took part either in the first, the second or both migrations to Abyssinia. This both adds to our confidence in the reliability of Ibn Isḥāq's information contained in the foregoing table, and fills our heart with sympathy and admiration for the sincerity and fortitude of those first Muslims. Falsehood rarely, if ever, breeds such a sincerity. For a believer in the Qur'ānic Truth, there could be no need for further proof than the Qur'ān itself. But for a would-be believer the willingness of those early Muslims to undergo any hardship in the cause of their religion should be a sign of faith at once genuine and profound.

(v) Also, the fine understanding, the ready willingness to sacrifice even their life, and the patience and serenity with which they endured hardship and suffering, strongly indicate the excellent quality of the training they received at the House of al-Arqam b. Abī al-Arqam. This house stands out as something more than merely a hiding and a meeting place for the early Muslims. It was a sort of School out of which the best cadres of nascent Islam graduated. If we recall, at this juncture, the amazing speed with which Islam swept the globe, then we may have some idea of the discipline and the high moral worth of those cadres. Saying this is to adopt the Muslims' interpretation of the events associated with the rapid military and cultural expansion of early Islam. This is not the place to justify this interpretation; suffice it to say that the Muslims' conduct both during the course of that expansion and in their subsequent management of the people and territories they controlled, represents a very bright chapter in the history of military conquests and the domination of one culture by another.

The First Muslims – Aspects of Their Character and Achievements

To attain some understanding of the phenomenon of those very first Muslims, it is essential not to view them as rare individuals with inherently extraordinary personalities. Such an approach is not only superficial but fails to take into account the factors that moulded and enhanced their spiritual and moral force – that important inward force that controls the ultimate springs of action in every man. Such an understanding can be achieved if we view them as the cardinal sociological phenomenon of their time, and of all times. To characterize this phenomenon in a few words would be to say that they were a 'Qur'ānic Generation' *(Jīl Qur'ānī)* as Sayyid Quṭb has put it.[23] It was the Qur'ān that exerted the primary educative influence upon the minds and souls of these early Muslims. Every time a set of verses were revealed to the Prophet he hurried to the Mosque; people were called to a special assembly, and the new verses read aloud by him. These Muslims then made it their urgent concern to understand the new revelation, memorizing it by heart, if possible. Most importantly, it was their major characteristic that they strove to apply the Qur'ānic guidance to their everyday affairs. They understood, better than any later generation, that following this guidance as closely as they could was the only way to procure God's pleasure and blessings and only by satisfying their Lord could they hope to succeed both in this life and in the Hereafter. Prompted by this understanding they sought to realize the Qur'ānic vision in their daily lives. The Qur'ān was never viewed by them as something to be chanted and recited only. This became the practice of later generations who sank much below the high level of the true Qur'ānic vision and design for the Muslims. An essential property of this vision was a dynamic spirit which eagerly sought to transform the social environment and engineer it so that it conformed to the Islamic pattern and scheme of things. Precepts for such social change are given in reasonable detail in the Qur'ān itself. The degree of excellence which those early Muslims were able to realize in their lives was due to their finding out those precepts and applying them in actual practice. In the early days, faced with the harsh opposition of the Quraysh idolaters, they would resort to the House of al-Arqam b. al-Arqam. Huddled together they would, joyfully and serenely, embark on the reading of the Qur'ān. The sound of it imparted calmness and peace to their agitated souls, and the explanation it rendered to them relieved and expanded their depressed and burdened hearts. The practical guidance they found in it was like a torch handed to them whilst standing in the wilderness of *Jāhiliyyah* (ignorance) and not knowing whither to turn. What was the nature of this guidance?

A cardinal requirement of Qur'ānic guidance *(Hudā)* is acceptance of, compliance with, and complete obedience to the will and order of God. This is implicit in the primary doctrine of monotheism. A sincere Muslim is required to resign and submit everything to God. And it is only through this submission that he can escape alienation and attain true peace and reconciliation.

A corollary of the cardinal monotheistic precept of submitting to God is the rule of following and strictly observing the orders and decisions of the Messenger of Allah, *ṣallā Allāhu 'alayhi wa sallam.* This is implicit in the *Shahādah* or declaration of faith:

Ashhadu al lā ilāha illā Allāh
Ashhadu anna Muḥammadar Rasūlullāh

Meaning:

I witness that there is no god excepting Allah;
I witness that Muḥammad is His Messenger.

Acceptance of and instant compliance with the rulings, judgements, recommendations and prohibitions of the Messenger of God is a mark of obedience and compliance with God's commandments. The Messenger did not speak for himself; he merely unfolded God's Word, Will and Purpose for man, as it had been revealed to him. Those early Muslims had completely assimilated this fact concerning the role of the Prophet in deciding their entire affairs.

Essentially, it was the role of the Messenger of Allah, Muḥammad, *ṣallā Allāhu 'alayhi wa sallam,* to expound the monotheistic concept to people in all its far-reaching and liberating implications and give practical directives for their realization. In order to perform this role, the Prophet was uniquely blessed. He is the Mercy of Allah to mankind. God made him a personification of His guidance, and an embodiment of all the high ideals necessary for the elevation of man. He bestowed upon him His grace and blessings, as several verses of the Qur'ān testify:

> Surely you are of a character sublime![24]
> Surely you are a noble Messenger.[25]

Most important of all, he was given the Qur'ān and 'the seven oft-repeated verses' therein:

> And verily, We have given you the seven oft-repeated (verses)[26] and the Great Qur'ān.
> So, stretch not your eyes towards that which We made some (wedded) pairs among them to enjoy, and be not grieved because of them, and lower thy wing (in tenderness) for the believers.[27]

Having been given the Qur'ān, Muḥammad, *ṣallā Allāhu 'alayhi wa sallam,* could not possibly desire anything also pertaining to the material riches and comforts of this world. And this is how the early Muslims too viewed the Qur'ān – as the greatest of all riches that they could possibly possess. If we study the elaborate contents of the Qur'ān, and the comprehensive detailed directives it contains about every aspect of life and man's purpose in this life then we may begin to appreciate the force and the relevance of the Qur'ānic education which the graduates of the Arqam Academy attained. The record of their achievement and the high moral civilizing mission which they sought to impart to humanity is a superb testimony and vindication of the training they received.

The first Muslims then constituted a whole generation that was carefully and patiently nurtured on the Qur'ānic revelations, and this nurturing continued throughout the Makkan phase (about thirteen years) and the Madinan phase (lasting for another ten years). The result was that they developed dispositions, attitudes and behavioural patterns which were superb examples of the guidance and the spirit of the glorious Qur'ān – hence the description, the Qur'ānic Generation.

The quality of the Qur'ānic guidance itself was intrinsically conducive to the creation and fostering of all that could be beautiful or desirable in the human personality. It is guidance which in both form (language) and content is precise and persuasive. It is not vague, cryptic or couched in unintelligible generalizations or metaphors. It is characterized by a sagacious admixture of common sense, based on the observed facts of Nature, and a rational metaphysical mysticism which never asserts anything that is demonstrably counter to reason. Moreover, it contains sometimes quite minute, practical details pertaining to almost every facet of human conduct and everyday life. The injunction that whoever disobeys the Messenger of Allah thereby disobeys Allah Himself is explicit in the Qur'ānic text. It effectively ensured the execution of the commandments of the Qur'ān.

This was the doctrine to which those first Muslims were effectively exposed in the Arqam Academy and which produced the unique Qur'ānic Generation.

With these remarks, we come to the end of our discussion on the private stage in the Prophet's career. Altogether this stage lasted for the first three years of the Prophetic mission from 610 to 613 C.E. During this stage, the Prophet spared no effort in inviting chosen individuals to the new religion. All this was conducted in absolute secrecy, good care being taken not to arouse the suspicion of the idolatrous Quraysh. Then he received his Lord's commandment to proclaim Islam publicly regardless of the consequences. As we shall see later, those consequences were very grave indeed.

Notes and References

1. Qur'ān, 26 *(Ash-Shu'arā')*: 215–16.
2. Qur'ān, 15 *(Al-Ḥijr)*: 94–6.
3. Bukhārī (Cairo edition), Bk. VI, p. 140.
4. 'Abū Lahab' was merely a nickname of this dissident uncle of the Prophet. His real name was 'Abd al-'Uzzā – the slave of 'Uzzā, one of the Makkan goddesses. Abū Lahab literally means 'Father of Flame'; he had a very ruddy complexion and a fiery temper.

5. Abū Lahab's wife, Umm Jamīl bint Ḥarb ibn Umayyah, was the sister of Abū Sufyān, one of the chief opponents of the Prophet before Allah guided him to Islam.
6. Abū Lahab's wife used to carry thorny wood and place it at the threshold of the Prophet's house. Abū Lahab was the next-door neighbour of the Prophet.
7. Qur'ān, 111 *(Al-Masad)*: 1–5.
8. Toynbee is here using the word '*Rūm*' which the early Muslims used to employ when referring to the Byzantines.
9. Arnold J. Toynbee, *Civilization on Trial,* Oxford University Press, 1948, p. 76.
10. Qur'ān, 112 *(Al-Ikhlāṣ)*: 1–4.
11. Qur'ān, 103 *(Al-'Aṣr)*: 1–3.
12. Qur'ān, 104 *(Al-Humazah)*: 1–9.
13. Qur'ān, 107 *(Al-Mā'ūn)*: 1–7.
14. Al-Wāḥidī, *Asbāb Nuzūl al-Qur'ān,* p. 502.
15. Qur'ān, 102 *(At-Takāthur)*: 1–8. This is a very early Makkan revelation.
16. Qur'ān, 1 *(Al-Fātiḥah)*: 1–7.
17. See Ibn Hishām, pp. 244 ff.
18. The full name was Abū Bakr ibn Abī Quḥāfah, nicknamed 'Aṭīq because of his comely face and because he survived despite the high infant mortality of his family.
19. The information contained in the table is that given by Ibn Isḥāq. See Ibn Hishām, pp. 244–62. The remarks are based mainly on the notes of the editors and Ibn Hishām.
20. 'Uthmān expressed his view concerning wine in the following acid statement: 'I do not drink what does away with my consciousness, causes my inferiors to ridicule me and prompts me to fornicate with my daughter.' When Islam later on prohibited wine, he commented, 'Blast it! My insight concerning it was correct.' Ibn Hishām, p. 252.
21. Ibn Hishām, p. 252.
22. *Ibid.*
23. Sayyid Quṭb, *Ma'ālim fi'ṭ-Ṭarīq (Milestones),* Cairo, 1966. The author attempted to set out the direction for change in the Muslim world. He was executed in August 1966 after being sentenced to death by an Egyptian court on charges of plotting against the Nasser regime in Egypt. The book *Ma'ālim fi'ṭ-Ṭarīq* was one of the documents produced by the prosecution against him.
24. Qur'ān, 68 *(Al-Qalam)*: 4.
25. Qur'ān, 33 *(Al-Aḥzāb)*: 21.
26. i.e. *Sūrah al-Fātiḥah.*
27. Qur'ān, 15 *(Al-Ḥijr)*: 87–8.

CHAPTER 6

The Call to Islam in Makkah – the Public Stage

The list of the first Muslim converts given above does not exhaust the number of persons who accepted Islam during the three years of the private stage according to Ibn Isḥāq. After mentioning all the names, up to Ṣuhayb which we included in the above list, he added:

'Then people entered into Islam, groups of men and women, until the mention of Islam became widespread in Makkah, and people talked about it. Allah, the Highly Exalted, ordered His Messenger to proclaim publicly what had come unto him from his Lord.'[1]

Until then, the Muslims conducted their devotions secretly. They might go into parts of the valley of Makkah which nobody frequented and perform their prayers. One day, Sa'd b. Abī Waqqāṣ (the future commander of the Muslim armies against the Persian Empire) was praying with a small company of the Prophet's Companions in a remote corner of the valley, when a group of idolaters saw them. The idolaters criticized and vilified their practice of praying, and the groups fought each other. Sa'd hit one of the idolaters on the head drawing blood; this 'was the first blood shed in the cause of Islam.'[2]

The Prophet as a Warner

We have already seen that in his first public statement from the summit of aṣ-Ṣafā the Prophet emphasized that he was a warner sent by God to deter people from 'a severe chastisement' which would be the inevitable consequence of their heedlessness. According to Ibn Sa'd,[3] he went on to state that no benefit would accrue to them in this life nor would they be able to attain the bliss of the Hereafter until they said, *'Lā ilāha illā Allāh'*. There was then no direct condemnation of the Arabs' idols on the part of the Prophet. We also noted the indignant aggressive response of Abū Lahab, an uncle of the Prophet, but this response was not immediately imitated by others. The general reaction was one of indifference, albeit of an arrogant nature. It was the indifference of an unaware, naive Quraysh who did not as yet appreciate any of the very grave implications of the Prophet's apparently quite innocuous call for them to say *'Lā ilāha illā Allāh'*. Being alert and having considerable interests at stake, Abū Lahab alone immediately grasped the true importance of the monotheistic dictum; it was the first cry of destruction for the heathenistic, aristocratic institutions of the Quraysh.

Condemnation of Quraysh Attitudes and Institutions

Thereafter, but not until he had made similar appeals to that at Mount Ṣafā, the Prophet launched a vigorous attack on the Quraysh attitudes and institutions. Worship of inanimate idols was strongly condemned as a terrible insult to human reason and dignity. The heathenistic legacy of taking excessive pride in the forefathers, chiefs and ancestors of the Quraysh was similarly condemned and insofar as those ancestors were unbelievers who paid no attention to the previous scriptures, they would be consigned to Hell-fire. Also, the Prophet sharply criticized their chiefs and the way they conducted their lives at Makkah. Their keen money-mindedness and their practice of accumulating wealth at the expense of the poor and the outcast was severely denounced; and so was their clanish arrogance and the injustice which they used to inflict on their slaves and non-Quraysh Arabs. Not only did he tell them that they were wrong about many things, but he also authoritatively demanded that they abandon their gods, give up their aristocratic privileges and attitudes, treat as equals both their venerated chiefs and dignitaries and the dispossessed and under-privileged, and conduct their affairs in such a manner as to provide for the orphans, the needy and wayfarers. These demands from the Prophet irritated them at first, then the irritation gradually developed into fury, as he continued arguing without respite. Then, as they saw his cause gaining ground and the number of his followers and disciples increasing every day, they became vindictive and violent. When they failed to restrain the Prophet with reason and argument, they sought to confine him by negotiation, compromise and even bargaining. When those tactics failed, they resorted to applying pressure on his uncle and protector Abū Ṭālib; but this too was unsuccessful. Finally, they resorted to outright and hysterical violence.

Quraysh Pressure on Abū Ṭālib

Ibn Isḥāq asserts that a delegation of the chiefs of the Quraysh visited Abū Ṭālib three times in a desperate effort to persuade him to forsake his nephew. They complained that he was a dissident who undermined their fathers' legacy, insulted their gods and degraded their established institutions. On the first occasion, Abū Ṭālib gently pacified them and they dispersed. On the second occasion, they succeeded in making him sympathize somewhat with their predicament and when they departed he called in his nephew and said:

'O son of my brother, your people have come to me and said so and so (he told him that they were utterly sickened by his attacks on their beliefs and social ways, and asked him to give up attacking them) and if you do not cease there would be war between Banū Hāshim and the rest of the Quraysh. So spare me and yourself and for God's sake don't make me suffer what I cannot bear . . .'[4]

When he heard these words, the noble, embattled Muḥammad, *ṣallā Allāhu 'alayhi wa sallam,* thought that his uncle had changed his stand about his pledge to protect him and that he was about to forsake and surrender him to the Quraysh idolaters. He promptly stood up and said:

'O my uncle, by God, if those people place the sun in my right and the moon in my left, so as to (deter me from) abandoning this matter I would not do that (but strive) until it prevails or I perish in the attempt.' Then being greatly moved in the meanwhile the Prophet sobbed passionately and turned to go away. But Abū Ṭālib in a tender voice called him back and said:

'Come back, son of my brother.' And when the Prophet came back, he added:

'Go out, son of my brother, and do whatever you like, for by God, I will not surrender you for anything.'[5]

On the third occasion the chiefs of the Quraysh took with them one of the finest and most handsome of their youths, 'Umārah ibn al-Walīd ibn al-Mughīrah, son of the aged but influential chief of Makhzūm. They offered to exchange 'Umārah for Muḥammad, *ṣallā Allāhu 'alayhi wa sallam.* This time Abū Ṭālib was very annoyed. He replied stiffly: 'What an unfair obligation you are imposing upon me. You give me your son to feed him for you, and I give you my son to be killed by you. This, by God, is what can never be.'

The Quraysh Seek a Compromise

Ibn Sa'd gives much the same story as that of Ibn Isḥāq except he did not mention:

(a) that they visited him a number of times.

(b) the statement that Abū Ṭālib sought to apply pressure upon the Prophet to stop calling upon the Quraysh to abandon their heathenistic practices, and the Prophet's reply that he would persist in his mission whatever the inducements to give it up. Besides, Ibn Sa'd's version is significantly different in that it asserts that the Prophet himself was present when the Quraysh chiefs called on Abū Ṭālib. He – the Prophet – is alleged to have addressed them himself. After mentioning the offer of the exchange of 'Umārah for Muḥammad, *ṣallā Allāhu 'alayhi wa sallam,* Ibn Sa'd's version reads:

'They said: Send for him (Muḥammad) and we shall give him a fair offer. Abū Ṭālib sent for him and when the Messenger of Allah came, he said to him: "O son of my brother, those are your uncles and the chiefs of your people and they want to deal fairly with you." The Messenger of Allah then said: "Speak, I am listening." They said:

"You leave us alone and our gods, and we leave you alone and your God."

Abū Ṭālib commented on their offer favourably, saying that the chiefs had treated his nephew fairly. But the Prophet replied as follows:

"Well, would you grant me a word, which if you adopt it you would thereby rule over the Arabs, and with it the non-Arabs would submit to you?"

Abū Jahl replied: "This must be a winning word. Yes, by your father, we would say it, and say even ten words like it." The Prophet then said:

"Say *Lā ilāha illā Allāh.*" When the Prophet uttered this monotheistic dictum, the idolaters were repelled by it. They shrank away from him and said to one another with displeasure:

"Cling to your gods, and be steadfast and patient with this belief." This last statement is ascribed to 'Uqbah ibn Abī Mu'ayṭ.'[6]

Once again, the Prophet here insisted on the monotheistic declaration as he did in his public speech on aṣ-Ṣafā. That the Prophet once again reiterated and insisted on this declaration in this important meeting must have impressed on those Arabs that he was in deadly earnest about his mission. It also makes the statement of Ibn Sa'd, who alone has cited it, more credible, since one would naturally expect the Prophet to reiterate it in public as he did in private. Another aspect of interest in Ibn Sa'd's statement is the information it contains about the compromise offer which the idolaters made to the Prophet and which he instantly rejected by insisting on the monotheistic declaration.

The main interest of Ibn Sa'd's statement, however, is the fact that it mentions the actual presence of the Prophet when that third meeting took place between the Quraysh chiefs and Abū Ṭālib.

When it became apparent that the meeting was about to end in failure and that Abū Ṭālib was not going to yield to their pressures and forsake his beloved nephew, they resorted to negotiation and bargaining with the Prophet personally. Ibn Sa'd's account is confirmed by Ibn Isḥāq. The latter reported a meeting that took place between the Prophet and one of the idolaters' chiefs, 'Utbah ibn Rabī'ah, a notable of 'Abd Shams and father of Hind who was the wife of Abū Sufyān, another chief of 'Abd Shams and a bitter opponent of the Prophet, that is before Allah blessed him with guidance to become a Muslim.

When it became clear that Abū Ṭālib would never abandon the Prophet, 'Utbah ibn Rabī'ah asked his people to give him leave to speak to him personally. Ibn Isḥāq asserts that this incident took place shortly after the conversion of Ḥamzah in the fifth year of the mission. Once in the Prophet's house, 'Utbah declared:

'You are, as you know, in an honoured position in your tribe and possess a high status in our lineage. But you have innovated amongst your people a grave matter by which you have created dissension in their community, undermined their prudence, vilified their gods and religion and declared their forefathers unbelievers who are doomed to Hell. So listen to me, I am going to offer you some options to consider so that you may accept some of them.'

Ibn Isḥāq narrates that the Prophet asked him to go on; 'Utbah continued:

'O son of my brother, if you want money by this matter which you have brought unto us, we will collect for you of our money till you become the richest amongst us. And if you want honour, we will make you chief and overlord over us, deciding on nothing without you. And if you want dominion, we will make you a King over us. But if it is a (vicious) vision which you see and which you cannot send away from you, we will arrange medical treatment for you, and we will spend generously until we cure you of it, since it is sometimes the case that the spirit dominates the man, till he is treated and cured of it.' 'Utbah went on till he had finished, with the Prophet listening patiently to him. Then the Prophet said:

'Have you finished, O father of al-Walīd?'

'Yes', said 'Utbah.

'Then listen to me!' said the Prophet.

'I will', said 'Utbah.

Then the Prophet began (reciting the Qur'ān):

> 'In the name of Allah, the Compassionate, the most Merciful.
> *Ḥā mīm.*
> A revelation from the Compassionate, the most Merciful,
> A Book whose verses are (well) expounded, a Recitation in Arabic for people who have knowledge.
> (Bringing) good tidings and a warning, but most of them turn away so that they hear not.
> And they said: Our hearts are (sealed) in covers from what you (O Muḥammad) call us to, in our ears there is a deafness, and between us and you there is a veil; act then, for verily we shall also be acting.'[7]

The Prophet continued reciting from *Sūrah Fuṣṣilat*[8] in a deep pious voice, and 'Utbah listened intently until he came to the verses where a prostration is prescribed. After prostrating he turned with a serious face to 'Utbah and said:

'You have heard, O father of al-Walīd, what you have heard. I will leave you then with that.' 'Utbah went back to his people with a changed face. They said: 'What do you have, O father of al-Walīd?' He replied: 'I have heard a speech, and by God, I have never heard anything like it. For, by God, it is not poetry, nor is it magic or soothsaying. O tribe of Quraysh, obey me. Place it (the responsibility) on me: and leave this man and what he is about. Leave him alone, for by God, the statement which I just heard from him will be something of great consequence. If the Arabs manage to get rid of him, you have been spared by others, but should he prevail over the Arabs, then his dominion is your dominion, and his honour is your honour and you would then be the happiest people because of him.'

They said: 'By God, the man has charmed you with his speech.'

'Utbah replied: 'This is my opinion but you are free to do what you think.'

Islam Continues to Spread: Quraysh Persecution

After the 'Utbah episode, Islam continued to spread in Makkah amongst the clans of the Quraysh. The chiefs of the idolaters had tried every tactic. They had applied pressure on Abū Ṭālib, sought to strike a bargain with him and had tried to negotiate and bargain with the Prophet himself. But none of these tactics had worked. Islam continued to gain followers, men and women, day by day. Muḥammad, *ṣallā Allāhu 'alayhi wa sallam,* must be stopped, the leaders of the Quraysh resolved, or there would be a monotheistic egalitarian revolution hanging over their heads. But then, what could be done? Nothing whatever seemed to work against the 'epidemic' of the 'renegades'. Every new success which the Prophet was able to secure filled their hearts with hatred and fury. When their best arguments failed they gave themselves up to irrational passions. They believed that they must resort to naked force and violence in order to destroy Muḥammad, *ṣallā Allāhu 'alayhi wa sallam,* once and for all. A policy of fighting the sincere and youthful religious faith with brutal force was launched. A new phase of persecution of Muslim converts began. They decided to apprehend those who were not well-protected by the existing social system which only safeguarded those who were members of the strongest Quraysh clans, respected confederates or allies of those clans or persons who enjoyed the personal protection of some powerful chief or chivalrous individuals. The slaves, the outcasts and persons who were non-Quraysh aliens living in Makkah, were those who, for the most part, did not enjoy these special privileges. Many such persons were seized and imprisoned, tortured and sometimes killed.

As for the Prophet, the Quraysh brought more pressure to bear on him. The idolaters would go to him with grotesque arguments and demands. They would demand that, if he was truly a Prophet sent from heaven, he ought to change the mountains and hills which surrounded Makkah into mountains of gold and silver. Failing that, then why could he not ask his God to cause them to move elsewhere, giving more plains and more space for Makkah to be used in agriculture. They also asked for rivers like those of Syria and Iraq. Then, they would demand to see their dead ancestors and forefathers come to life again. In particular they wanted to see the celebrated founder of Makkah, Quṣayy ibn Kilāb, who had died long before.

A delegation consisting of the leaders of the idolaters went to the Prophet and in addition to putting forward the foregoing fantastic demands, also repeated much the same offer which ‘Utbah had previously made. This delegation consisted of:

1. ‘Utbah ibn Rabī‘ah.
2. Shaybah ibn Rabī‘ah, his brother, both of whom were among the chiefs of ‘Abd Shams killed at Badr.
3. Abū Sufyān ibn Ḥarb (also of ‘Abd Shams).
4. an-Naḍr ibn al-Ḥārith (‘Abd ad-Dār).
5. al-Walīd ibn al-Mughīrah (prestigious chief of Makhzūm).
6. Abū Jahl ibn Hishām (a major chief of Makhzūm).
7. Umayyah ibn Khalaf (of Jumaḥ) and others.

Their offer to make him a King or a wealthy man was instantly rejected by the Prophet in much the same way that the similar offer from ‘Utbah had been rejected. In reply to the fantastic demands mentioned above, he frankly and plainly disavowed possessing any supernatural powers. He stressed that he was only a plain warner and reminder before a severe chastisement, conveying the commandments and injunctions of God as they were revealed to him through the mediation of the Archangel Gabriel. If they accepted what he brought to them, they would surely procure the good and the benefits of this world and of the Hereafter. But, if they rejected it then he was to be patient and persistent until God decided between him and them. But the idolaters were in no mind to hear a sober, rational reply. They did not come seeking one in the first place. Their objective was to mock and ridicule the Prophet and the Muslims, and, in this way, relieve their acute sense of failure and exasperation at being unable to stop the sweeping successes of the new religion which the Prophet was boldly proclaiming in Makkah. They continued their verbal attacks on the Prophet and asked various questions and demanded information about them. They asked about a group of young men, who had deserted their people and had strange experiences. They also wanted to know whether a man who travelled a great distance would reach the western and eastern limits of the Universe. Finally they wanted to know about the essence of the soul. The Prophet promised to have his answer ready by the next morning. However, he forgot to say *'Inshā' Allāh'*, i.e. 'If God wills'. So the Angel did not reveal anything to him by the next morning, and indeed did not appear for the next fifteen days. During those long days, the Prophet grieved and the idolaters were jubilant, their attacks on the Prophet reaching new heights. Then God revealed *Sūrah al-Kahf* (The Cave), giving elaborate answers to those questions. This long, absorbing *sūrah* takes its name from the cave to which those faithful young men had resorted in order to seek refuge from persecution at the hands of the unbelievers. Pickthall asserts that Western writers (e.g. Gibbon) identify the story of those faithful youths with that of the Seven Sleepers of Ephesus.[9] It was the Jewish rabbis of Yathrib who suggested these questions to them to put to the Prophet as a test of his Prophetic claims.

The story of the 'People of the Cave' served as a prelude to the hard and cruel period of persecution which the idolaters of the Quraysh were about to launch against the Prophet and his followers. Persecution of those who opposed falsehood and injustice was not a consequence only of the struggle between

Muḥammad, *ṣallā Allāhu 'alayhi wa sallam,* and the forces of the Arabian *Jāhiliyyah.* It was and still is, a sociological, universal law, governing such conflicts. The story of those youthful believers provided pertinent education for the Muslims in respect of the Divine laws.

Persecution of the Prophet himself and the early Muslims was now fully under way. However, the degree of the persecution depended on the prestige enjoyed by each persecuted individual. The social system of the Quraysh was based on privilege. The less the prestige, the greater was the degree of persecution. The worst persecution was inflicted upon slaves and persons with weak tribal links. Banū Hāshim and their allies, the Banū al-Muṭṭalib, were also persecuted, though to a lesser degree, and ultimately the Prophet himself was insulted and physically assaulted a number of times. However the protection given to him by Abū Ṭālib, and Banū Hāshim in general, acted as a strong deterrent to the aggression of the Quraysh against him. Members of strong clans such as 'Abd Shams or Makhzūm also enjoyed a reasonable protection. Nevertheless, a substantial degree of persecution was inflicted upon them. The entire clans of Banū Hāshim and Banū al-Muṭṭalib were exposed to a policy of the most harsh ostracism and social exile that history has ever seen. The entire membership of two clans, irrespective of whether they were Muslims or non-Muslims, were obliged to retreat to the Shi'b (an isolated portion of the valley of Makkah) of Abū Ṭālib. But before we give more details about this social exile, let us see what the gracious, magnanimous Prophet himself suffered in the cause of the struggle to carry out the order and commandments of his Lord.

The Prophet Leads the Struggle

There could be no doubt that the brunt of the idolaters' opposition was directed against the person of the Prophet himself. This was inevitable since it was Muḥammad, *ṣallā Allāhu 'alayhi wa sallam,* more than anyone who insisted upon a whole range of measures that were precisely designed to overthrow their social system and end their unjust aristocratic domination in Makkah. He was the spearhead of the Monotheistic Revolution which, in their own words, had succeeded in creating dissension and strife in their community and, as a result of this denunciation of their worthless gods, undermined their prestige and honour in Arabia. It was then quite natural that the very first concern of the Quraysh, at this juncture, was to be rid of him by any means and at any cost.

The ringleaders of the idolaters' offensive against the Prophet were:

	Name	*Clan*
1.	'Amr ibn Hishām (Abū Jahl)	Makhzūm
2.	'Utbah ibn Rabī'ah	'Abd Shams
3.	Shaybah ibn Rabī'ah	'Abd Shams
4.	Umayyah ibn Khalaf	Jumaḥ
5.	Ubayy ibn Khalaf	Jumaḥ
6.	Al-Walīd ibn al-Mughīrah	Makhzūm
7.	Abū Lahab	Hāshim
8.	'Uqbah ibn Abī Mu'ayṭ	'Abd Shams
9.	an-Naḍr ibn al-Ḥārith	'Abd ad-Dār
10.	Umm Jamīl (wife of Abū Lahab)	'Abd Shams

The first five enemies of God, belonging to Makhzūm, 'Abd Shams and Jumaḥ respectively, must have led the persecution against the Prophet and his followers. In an authentic *Ḥadīth,* narrated by al-Bukhārī, the Prophet is reported to have complained to his Lord of the harm they were doing him. He asked that God should punish them for their misdeeds against him and his followers. Five of them were killed at Badr, and two of them were killed by Muslims whom they had tortured at Makkah. The *Ḥadīth* runs as follows:

'On the authority of 'Abdullāh (Ibn 'Umar) who said:

As the Prophet was prostrating and some people of the Quraysh were not far away, 'Uqbah ibn Abī Mu'ayṭ came along with the entrails of a goat and flung them on his back. Fāṭimah, his daughter, came out and removed the unclean stuff and angrily cursed the wrong-doers and prayed that God might punish them. Then the Prophet raised his head, finished his prostration and then prayed passionately:

"O Lord, deal unkindly with the *Mala'* (the notables) of the Quraysh, Abū Jahl ibn Hishām, 'Utbah ibn Rabī'ah, Shaybah ibn Rabī'ah, Umayyah ibn Khalaf and Ubayy ibn Khalaf." '[10]

Apparently, the Prophet did not mention the direct culprit

‘Uqbah ibn Abī Mu‘ayṭ among those whose punishment he prayed for because, despite his evil-doing and meanness, he was a weak, docile man who was very much under the influence of his close friend, Ubayy ibn Khalaf.[11]

Apart from this ugly incident involving ‘Uqbah ibn Abī Mu‘ayṭ, the noble Muḥammad, *ṣallā Allāhu ‘alayhi wa sallam,* had suffered a great deal of harsh ill-treatment at the hands of the unbelievers. But according to Ibn Isḥāq,[12] the worst incident of persecution which the Prophet had suffered in the cause of carrying out his Lord’s commandments was the following:

‘Urwah ibn az-Zubayr asked ‘Abdullāh ibn ‘Amr ibn al-‘Āṣ about the worst incident of persecution which he had seen the Quraysh inflict upon the Prophet of Islam. ‘Abdullāh then narrated that he was present when a group of the Quraysh were assembled in the courtyard of the Ka‘bah. They talked about the Prophet and what he had innovated in the affairs of the Quraysh and about matters which they did not find to their liking. As they were thus assembled the Prophet himself appeared in the courtyard of the sanctuary. When he came past them, they made slanderous remarks about him. ‘Abdullāh said that he noticed the effect of those slanderous remarks on the face of the Prophet. When he passed by for the second time, they repeated their remarks. Again ‘Abdullāh noticed a change in the Prophet’s face. When they did that for the third time, the Prophet stood facing them and said, ‘Do you know, O tribe of Quraysh, for by Him in whose hands is my life I have come to you with destruction.’ They were so taken aback by his statement that they were utterly silenced (as if there were birds in their heads). Some of those who had treated him the worst, now addressed him very politely, saying that they had previously known him not to be provocative or ignorant (of good manners) and politely entreated with him to leave. Then the Prophet left peacefully.

The next day, the same people assembled in the Ka‘bah, and when the Prophet appeared, accompanied by Abū Bakr, they attacked him, as if they were one man, saying: ‘Is it you who say so and so?’ and the Prophet answered in the affirmative every time. One of the men took him by the mantle and pulled him violently. Abū Bakr intervened angrily, protesting, ‘Do you kill a man because he said: “God is my Lord”?’ Then the men left him and dispersed. Abū Bakr went home with an acute headache due to the fact that his long hair was pulled very hard during the scuffle.

The above version of what the Prophet suffered at the hands of the unbelievers received additional confirmation from al-Bukhārī[13] who cited the incident without giving all the details which Ibn Isḥāq gives in his version. However, al-Bukhārī gives an item of information which we do not find in Ibn Isḥāq, namely that the man who pulled the Prophet's mantle was none other than the mean enemy of God, 'Uqbah ibn Abī Mu'ayṭ. According to Bukhārī's version, 'Uqbah tried to strangle the Prophet but Abū Bakr took him by the shoulder and pushed him away.

In addition to Abū Lahab, his wife and 'Uqbah ibn Abī Mu'ayṭ, Abū Jahl also sought to inflict bodily harm on the Prophet. On one occasion, he took a big stone and attempted to let it fall on the Prophet's head while he was prostrating in the courtyard of the Ka'bah. But as he drew near, he saw an enormous camel charging in his direction, so he threw the stone down and fled to tell the strange story to his fellow idolaters. In a second incident, he insulted the Prophet, *ṣallā Allāhu 'alayhi wa sallam,* using profane and provocative language as he was worshipping at the Ka'bah. But the Prophet chivalrously restrained himself and was quite unmoved by the ugly provocation. This latter incident led to the conversion of the noble uncle of the Prophet, Ḥamzah ibn 'Abd al-Muṭṭalib. His conversion not only helped to relieve the suffering and the persecution but it almost tipped the balance of power in favour of the Muslims.

Abū Ṭālib's Protection

Despite the fact that the Prophet, *ṣallā Allāhu 'alayhi wa sallam,* actually suffered a lot at the hands of the ringleaders of the idolaters, it could not be disputed that, had it not been for the protection which he received from Banū Hāshim and Banū al-Muṭṭalib and their senior patriarch Abū Ṭālib, things could have been much harder for him. The following incident, narrated by Ibn Sa'd[14] amply demonstrates that the protection was most effective.

One day, Muḥammad, *ṣallā Allāhu 'alayhi wa sallam,* could not be found anywhere in Makkah. Abū Ṭālib thought that he had perhaps been harmed by the idolaters. He hastily gathered together an armed contingent of Banū Hāshim youths and set out to look for him. But he was soon assured that Muḥammad, *ṣallā Allāhu 'alayhi wa sallam,* was quite safe in a nearby house. However, Abū Ṭālib did not let the incident pass by without making it well known to everybody that when it came to Muḥammad's safety and protection, he was in deadly earnest. The next morning he appeared with his armed contingent before the assembly of the Quraysh. He explained why they were there and solemnly told them that had Muḥammad, *ṣallā Allāhu 'alayhi wa sallam,* been killed, they were resolved to kill them all or die themselves in the attempt.

But despite this strong protection, the Prophet suffered as we have seen. Of course, God could have absolutely protected His Prophet, so that nothing at all could harm or insult him. But, suffering in the cause of truth and in the way of the Lord was the School in which his people, and those who stood for his cause, were receiving their education and training. The Prophet himself was perhaps in no need of such training, having been chosen and prepared for his high prophetic office since his early childhood. But it was important that he should give an example to his people in this respect. Not only did it become absolutely clear to those early Muslims that persecution is an essential and inevitable consequence of the call to the way of God, a universal experience of those who sincerely follow this way, but that it is God's way of examining those followers themselves and separating the sincere from the mere pretenders:

> Or think you that you will enter Paradise while yet there has not come unto you the like of (that which came to) those who passed away before you? Affliction and adversity befell them, they were shaken as with earthquake, till the messenger (of Allah) and those who believed along with him said: When shall Allah's help come? Now, surely Allah's help is nigh . . . [15]

Persecution is also God's way of strengthening the ranks of the believers, since hardship and suffering discourage the timid, the weak and the opportunist from continuing in the membership of the new movement.

The Conversion of Ḥamzah

It is hardly an exaggeration to say that the conversion of Ḥamzah was a major development in the history of Islam. Ḥamzah was roughly the same age as his nephew, Muḥammad, *ṣallā Allāhu ʻalayhi wa sallam.* But Ḥamzah was a man with an enormous, towering physique and a fighter of tremendous courage. He had fine manners and tastes, he was chivalrous, fond of hunting and had a keen sense of justice and fair play.

One afternoon he entered the city after spending a day hunting wild game. He visited the sanctuary to circumambulate the Kaʻbah. As he was getting ready to go home, a slave girl called out loudly to him:

'You have not seen, O Ḥamzah, how Abū Jahl insulted your nephew, just a few hours ago!'

'Oh really! and what did he say to him?'

'O dear! O dear, it was a very ugly insult! It is unrepeatable!'

'And then what happened?'

'Nothing! The Prophet said absolutely nothing. But he went home as soon as Abū Jahl disappeared.'

Ḥamzah, who was a friend of the Prophet, was furious. He went directly to the Assembly House of the Quraysh. There Abū Jahl was sitting among the dignitaries. Ḥamzah went straight to him and hit him on the head with his bow, hard enough to cause it to bleed:

'You insulted him, and I am also of his religion,' said Ḥamzah, not meaning precisely what he said since he was actually not a believer at that time. He merely said these words to hurt Abū Jahl.

When Abū Jahl's relatives and tribesmen stood up to confront Ḥamzah, Abū Jahl pacified them by admitting that he had badly insulted his nephew. Actually, Abū Jahl might have been apprehensive lest Ḥamzah be killed and a blood feud develop in Makkah. When his anger had subsided and he was alone at home, Ḥamzah indicated that he was sorry that he had gone to such lengths in order to hurt Abū Jahl. In particular, he was not easy in his mind at having asserted that he was a convert to the cause of the Prophet when, in fact, as yet he was not. He spent a sleepless night, asking God to guide him in the matter. But in the morning he felt assured that he had done the right thing by declaring his intention of becoming a Muslim. So he went to the

Prophet and declared himself a believer and there was rejoicing and jubilation in the House of al-Arqam. Throughout Makkah, the Quraysh received the news of his conversion with deep dismay. It had a profoundly demoralizing effect upon them. They knew that the cause of Islam had been tremendously strengthened, and that it would no longer be possible for individual members among them to publicly vilify the Prophet. And, indeed, their anticipation was right. Ḥamzah devoted all his tremendous energy and courage to the defence and advancement of the new religion.

Later he played a major role in the decisive Battle of Badr. He, more than anyone, was able to inflict heavy casualties on the polytheists from the Quraysh and especially amongst the leading house of 'Abd Shams. At Uḥud, the next battle in which the Quraysh sought to take their vengeance on the Prophet and his followers, to kill Ḥamzah was therefore their first objective. So keen and intent were 'Abd Shams on killing Ḥamzah that Hind, whose father 'Utbah ibn Rabī'ah, uncle Shaybah ibn Rabī'ah and brother al-Walīd were all killed at Badr, recruited a special agent to kill him at Uḥud. He was one of her ambitious bondmen who was eager to be freed:

'Wouldn't you like to be free, Waḥshī (for that was his name)?'

'And who doesn't desire freedom, my lady Hind?'

'Then you will be free, if you can get me the head of Ḥamzah ibn 'Abd al-Muṭṭalib.'

'But where shall I find him?'

'Don't worry. We shall soon go to war against these renegades and Ḥamzah is sure to be there.'

'Then I bet I shall be free as soon as the battle takes place.'

So Waḥshī began to prepare for his ugly mission. He purchased a special weapon, and kept it ready. At Uḥud, the wretched Waḥshī never took part in the fighting, but he kept Ḥamzah in view, until he got his opportunity to bludgeon to death the 'Chivalrous Knight of Islam and Lion of God'. Since the idolaters were victorious that day, Hind got hold of the corpse of the noble fighter, cut open his abdomen and chewed his liver.

The Prophet was deeply grieved at the news of Ḥamzah's martyrdom and Hind's vicious profanity. He declared that she should be taken prisoner dead or alive. However, Hind later became a Muslim and the Prophet forgave her – a truly great example of magnanimity and forgiveness and a superb illustration of the nature of relationships in Islam.

The Conversion of 'Umar

After the conversion of Ḥamzah, the biggest victory for the Prophet was the conversion of 'Umar ibn al-Khaṭṭāb, the second man to assume power after the Prophet. 'Umar's conversion was also hailed as a great victory for the cause of Islam. Like Ḥamzah, 'Umar was a tall, imposing figure, and like the 'Lion of Allah', he possessed unquestionable courage. 'Umar's conversion took place only a few months after the conversion of Ḥamzah, and these two major events took place either in the fifth year of Muḥammad's mission or at the beginning of the sixth.

Ibn Isḥāq[16] gives more than one version of 'Umar's conversion. According to one account, he embraced Islam some time after the first migration to Abyssinia. But a second version has it that the conversion happened as the immigrants were preparing to leave for Abyssinia, the 'land of righteousness'.[17] Since the first migration took place towards the end of the fifth year of the Prophet's mission,[18] then if the second version is true, the conversion must have taken place in the fifth year. But if the first version of Ibn Isḥāq is true, then the conversion took place some time at the beginning of the sixth year of the Prophet's mission, a short time after the return of the Quraysh delegation to the Negus, requesting, without success, the extradition of the immigrants.

Be that as it may, 'Umar's conversion was an historic event. It deeply shocked everybody in Makkah. The Muslims were jubilant and the unbelievers dismayed. Until 'Umar's conversion, the Muslims could not hold their prayers in public. Now, after the accession of 'Umar to Islam, they held them in the courtyard of the ancient sanctuary. Entering Arqam's house, he found the Prophet and his Companions, including Ḥamzah and Abū Bakr, still reciting and studying the Qur'ān in secrecy, lest the Quraysh should harm them. But the outspoken, exuberant 'Umar did not find secrecy and timidity to his liking. He did not rest content until he had persuaded the Prophet and his followers to appear in public and declare their faith and its doctrines before everybody. So, the Muslims formed up into two columns, with Ḥamzah heading one column and the newcomer, 'Umar, heading the second. It was the first Muslim public demonstration in history. The effects of this demonstration were remarkable. The Quraysh were overawed by the bold and aggressive attitude of the small company of Muslims. They were confronted with the reality of the solid basis of the new movement in their midst. It was a manifest challenge to the continuation of the oppressive domination of the Quraysh both in Makkah and in Arabia at large.

The conversion of 'Umar was described as a 'succour', his migration later to Yathrib was termed a 'victory' and his rule after the death of the Prophet a 'mercy'.[19] It was because of the great role he played in the success of Islam, that 'Umar was called al-Fārūq[20] or 'the Distinguisher', i.e. the one who distinguishes between truth (Islam) and falsehood.

Different versions are given about the manner in which the conversion of 'Umar took place. The following is the most widespread and the most reliable:[21]

Anas ibn Mālik said: 'Umar went out of his house carrying a sword. A man met him who asked about his destination.

I want to kill Muḥammad.

Do you think that Banū Hāshim and Banū Zuhrah would leave you in peace if you killed Muḥammad?

What! You have also become a renegade and left your religion?

Could I tell you something that would surprise you? Your brother-in-law and your sister Fāṭimah have both become renegades and have abandoned the religion to which you adhere!

'Umar hurried to their house in great agitation and anger. He confronted his sister and her husband.

What is the strange humming which I have just heard? (He had actually heard them reciting the Qur'ān as he approached their house).

Only something that has been talked about between us.

Perhaps you have become renegades?

O 'Umar, what if the Truth is in something other than your religion? said Fāṭimah's husband.

'Umar leapt upon him, hitting and kicking him as hard as he could. Fāṭimah stepped in between the two men in an attempt to protect her husband against 'Umar's blows, but she was badly hit in the face, and bled profusely. She said angrily:

Yes, 'Umar, what if Truth is *not* in your religion? I give witness that there is no god, except the One True God *(Ashhadu al lā ilāha illā Allāh)* and that Muḥammad is His Messenger (*Wa Ashhadu anna Muḥammadar Rasūlullāh*).

'Umar was greatly moved and shaken by the bloody incident. His sister's wound moved him to pity and affection:

May I look into what you have been reciting just now?

But you are impure *(Najis),* and it (the Qur'ān) is only touched by the pure ones; so go and wash yourself or wash your limbs, said his sister.

'Umar complied at once. Then she gave him the sheet and he read:

> In the name of Allah, the Compassionate, the most Merciful,
> *Ṭā Hā*,
> We have not revealed unto you (O Muḥammad) the Qur'ān that you should be distressed,
> But as a reminder unto him who fears,
> A revelation from Him who created the earth and the high heavens,
> The Compassionate One, Who is established on the Throne.
> Unto Him belongs whatsoever is in the earth, and whatsoever is between them and whatsoever is beneath the sod.
> And if you speak aloud, then verily He knows the secret (thought) and (that which is yet) more hidden.
> Allah! There is no God save Him. His are the most beautiful names . . .
> Verily I am Allah, there is no god save Me.
> So serve Me and establish prayer for My remembrance.[22]

When he reached the fourteenth verse, 'Umar expressed a wish to go and see the Prophet. He wanted to declare himself a Muslim and to admit that there is no god except the One, True God, *'Lā ilāha illā Allāh'*. When he knocked at the door of the House of al-Arqam, there was a deep hush inside – 'Umar, the staunch enemy of God, was at the door armed with his famous sword. But the Prophet firmly gave the order that 'Umar be admitted. Ḥamzah, who was at the side of the Prophet called out loudly:

'If he means well, then we will treat him well, but if he wants evil, we shall kill him with his sword and that will be easy for us.'

As 'Umar was crossing the threshold, the Prophet leapt forward and seized him by his mantle and the straps by which his sword was attached:

'O 'Umar, aren't you going to end (your unbelief and enmity towards the Muslims) until God causes to descend upon you indignity and torment as He did upon al-Walīd ibn al-Mughīrah? O Lord, this is 'Umar ibn al-Khaṭṭāb! O Lord, strengthen the religion with 'Umar ibn al-Khaṭṭāb.'

Notes and References

1. Ibn Hishām, p. 262.
2. *Ibid.,* p. 263.
3. Ibn Sa'd, p. 200.
4. Ibn Hishām, p. 266.
5. *Ibid.*
6. *Ibid.*, p. 417; Ibn Sa'd, p. 202.
7. Ibn Hishām, p. 294.
8. Qur'ān, 41 *(Fuṣṣilat)*.
9. The identification of the 'People of the Cave' with the 'Seven Sleepers of Ephesus' is doubted by Pickthall who maintains that the story probably belongs to the rabbinic tradition. See his introduction to *Sūrah al-Kahf* (18), *The Meaning of the Glorious Qur'ān.*
10. *Ṣaḥīḥ al-Bukhārī* (Cairo), Vol. II, Bk. 5, p. 58.
11. See Ibn Hishām, p. 361.
12. *Ibid.,* p. 289f.
13. *Ṣaḥīḥ al-Bukhārī,* Vol. II, Bk. 5, p. 58.
14. Ibn Sa'd, p. 202 f.
15. Qur'ān, 2 *(Al-Baqarah)*: 214.
16. See Ibn Hishām, p. 342.
17. This is how the Prophet referred to Abyssinia when he recommended migration there.
18. Ibn Sa'd, Vol. I, p. 204.
19. *Ibid.,* Vol. III, p. 270.
20. It was the Prophet who gave 'Umar this name. See Ibn Sa'd, Vol. III, p. 267 f.
21. This version is favoured by Ibn Hishām, Vol. I, pp. 343–5; Ibn Sa'd, Vol. III, p. 267 f.
22. Qur'ān, 20 *(Ṭā Hā)*: 1–14. This version is given in Ibn Sa'd, Vol. III, p. 267 f.

CHAPTER 7

Persecution

The conversion of 'Umar added substantially, as we have seen, to the power and prestige of the emerging faith. The Prophet himself was further protected from harm and harassment by these new important conversions. On the other hand, the Quraysh felt more and more vindictive at the Prophet's continued progress and the inroads he was making among the Quraysh. They intensified their efforts to repress the new faith, and to oppress the new Muslim converts. The noble and considerate Prophet was moved when he saw the trials and persecutions to which his followers were exposed and from which he was unable to protect them. He is reported to have suggested to them:

'Perhaps you should go to the land of Abyssinia, for there is a King there under whom no injustice is done to anyone, and it is a land of truth and righteousness, and until Allah provides you a relief from your present circumstances.'[1]

The First *Hijrah* to Abyssinia

The Prophet's suggestion gave rise to the first *hijrah* or migration to Abyssinia. It has sometimes been assumed that the migration to Abyssinia was a single event but the bulk of the evidence suggests that it took place in two successive and distinct stages. In the first stage a small number of persons participated – ten or eleven men, four of whom were accompanied by their wives. These included a daughter of the Prophet, Ruqayyah, who was the wife of 'Uthmān ibn 'Affān. According to Ibn Sa'd, this migration took place in the fifth year of the Prophet's mission in the month of Rajab. The migrating Muslims led by 'Uthmān ibn

Maẓ'ūn were hotly pursued by the Quraysh but they managed to catch a boat at the port of Shu'aybiyyah near the site of the present port of Jeddah. They stayed in Abyssinia for only three months. Their return to Makkah was probably prompted by rumours of the mass conversion of Makkans to Islam,[2] which turned out to be false. The story behind the alleged mass conversion of Makkans has been related in the so-called 'Satanic Verses' – verses which allegedly spoke favourably of the idols of Makkah (see pp. 171–7).

The Second *Hijrah* to Abyssinia

The second group of Muslims migrated to Abyssinia after the first group had returned to Makkah. In fact some who were in the first group were included in the second which was led by Ja'far ibn Abī Ṭālib.

When the Quraysh saw that they were unable to check the Muslim exodus to Abyssinia, they decided to send an official delegation to the Abyssinian ruler, the Negus, to make a request for their extradition. The delegation consisted of the Quraysh's foremost diplomat, the crafty 'Āmr ibn al-'Āṣ, a man well known for his inventiveness, and a certain 'Abdullāh ibn Abī Rabī'ah. The two men went loaded with valuable gifts of fine leather for the Negus and his notables. Umm Salamah bint Umayyah ibn al-Mughīrah narrated that the two envoys arrived in Abyssinia to find the Muslims living peacefully under the protection and hospitality of the Negus. They gave a gift to each of the Negus' courtiers to win them over to the task of persuading the Negus to agree to the extradition of the Muslim refugees. They argued that although the Muslims had deserted the religion of their own people they had not accepted the religion of the Negus' court (Christianity) but instead had brought into being a religion of their own – the obvious implication being that the Muslims were subversive elements in both Makkah and Abyssinia and as such the Abyssinians would do well to extradite them.

The courtiers supported the delegation's request for the extradition of the Muslim refugees. When the Quraysh envoys formally put forward their demands before the Negus, he hesitated, wanting to hear what the refugees themselves had to say. It was Ja'far ibn Abī Ṭālib, a cousin of the Prophet, who spoke on behalf of the emigrants as follows:

'O King! We have been a people of Ignorance *(Jāhiliyyah)* worshipping idols, eating the flesh of dead animals, committing abominations, neglecting our relatives and doing evil to our neighbours. The strong among us would oppress the weak. We were in this state when God sent to us a Messenger from among us whose descent and sincerity, trustworthiness and honesty were known to us. He summoned us to worship the One True God and to reject the stones and idols we and our fathers had been worshipping in addition to God. He ordered us to be truthful of speech, to fulfil all the duties that were entrusted to us, to care for our relatives, to be kind to our neighbours, to refrain from unlawful food and the consumption of blood. He forbade us to engage in lewdness and lying, the devouring of the money of the orphan and the defamation of married women. He commanded us to worship the One God and to assign no partners unto Him, to pray, to pay the purifying tax and to fast. We deem him truthful and we believed him, and we accepted the message he brought to us from God . . .'[3]

Umm Salamah said that Ja'far continued to enumerate matters pertaining to Islam. He told the Negus that when they accepted the Prophet's message and followed his doctrine, the people of the Quraysh showed enmity and bitterness towards them, persecuting them because of their new religious faith. Life had become unbearable for them in Makkah, so they had come to the Negus' land – the land of righteousness and truth – looking for peace and tranquillity. They honoured him above all other kings and placed their trust in him and desired his protection. The Negus was touched and asked:

'Do you have with you some portions of his (the Prophet's) teachings?'

'Yes,' replied Ja'far.

'Then read it aloud to me.'

The youthful Ja'far began to recite *Sūrah Maryam*[4] in his pure, Quraysh accent and in a voice full of feeling and conviction. The *sūrah* relates the story of Mary (Maryam) and the Divine miracle of her conceiving a child without being touched by any mortal – as 'a sign to the people, a mercy from (God) and a thing ordained'. It tells of her pangs of childbirth and her painful plea, 'O would that I had died before this and had become a thing forgotten.'

But her Lord provided for her and consoled her. Even so, on presenting the child to the people, she was charged with having done a 'despicable' thing and of virtually being a harlot. In defence she meekly pointed to the new-born baby Jesus in the cradle. Miraculously the baby spoke and said, 'Indeed I am the servant of Allah. He has given me the scripture and has appointed me a Prophet.'

Ja'far, who greatly resembled the Prophet both in manners and appearance, went on reciting the beautiful *sūrah*. When he had finished his moving recitation, the Negus and his notables were reported to have been overcome with tears.

'Indeed, this (scripture) and what Jesus brought,' said the Negus, 'arise from the same source. Go in peace, for by God, I will never surrender you to them.'[5]

Umm Salamah reported that 'Āmr was furious at his failure to win the Negus over to his side. He determined to try once more the next day. He told everyone that he had worked out a plan which would enable him to eradicate them (the Muslims) from Abyssinia. 'Abdullāh, his fellow envoy, tried to dissociate himself from making a fresh attempt to obtain their extradition, saying that, after all, there existed bonds of kinship between them and the Muslim emigrants. But 'Āmr was adamant: 'By God, I am going to tell him (the Negus) that they (the Muslims) claim that Jesus is a slave.'

The next day, 'Āmr came early to the royal court of the Negus and said:

'O king! They make terrible accusations against Jesus. Perhaps you could send for them and ask them what they say about him (Jesus).'

When the Negus' summons reached the Muslims they held a special council. What were they going to tell the Negus if he asked them about the nature of Jesus? They decided that they would just tell him without any hesitation what the Qur'ān says about him. They could not distort their religion under any circumstances. When they entered the royal court, the Negus asked what they had said about Jesus.

Ja'far again came forward and said: 'We will say concerning him what our Prophet has told us about him. He is the servant of Allah, and His Spirit and Word, which he cast upon Mary, the virgin Immaculate.' Much to the dismay and resentment of his courtiers the Negus emphatically concurred with the statement of Ja'far concerning the nature of Jesus. 'Go in peace,' he told them. 'Whoever insults you shall be punished. Go in peace, wherever you wish. In my land, you will be secure.'

Thus 'Āmr's mission ended in utter failure. The two envoys returned to Makkah. The Quraysh received the news of the Negus' determination with exasperation. Their hatred towards the Muslims in Makkah was intensified and they resorted to open persecution and violence.

Now, having recounted what happened in the court of this compassionate ruler, let us return with the Quraysh emissaries to Makkah and examine more closely the motives and reasons that had promoted Ja'far and his companions to come to Abyssinia in the first place. We leave the just Negus to face the agitation of the crowds, stirred by religious fanatics and bigots who were angered by his inclination towards the Muslim position on the nature of Jesus. Ibn Hishām reported that the Negus was ultimately converted to Islam and died a Muslim. The Prophet is reported to have said a special prayer for his soul when news of his death reached him some years later in his new administrative capital at al-Madīnah.[6]

That the fear of further persecution and even of outright annihilation was the cardinal motive behind the Muslims' migration to Abyssinia, is suggested by our major sources. There is nothing to make us doubt the standard accounts of these events or to suspect that they were in any way fabricated.[7] A careful analysis and survey of the circumstances in which the emigration took place clearly support the view that the major motive behind this exodus was to escape persecution and oppression. First of all, Abū Jahl had become so arrogant and aggressive against the Muslims that he even seriously insulted the Prophet himself. We have seen how this incident had led to the conversion of the formidable Ḥamzah. Secondly, 'Umar ibn al-Khaṭṭāb's conversion also took place in similar circumstances. He was looking for the Prophet to kill him, and having been diverted to the house of his sister and brother-in-law, who had recently converted to Islam, he almost killed both of them in his rage at their conversion. These two incidents clearly show the existence of active persecution towards the end of the fifth year and the beginning of the sixth year of the Prophet's mission, i.e. the time at which the first emigration to Abyssinia took place. Of course, the principal reason why the Quraysh persecuted the Muslims was their fear of the spreading and ultimate victory of the new faith. Such success would bring about the downfall and disappearance of their vested interests and their social order. It was this fear which prompted the Quraysh to seek their repatriation from Abyssinia. Finally, the boycott of Banū Hāshim and Banū al-Muṭṭalib, which took place shortly after the Muslim migration to Abyssinia, goes a long way to prove our contention that it was to escape trials and persecution and to secure religious liberty that the Muslims migrated.

The Prophet seeing that he himself was protected and relatively unharmed by the malpractices of the Quraysh, felt morally obliged to help his followers escape suffering and indignities at the hands of their Quraysh enemies. While it was, no doubt, this desire to help his beleaguered followers escape persecution that motivated the Prophet to suggest the emigration to Abyssinia, it would not be out of place to speculate about the existence of other motives for the Prophet's action. From his efforts, at this time, to elicit support from tribes and cities beyond the immediate sphere of the Quraysh's influence, it can be inferred that he had reached the conviction that his call to Islam would not be honoured in Makkah, at least for some years, and that he must look elsewhere, beyond that city, for such support. It was towards this end that he undertook the journey to the city of aṭ-Ṭā'if which took place immediately after the termination of the boycott (see pp. 182–5).

If this theory is correct, then it seems very likely that he was probably, also, investigating the possibility of gaining support from 'the land of truth and righteousness' which was the Negus' Abyssinia. Though the Prophet had not been to that land, he clearly possessed a fair idea of what was going on there. Moreover, Abyssinia was a household word in Makkah due to the frequent trade visits which the Quraysh merchants used to make to its markets and fairs. On their return these merchants brought back favourable impressions about the land, its just and compassionate King and its urbane and civilized people who seemed to enjoy a substantial measure of prosperity and social and political stability. These features must have aroused a certain envy in the hearts of the Makkans because of the state of social instability and civil strife which characterized Makkan society at that time. In the eyes of the oppressed Muslims, this picture of the African land across the Red Sea presented a very appealing contrast to the chaos and disorder in Arabia.

Rumours About Mass Conversion of Makkah (or the 'Satanic Verses')

The rumours that mass conversion of the people of Makkah to Islam had taken place at the beginning of the sixth year of the Prophet's mission is important because of its connection with the return of the first company of Muslim emigrants from Abyssinia. It is also important because of its connection with the so-called *Ḥadīth al-Gharānīq al-'Ulā* (the Talk of Exalted Damsels or the Talk of the Exalted Swans). What is the background to this 'talk'? The Prophet was no doubt deeply concerned that the Quraysh had rejected his call to monotheism. He was profoundly grieved by the enmity and opposition which they had shown towards him and his followers. He tried every possible way to effect a reconciliation with them. One day, so runs the *Ḥadīth al-Gharānīq al-'Ulā,* he was sitting with the people as they assembled around the Ka'bah. They talked to him and he responded with great sympathy. Then he started to recite, in their hearing, *Sūrah an-Najm.*[8] Some commentators of the Qur'ān say that the opening verses of this *sūrah* are related to Muḥammad's ascent to Heaven, in the famous episode of the *Isrā'* and *Mi'rāj* (see pp. 187–9). The recitation (from verse 13) went as follows:

> And he saw him (Gabriel) yet another time,
> By the lote-tree at the farthest boundary,
> Near unto which is the Garden of Abode,
> When that which covers the tree does cover it.
> The sight turned not aside, nor did it extend beyond the limits.
> Indeed he saw some of the greater signs of his Lord.
> Have ye seen al-Lāt and al-'Uzzā?
> And Manāt the third one besides? . . .

Here, the propounders of *Ḥadīth al-Gharānīq* maintain that the Prophet's recitation was tampered with by Satan (hence the name 'Satanic Verses')[9] who managed to put into his speech the false words:

These are the Exalted *Gharānīq* (Damsels or Swans)
And verily their intercession (with God) is to be hoped for.

The Quraysh were wildly excited at the unexpected acknowledgement of their three major idols, so goes the tale of the Satanic Verses. When the Prophet reached a place where prostration is mandatory in the recitation, the Quraysh idolaters followed him in his prostration. The incident allegedly gave rise to rumours that mass conversion to Islam had taken place in Makkah. The rumour reached the emigrants in Abyssinia, so goes the tale, and they hastily returned to Makkah. When they drew near to the city, they discovered that the rumour was false. Gabriel came that night to the Prophet, told him what Satan had done during his morning recitation, and the Satanic Verses were discredited. Muḥammad, *ṣallā Allāhu 'alayhi wa sallam,* greatly depressed, summoned the Muslims and related to them the Revelation concerning the Satanic Verses, and added the genuine Qur'ānic continuation of *Sūrah an-Najm* from 'And Manāt the third one besides?':

Could it be that you have the male progeny unto you, and unto Him the female?
That, indeed, were an unjust partition.
Verily, they are but names you have named,
You and your fathers. Allah has not revealed concerning it (any) Warrant.

Now, the facts of the situation concerning the Satanic Verses (or *Ḥadīth al-Gharānīq*) are as follows:

(1) No mention of them is to be found in any of the authentic books of the sayings (or traditions) of the Prophet.[10]

(2) Ibn Isḥāq, the leading author of the life of the Prophet, dismissed them as 'the invention of the heretics'.[11]

(3) Ibn Hishām completely ignored them in his edition of Ibn Isḥāq. What Ibn Hishām[12] gives, in connection with the return of the first refugees to Abyssinia, is the rumour about the mass conversion of the people of Makkah to Islam. No details are given, nor what was the substance of this rumour, except that it turned out to be false.

In a comment on this quotation from Ibn Hishām, as-Suhaylī, a leading commentator and expounder of Ibn Hishām, gives the following notes:

'The reason for that (the return of the emigrants from Abyssinia) is that the Messenger of Allah recited *Sūrah an-Najm*; then Satan added the remark about al-Lāt and al-'Uzzā, that they were 'the Exalted Damsels', and that their intercession (with Allah) was to be hoped for. This became widely known in Makkah and the polytheists were delighted and said: "He (Muḥammad) has mentioned kindly our deities." When the Prophet prostrated himself at the end of the *sūrah* both the polytheists and the Muslims prostrated after him. And Allah revealed (verses 52–3 of *Sūrah al-Ḥajj*):

> Never have We sent a Messenger or a Prophet before you but when he recited (the Scripture) Satan proposed (something) in his recitation, but Allah abrogates that which Satan proposes; then Allah perfects His revelations. Allah is all-Knowing, all-Wise.[13]

Because of this, news reached them (the emigrants) in the land of Abyssinia that the Quraysh had professed Islam. Mūsa ibn 'Uqbah mentioned it (the story of the Satanic Verses) and Ibn Isḥāq[14] also mentioned it, but not through the chain of al-Bukhārī. Authorities of the foundation (of Islamic jurisprudence) refute it (the talk of the Satanic Verses) by (valid) arguments. But even those who accept it as authentic, interpret it in different ways: (a) one of them is that it was Satan, in the first place, that uttered those verses and spread them. The Prophet himself never spoke those words. This may be so, but part of their statement mentions that Gabriel said (reproachfully) to the Prophet: I did not come to you with these words (an obvious implication that the Prophet said them himself);[15] (b) the Prophet actually said them (the verses) himself but meant by "al-Gharānīq" the Angels; (c) that the Prophet repeated them as a quotation of a statement of the polytheists, in order to express his misgivings about it. But the whole affair, according to my opinion, is unauthentic but Allah knows best.'[16]

(4) The major sources which give elaborate details about the *Ḥadīth al-Gharānīq* are: (a) al-Wāqidī and his secretary Ibn Sa'd[17]

and (b) aṭ-Ṭabarī.[18] We have already given an outline of the story of the Satanic Verses, as it is narrated by these sources.

It does not appear that aṭ-Ṭabarī, being a much later authority, since he died in 310 after the *Hijrah* (922 C.E.), was drawing on the same sources as Ibn Sa'd or al-Wāqidī. He could not be drawing on either Ibn Isḥāq or Ibn Hishām, both of whom have rejected the Satanic Verses as spurious. Nor is he drawing upon 'Urwah ibn az-Zubayr, an early authority who seemed to have been sometimes ignored by Ibn Isḥāq, but whom aṭ-Ṭabarī was always keen to quote whenever he could. In two versions of his account of the Satanic Verses, aṭ-Ṭabarī quotes an apparently anonymous authority by the name of Abū al-'Āliyah. We cannot place much confidence in aṭ-Ṭabarī, not only because he wrote so long after the event, but also because he was not a specialist on the *Sīrah* (or life) of the Prophet. He was a general historian who included in his works some chapters on the life of the Prophet. Our confidence in the authenticity of the incident relating to the Satanic Verses is further weakened by its rejection by the principal *Sīrah* authorities, Ibn Isḥāq and his disciples, Ibn Hishām and as-Suhaylī. We are thus only left with al-Wāqidī (and his secretary Ibn Sa'd) as the ultimate source of the tale of the Satanic Verses. But al-Wāqidī, who died in 207 A.H. is also a later authority compared to Ibn Isḥāq, who died in 150 or 153 A.H. Moreover, al-Wāqidī is chiefly referred to in connection with the Madinan period of the life of the Prophet, although he is also of interest when he quotes 'Urwah ibn az-Zubayr in connection with the Makkan era. Similarly, Ibn Sa'd also relies on a little-known authority by the name of al-Muṭṭalib ibn 'Abdullāh ibn Ḥanṭab.

Ibn Kathīr, the famous commentator on the Qur'ān, asserted that 'they (various versions of the alleged verses) are all loose (in the chain of authorities) and I have not found them supported in any authentic way, but Allah knows best.'[19] According to Ibn Kathīr and the majority of authorities on the science of *Ḥadīth* (or the Prophet's sayings), the traditions on the Satanic Verses are weak in their *Isnād* (or chain of authorities); for example, Abū Bakr al-Bazzār said: 'We do not know that this tradition has been related on the (direct) authority of the Prophet (i.e. there is a break in the chain of authorities reporting the *Ḥadīth,* in the sense that the last person who related it was not a Companion of the Prophet). It does not possess an *Isnād* which is worth mentioning. As to its subject matter or content, it contradicts a basic doctrine of the religion, namely the infallibility of the Prophet and his immunity against the intrigues of Satan.'[20]

I think that talk about the inconsistency between the doctrine of the infallibility of the Prophet and the alleged Satanic Verses given that they were genuine, can be completely refuted. Even aṭ-Ṭabarī's[21] account ascribes the 'Satanic' verses to Satan. Satan is supposed to have put the alleged verses into the Prophet's mouth. But other authorities are quite explicit in ascribing the verses to Satan without mentioning anything about the Prophet having uttered them. These authorities maintain that Satan himself uttered these verses in the hearing of the Prophet's audience, and without the intervention of the Prophet.

But quite apart from the considerations of the sources, there are weighty problems which bar any critical acceptance of the Satanic Verses as authentic. (a) First of all, it is not inevitable that we connect the rumour of mass conversion of the people of Makkah with the talk of Satanic Verses. In fact, it has been suggested by Haykal[22] that this rumour was generated by the startling conversion of 'Umar ibn al-Khaṭṭāb. Haykal also ascribes the return of the first batch of emigrants from Abyssinia to the threat of revolt against the Negus. (b) It has been remarked by Muḥammad 'Abduh, the famous Egyptian scholar of the nineteenth century, that the Arabic word *'Gharānīq'* does not in any way refer to the idols. It could only mean (i) a kind of bird, namely the swan or a crowned-crane; (ii) a handsome young man who is particularly careful about his looks, a kind of dandy. Now clearly none of those meanings has anything to do with the Arabian idols – no third meaning can be found for the word *'Ghirniq'*, which is the singular of *'Gharānīq'*. (c) Lastly, we have to deal with the contention of various authorities that verses 52 and 53 of *Sūrah al-Ḥajj* (the Pilgrimage) mentioned by as-Suhaylī in the quotation we gave above were actually revealed in connection with the so-called Satanic Verses. First of all, the verses in question obviously have a perfectly general import; they express a valid statement about all Prophets and all Divine Messengers – that they in their capacity as human beings, despite their infallibility, are sometimes misled in their judgements and conduct by Satan. But Allah soon denies what Satan foists on them and so He perfects His designs for mankind. In the case of the Prophet Muḥammad, *ṣallā Allāhu ʻalayhi wa sallam,* there are instances in the Qur'ān where the Prophet's judgements are sharply criticized. *Sūrah ʻAbasa* – 'He frowned' – deals with the Prophet's slighting of a poor blind man who came to him seeking guidance. The Prophet was then engaged in trying to persuade certain leaders of the Quraysh to adopt Islam and showed his displeasure at the blind man's interruption by frowning and turning away from him. *Sūrah ʻAbasa* was then revealed pointing out and correcting the Prophet's error of judgement. A similar incident occurred when the Prophet was inclined to show deference to a group of Quraysh aristocrats who had objected to sitting with a group of Muslims of lowly social status, some of whom were former slaves of the aristocrats. But Allah revealed the following verse:

> Repel not those who pray to their Lord in the morning and in the evening, seeking His countenance. You are not all accountable for them nor are they accountable for you that you should repel them and be of the wrong ones.[23]

Again the Prophet's conduct was reproved concerning the uneasy marriage relationship that existed between his adopted son Zayd ibn Ḥārithah and his cousin Zaynab bint Jaḥsh. The Prophet had consistently advised against divorce, because he feared the possible public reaction.

> And you concealed within yourself what Allah was to bring to light, fearing people whereas Allah had a better right that you should fear Him.[24]

Verses 52 and 53 of *Sūrah al-Ḥajj* do not therefore refer to *Ḥadīth al-Gharānīq* but to incidents like the above-mentioned ones where the Prophet's judgements were not confirmed by the Qur'ān.

Secondly, and in keeping with the above interpretation, the word 'tamanna' in verse 52 of *Sūrah al-Ḥajj* could not be taken to mean 'recite' as some sources have taken it to mean. Rather it means 'desire' or 'hope'. The meaning of the verses then is that whenever a Prophet or messenger strongly desired or hoped for something, Satan exploited his longing and attempted to lead him into error and falsehood.

The above remarks on the so-called 'Satanic Verses' should suffice for our present purposes but for further explanation and details see Appendix 2.

The Boycott of Banū Hāshim

If the Prophet's directive to his persecuted Companions to emigrate to Abyssinia was a major initiative on his part in order to alleviate their suffering, the boycott was the spontaneous response of the Quraysh to this initiative. It expressed their frustration and indignation about this successful initiative by which the Prophet neutralized their attempts to repress the new movement. Whereas the Prophet's initiative was the positive action of a man with a mission, the idolater's reaction represented the frustration and negative attitude of people fighting a losing battle. They could command no cunning or power to stop the advance and spread of Islam. Seeing the gracious reception which the Muslim emigrants found in the 'land of righteousness' the polytheists became even more angry and spiteful. In their poverty of mind and purpose, they resorted to hysterical violence against the adherents of the new religion. They intensified their efforts to repress the Muslims and to force them to recant their monotheistic faith. It was these efforts that led to the long and bitter boycott of the Muslims and their Banū Hāshim supporters and protectors. Ibn Isḥāq describes the circumstances leading up to the boycott as follows:

'When the Quraysh saw that the companions of the Prophet had landed in a country where they had found security and stability, and that the Negus had protected those who took refuge under him, and that 'Umar had become a Muslim, and that he and Ḥamzah sided with the Messenger of Allah and that Islam continued to spread among the tribes (of Arabia), they held a meeting and after some deliberation decided to write a document in which they made it binding upon themselves with respect to Banū Hāshim and Banū al-Muṭṭalib that they would not marry with them nor give their girls in marriage to them; neither would they sell them anything, nor buy anything from them. They wrote this in the document and vowed to observe its terms. They then hung the document inside the Ka'bah, in order to impress it even more upon themselves.'

Ibn Sa'd roughly gives the same account, quoting a number of authorities, except that he mentions that the Quraysh also agreed to kill the Prophet.

When Banū Hāshim and Banū al-Muṭṭalib saw what the other Quraysh clans had done with this document, they sided with the Prophet and Abū Ṭālib and assembled in the Shi'b (defile) of the latter. Only Abū Lahab, the Prophet's uncle, dissented from his Banū Hāshim clan and sided with the Quraysh, no doubt influenced both by his financial interests, which were considerable, and also by his wife, who was from the generally hostile clan of 'Abd Shams. Thus the boycott was fully enforced against the Prophet, his followers and their protectors from Banū Hāshim and Banū al-Muṭṭalib, both Muslims and idolaters alike. The Shi'b of Abū Ṭālib was a rugged little valley enclosed by hills on all sides which could only be entered from Makkah by a narrow defile. In this arid valley, Muḥammad, *ṣallā Allāhu 'alayhi wa sallam,* his followers and the entire clans of Banū Hāshim and Banū al-Muṭṭalib, were obliged to retire with limited supplies of food and necessities. Their banishment from Makkah took place in the beginning of the seventh year of the Prophet's mission.[25] Soon the supplies of food and basic necessities began to run short, and the people of the Shi'b had to wait for foreign merchants, who came to Makkah only occasionally, to obtain fresh supplies. Thus hardship and suffering became their lot. As the months and the years of their confinement dragged along the wailing of hungry children and women in the Shi'b could be heard in Makkah. A few, known for their spite and cruelty, were well satisfied with the effect of the boycott which they had imposed upon the Muslims. Many were moved by pity and sympathy and others were impressed by the devotion, courage and dedication of the Muslims to their cause. According to the best accounts, the isolation and boycott lasted for two years,[26] during which Muḥammad, *ṣallā Allāhu 'alayhi wa sallam,* and the inmates of the Shi'b could only venture outside their place of confinement during the season of Pilgrimage. At those times, which were sacred, they would go out, mingle freely with their oppressors and perhaps secure some supplies, either by purchase from foreign merchants or as gifts, which some sympathetic souls in Makkah delivered to them in secret.

At length, the majority of the Quraysh became exasperated

with the senseless banishment of Banū Hāshim and Banū al-Muṭṭalib from Makkah and the Muslims were allowed to return to their homes. When the Muslim sympathizers from the Quraysh went to the Ka'bah to take down the boycott document, they found it had been completely consumed by white ants, except for that portion in which the name of Allah was written. Abū Ṭālib himself is reported to have drawn the attention of the Quraysh to the activity of the ants. Naturally, he interpreted this incident as a further demonstration of the injustice and aggression against the Prophet and his clan. His views succeeded in creating a division within the ranks of the Quraysh; a group of them, led by five distinguished men, were of the opinion that the ban should be lifted at once. When they saw that their opinion was not heeded, they put on their swords and proceeded to the Shi'b and encouraged the Muslims to return to their homes in Makkah under their protection. The Muslims did so and the Quraysh determination to enforce the boycott was at last broken. The instigators of the boycott had been morally defeated. The five distinguished men were: Zam'ah ibn al-Aswad, Abu'l-Bukhtarī ibn Hāshim, Zuhayr ibn Abī Umayyah, 'Adī ibn Qays and Muṭ'im ibn 'Adī.

The boycott of the early Muslims, and their gracious Prophet is a useful reminder of the hardship and suffering which they had to bear in the cause of their faith. It also shows that the method of boycott was a weapon which enemies of Islam have long used in their vain efforts to extinguish the light of God.

The end of the boycott marked the tenth year of the Prophet's mission. The embattled Muḥammad, *ṣallā Allāhu 'alayhi wa sallam,* returned to face yet new trials and difficulties.

The Year of Grief

Hardly had the Prophet settled in Makkah after the end of the boycott than two events took place that were particularly hard for his sensitive nature to bear. First, Khadījah bint Khuwaylid, the Prophet's much-loved wife who had always helped and consoled him in times of hardship and distress, died unexpectedly. Perhaps the harsh and uncomfortable life in the arid Shi'b during the difficult years of boycott, with so little to eat had badly affected her health, for she had not been used to such painful living conditions. Her death left the Prophet without that affectionate support which had for so long helped to sustain him in the face of trial and persecution. To the many sorrows and bereavements of his childhood there was now added this sad experience. Khadījah, faithful and loving Khadījah, his comfort and help, had now gone from his life. The Prophet deeply grieved and, almost overwhelmed by sorrow, kept to his quarters for many days, rarely appearing in public.

A month and ten days after the death of Khadījah, Abū Ṭālib, his uncle and protector, passed away. The Prophet's grief became yet deeper. He kept more and more to his house, seldom venturing outside. He was keenly aware that he was left not only without a spouse, but also without a protector. His idolatrous enemies saw in the death of Abū Ṭālib a long-awaited opportunity to harm and persecute him without provoking the wrath or the counter-offensive of Banū Hāshim, now that their influential patriarch had died. And this was precisely what happened. 'Abdullāh ibn 'Urwah ibn az-Zubayr on the authority of his father has related that the neighbours of the Prophet who were opposed to him, under the leadership of Abū Lahab and his wife, intensified their campaign of persecution. The Prophet used to remove the unclean refuse which they repeatedly threw inside his yard and in front of his door, complaining in a markedly restrained voice:

'What kind of neighbourhood is this, O Sons of 'Abd Manāf?'[27] But the worst incident of persecution which the Prophet experienced after the death of Abū Ṭālib is narrated by Ibn Isḥāq as follows:

'Then Khadījah bint Khuwaylid and Abū Ṭālib died in the same year. Misfortunes continued to befall the Messenger of Allah, *ṣallā Allāhu 'alayhi wa sallam,* as they could not hope to inflict upon him during Abū Ṭālib's life. One of their insolent mob even heaped dust and earth upon his gracious head. As he entered his home, one of his daughters wept passionately as she wiped the dust from her father's head.

'Do not cry, my daughter,' he said, 'for Allah shall protect your father.'

Then he added: 'The Quraysh could not have done this to me had Abū Ṭālib been alive.'[28]

Ibn Isḥāq narrates that when the leaders of the polytheists heard about Abū Ṭālib's illness, they hurried to his bedside. They included 'Utbah and Shaybah, sons of Rabī'ah, Abū Jahl,

Umayyah ibn Khalaf and Abū Sufyān ibn Ḥarb. They again complained about the activities of the Prophet in Makkah and the contacts which he was then establishing with the various tribes of Arabia. They appealed to him to send for the Prophet so that they might plead with him to desist from vilifying their (heathen) deities. The Prophet came and said:

> 'Only one word, if you say it, you would rule over the Arabs and by it the non-Arabs would submit to you. Say: *Lā ilāha illa Allāh*.'

They replied: 'O Muḥammad! Do you want to reduce the deities to only one Deity. Verily, your advice is fantastic.'

On this occasion Allah revealed the following Qur'ānic verses:

> *Ṣād.*
> By the Qur'ān containing the Remembrance (of Allah). Nay, but those who disbelieve are in false pride and schism . . . Is he making the gods one God? Verily, this is an astounding thing.
> The chiefs among them went about exhorting: Go and be staunch to your gods! Verily, this is a thing designed.[29]

When the polytheists declined the Prophet's demand that they accept the dictum that there was no God except Allah, Abū Ṭālib commented that the demand was not an excessive thing to ask. Ibn Isḥāq mentions here that when Abū Ṭālib made that comment, the Prophet aspired to win his conversion to Islam. Some sources even maintain that he actually uttered the monotheistic dictum, but the accepted opinion is that he died in unbelief.

The year in which Khadījah and Abū Ṭālib died became known as *'Ām al-Ḥuzn* (the Year of Grief), because of the tremendous loss to the already afflicted Prophet. The Muslims shared in Muḥammad's, *ṣallā Allāhu 'alayhi wa sallam,* sorrow and mourning but they were too weak and oppressed to provide the kind of protection he had lost due to the death of Abū Ṭālib. After the Prophet had spent some days confined to his home, he renewed his efforts and activities to proclaim his Lord's commandments to 'Rise and Warn'. However, some other place had to be found where the Muslims would be more responsive to Allah's call to pure monotheism.

The Trip to aṭ-Ṭā'if

The Prophet's hopes and aspirations for support, safety and protection were finally directed to the green and beautiful city of aṭ-Ṭā'if. Aṭ-Ṭā'if was neither remote nor hostile to the Quraysh, and particularly not to Banū Hāshim who had intermarried frequently with the people of the city. It lies some sixty or seventy miles from Makkah, but, in contrast to the low and excessively hot valley of the holy city, aṭ-Ṭā'if lies at a high elevation and enjoys a temperate climate, which made it a favourable summer resort for the wealthy Makkans. Moreover, the city is in the midst of a green and fertile valley, famous for its vineyards. Many well-to-do Makkans owned, and still own, property in this valley. In particular, the foremost leaders of the enemies of the Prophet, 'Utbah and Shaybah, sons of Rabī'ah ('Abd Shams), to whom is ascribed a major role in stirring up hatred and enmity against the Prophet, owned property in aṭ-Ṭā'if.

The Prophet's decision to proceed to aṭ-Ṭā'if in search of a new base for his faith and in protest against the molestation and oppression to which he and his followers were exposed in Makkah, must be regarded as a very positive and daring step. The Prophet became convinced, after the death of Khadījah and Abū Ṭālib, that he could no longer stay in Makkah with any hope of victory or security. Before things became too critical, he had to act vigorously to secure an alternative to Makkah. So, accompanied by Zayd, his trusted adopted son, he set out for aṭ-Ṭā'if, only a few weeks after the deaths of Khadījah and Abū Ṭālib. Once there, he went straight to a leading family in the city, in particular to the sons of 'Amr ibn 'Umayr, known as 'Abd Yālīl, Mas'ūd and Ḥabīb. But their response to his call to monotheism was disappointing. They too preferred their heathenistic sanctuary and their goddess, Al-Lāt, to the worship of the One True God. They asked the same pointless questions as their Makkan counterparts. Despairing of their conversion, he only requested them not to disclose the objective of his trip to aṭ-Ṭā'if. Even this they were not prepared to grant and with the treachery which is always characteristic of the enemies of Truth and goodness, they urged the rabble of the city to follow him and shout abuse at him. They even threw stones at him until his feet bled. Zayd, who did his best to shield him, received a painful wound in the head. The insolent mob continued to chastise the Prophet and his companion till they were driven to the outskirts of the city, where the Prophet and Zayd took refuge in a vineyard which happened to be owned by the two arch-enemies of Islam, ‘Utbah and Shaybah, sons of Rabī‘ah. When they saw the Prophet, breathless and bleeding, they were apparently moved to pity. They sent their slave, a certain ‘Addās, from Nineveh, with a tray of fresh grapes. ‘Addās is reported to have been deeply impressed by the noble bearing of the stranger, and by his pious prayers when he received and ate the grapes. When the Prophet knew that ‘Addās was from Nineveh, he mentioned the Prophet Jonas with sympathy and compassion. That mention completely won the heart of the Christian ‘Addās who is reported to have kissed the Prophet's head, hands and feet. It was a moving and comforting homage that must have somewhat reassured the troubled heart of the Prophet. And from this troubled heart came the following prayer, filled with pathos, yearning and hope, and absolute dependence on God:

> O Lord! Unto You do I complain of my frailty, lack of resources and my insignificance before (these) people. O Most Merciful of the Merciful, You are the Lord of the oppressed and You are my Lord. To whom will You abandon me? To one afar who looks askance at me or to an enemy to whom You have given mastery over me? If Your indignation is not against me, I have no worry. But Your security encompasses me. I seek refuge in the light of Your countenance, which (light) illumines the darkness and by which the affairs of this life and the Hereafter have been rightly ordered, lest Your wrath alight upon me, or Your indignation descend upon me. It is Yours to show anger until You are pleased, and there is no other resource nor any power but in You.[30]

When the Prophet felt somewhat refreshed, he set out towards Makkah, the city which had so far rejected him and his Divine call. But he could not go straight to the city for he had a serious problem to solve. The passing away of Abū Ṭālib left him completely without a protector. So he stopped at a place called Nakhlah in the midst of the empty desert. When he got up, in the middle of the night to pray, offer his passionate invocations and complain of his concerns and worries to his Lord, he witnessed an incredible spectacle. A huge crowd of *jinns* filled the limitless desert. They were attracted by the beautiful verse of the glorious Qur'ān which the Prophet was reciting with complete absorption, unaware of the extraordinary gathering around him. But Gabriel descended upon him with news of the extraordinary event that was taking place in Nakhlah:

> And (remember O Muḥammad!) When We caused a company of *jinns* to come unto you, listening to the Qur'ān. When they were present at its recitation, they said: Listen. When it was finished, they turned to their folk, warning.
>
> They said: O our people! Indeed we have heard a Scripture which has been revealed after Moses, attesting the truth of that which was before it, guiding unto the truth and unto a straight path.
>
> O our people! Obey the summoner of Allah and believe in Him, that He may forgive you (some of) your sins and save you from a fearful doom.
>
> And who does not obey Allah's summoner, he can in no wise escape in the earth, and he (can find) no protecting friend instead of Him. Such are in error manifest.[31]

Although Bukhārī narrates that *Sūrah al-Jinn* (*Sūrah* 72) was revealed on a different occasion, namely when the Prophet was on his way to the Fair of 'Ukāẓ accompanied by his followers, Ibn Isḥāq believes that it was revealed on the same occasion as *Sūrah al-Aḥqāf* (the Wind-Curved Sandhills) above. However, both versions assert that *Sūrah al-Jinn* was revealed at Nakhlah. This *Sūrah* opens as follows:

> Say (O Muḥammad): It is revealed unto me that a company of Jinns listened, and said: Verily we have heard a marvellous Recitation (Qur'ān), which guides unto righteousness, so we believe in it, and we will never (henceforth) take any partner with our Lord . . .[32]

After leaving Nakhlah, the Prophet stopped at Ḥirā' and sent a message to Muṭ'im ibn 'Adī, one of those who had resisted the boycott, asking if it was possible for him to extend his protection to him so that he could enter Makkah. The chivalrous Muṭ'im instantly agreed. Summoning his sons, he ordered them to take their weapons and assemble in the courtyard of the Ka'bah. When they were assembled in the Ka'bah, Muṭ'im called out loudly that he had extended his protection *(Jiwār)* to the Prophet and that whoever harmed him would have to bear the consequences. The Quraysh were overawed, and the Prophet managed to enter Makkah safely. After visiting the sanctuary, he was able to retire to his home in peace. Khadījah was no longer there, nor was Abū Ṭālib. The gracious Prophet, after his fruitless journey to aṭ-Ṭā'if, must have felt lonely and isolated. Moreover, he still had to find an alternative to Makkah.

Notes and References

1. Ibn Hishām, p. 321f.
2. Ibn Isḥāq wrongly gives these rumours as the reason for the return of the second group of refugees.
3. Ibn Hishām, p. 335.
4. Qur'ān, 19 *(Maryam)*.
5. Ibn Hishām, p. 336f.
6. *Ibid.*, p. 341. The editors add a note to the effect that when some people protested against the Prophet's prayer, saying, 'You pray for the infidel,' Allah revealed, 'Verily, from the people of the Book, there are some who believe in Allah and what has been revealed unto you and what has been revealed unto them.' Qur'ān, 3 *(Āl 'Imrān)*: 199.
7. Montgomery Watt suggests that part of Muḥammad's aim in sending the Muslims to Abyssinia may have been to develop a trade route not under the control of the Makkan monopolists. See his *Islam and the Integration of Society*, Northwestern University Press, 1961, p. 9.
8. Qur'ān, 53 *(An-Najm)*.
9. The term 'Satanic Verses' was first used by Sir William Muir.
10. Al-Bukhārī mentions the prostration of the Prophet in which he was followed by the polytheists but he makes no mention of any 'Satanic Verse'.
11. See M. H. Haykal, *Ḥayāt Muḥammad*, Cairo.
12. Ibn Hishām, p. 364.
13. Qur'ān, 22 *(Al-Ḥajj)*.
14. But Ibn Isḥāq in fact dismissed it as a fabrication.
15. Parentheses added.
16. Ibn Hishām, p. 304.
17. Ibn Sa'd, Vol. I, p. 205.

18. See Montgomery Watt, *Muhammad at Mecca,* p. 104f, who gives a full account of aṭ-Ṭābarī's version of the 'Satanic Verses'.
19. Ibn Kathīr, *Al-Bidāyah wa'n Nihāyah fi't Ta'rīkh.*
20. Sayyid Quṭb, *Fī Ẓilāl al-Qur'ān,* Vol. IV, p. 104.
21. Aṭ-Ṭabarī is clearly following Ibn Sa'd in this respect.
22. Haykal, *op. cit.,* p. 163.
23. Qur'ān, 6 *(Al-An'ām)*: 52.
24. Qur'ān, 33 *(Al-Aḥzāb)*: 37.
25. Ibn Sa'd, Vol. I, p. 208.
26. *Ibid.,* p. 209f.
27. Ibn Hishām, p. 416.
28. *Ibid.*
29. Qur'ān, 38 *(Ṣād)*: 1–6.
30. Ibn Hishām, p. 420.
31. Qur'ān, 46 *(Al-Aḥqāf)*: 29–32.
32. Qur'ān, 72 *(Al-Jinn).*

CHAPTER 8

The Tide Turns

Once he had launched his public ministry towards the end of the third year of his mission, the Prophet's efforts to win over the bedouin tribes of Arabia never abated. But in the new circumstances following the 'Year of Grief' these attempts acquired an added urgency. Ibn Isḥāq narrates that he contacted many tribes hoping to win them over. In particular, he made contact, in the season of Pilgrimage, with Banū Kalb and Banū Ḥanīfah, who were especially insolent in rebuffing him, and also Banū 'Āmir. None of them showed any interest in his call to them to abandon idolatry and worship the One True God. Abū Lahab, his polytheist uncle, followed him around in Minā, a valley not far from Makkah, in order to discourage the tribes from accepting what he advocated or even listening to him. Ibn Sa'd even narrates that Abū Lahab was most savage in his attempts to frustrate the endeavours of the Prophet to win over the bedouins. For instance, he would say, commenting on the Prophet's exhortation, 'Don't obey him. He is a lying renegade!' On such occasions the bedouins became insolent and would say:

'Your family and your tribe know all about you, but they have not followed you.' The Prophet would then pray: 'O Lord, if You will, it would not be so!'

The Isrā' and the *Mi'rāj*

It is in this period that the Prophet's night trip to Jerusalem *(Isrā')* and his ascent from there to heaven *(Mi'rāj)* took place (see Appendix 1). That memorable night, the Prophet was sleeping in the house of his cousin, Umm Hānī. Said 'Umm Hānī:

'The Messenger of Allah spent that night in my house. He performed the Night (*'Ishā'*) Prayer, then he slept, and we slept. Just before dawn we woke the Messenger of Allah, but when he performed the Dawn Prayer and we prayed with him, he said: "O Umm Hānī, I have prayed the Night Prayer with you in this valley, as you have witnessed, then I went to the House (Mosque) of Jerusalem and prayed therein, and I have prayed the Dawn Prayer with you now, as you see." I said: "O Prophet of Allah, do not tell it to the people, they may belie and harm you." He replied: "By Allah, I will tell it to them." '[1]

The question arises whether the Prophet's *Isrā'* (Night Trip) was spiritual or physical or both. Umm Hānī's version seems to imply that it was by his soul only, since his body never left the house. 'Ā'ishah also narrates that the Prophet's body never left the house that night. This interpretation is also supported by the description of *Isrā'*, cited in many versions, as a true dream or vision.

The *Mi'rāj* (or Ascent to heaven) is also narrated in our source books in a very vivid way. And the same question, that was raised in connection with *Isrā'*, can also be raised in connection with *Mi'rāj*, i.e. was it a spiritual or a physical journey? It is not our purpose in this study to plunge into the theological controversy that has raged around this question. I can only say that if one's belief in the free, limitless power and potency of God is firm and unshakeable, then the questions at issue lose much of their interest. Whether the Night Trip *(Isrā')* or the stupendous Ascent *(Mi'rāj)* were spiritual or physical, the two events were of the greatest significance and confirm that this honour conferred upon the Prophet by his Lord acclaims him as a Divine Prophet. Its impact upon Makkah was enormous. Some persons, who lacked belief and imagination and therefore could not conceive of the possibility of the two unusual events, became so shocked that they reportedly lapsed into apostasy. Only Abū Bakr refused to be overwhelmed by the extraordinary nature of the two achievements. When he was first told about the incident, he replied, 'By Allah, if he had said it, he must be truthful for I have believed him in his claims that revelation descends upon him from Heaven during the night. This latter matter is by far greater than what you are now wondering about.' Abū Bakr's reply showed his acute perception and natural common sense. When he met the Prophet in person and listened to him relating details of the *Isrā'* and *Mi'rāj,* he said to him, 'You have told the truth.' Because of this incident, Abū Bakr was called 'aṣ-Ṣiddīq' – the one who affirms the truth. No better testimony to the veracity of the Prophet could be imagined especially as it came from someone closely associated with him and who knew him very well over a long period of time.

The Winning of Yathrib

From there on, the Muslims never met with an obstacle which they were unable to overcome. The hardest years of trial and probation were over. The Muslims had been subjected to the test of the crucible and had survived. The strength of their faith and their determination to carry out the Divine mission in face of hardship, torture, exile, boycott and unjust persecution was sufficiently attested. Thus, by being utterly sincere in their persistent endeavours, the early Muslims were well qualified to deserve Allah's victory; and complete victory was indeed just within reach, as if it had an appointment with those noble seekers of the truth, and worshippers of the One, True God. Their just cause, and high moral excellence had won them the hearts of the inhabitants of Yathrib, and this proved a turning point in the history of Islam.

What was the background to the exciting events that led to the winning and conversion of the two leading Arab tribes of Yathrib, the Khazraj and the Aws? Those two tribes had been in conflict with each other for many years, and were bitter rivals of the Jewish inhabitants for financial and socio-political control of the city. The two secret meetings at which the Khazraj and Aws agreed to accept Islam and to extend support and protection to the Prophet and his persecuted followers came to be known as the first and second 'Aqabah Pledges.

'Aqabah was a place in the valley of Minā, not far from Makkah, which was used, and still is used, as an encampment for pilgrims.

Our sources agree that prior to the conclusion of the pledges at 'Aqabah, the Prophet had made successful contacts with the Arabs of Yathrib. There is disagreement as to the number and identity of the men with whom these contacts had been made. Both Ibn Isḥāq and Ibn Sa'd are of the view that contacts prior to 'Aqabah were made with six men (and, according to Ibn Isḥāq, a woman) of the Khazraj tribe. Their names were as follows:

As‘ad ibn Zurārah
‘Awf ibn al-Ḥārith
Rāfi‘ ibn Mālik
Quṭbah ibn ‘Āmir ibn Ḥadīdah
‘Uqbah ibn ‘Āmir ibn Nābī
Jābir ibn ‘Abdullāh

Ibn Isḥāq adds

‘Afrā’ bint (daughter of) ‘Ubayd.

The circumstances that led to their conversion is related by Ibn Isḥāq, as follows:

‘Who are you?’ asked the Prophet (who met them as he was soliciting the support of Arab tribes in the season of the Pilgrimage).[2]

‘A company of the Khazraj,’ they replied.

‘Are you of the confederates of the Jews?’ he asked.

‘Yes,’ they replied.

‘Would you then sit down so that I may talk to you?’

‘Yes,’ and they sat down.

The Prophet then proceeded to exhort them to the worship of the One True God, and expounded (the doctrines) of Islam to them, and recited portions of the Qur’ān. Some of the circumstances which Allah designed to render them more inclined to accept Islam were that the Jews of Yathrib who were a people with a Scripture, in contrast to them (the Khazraj), who were idolaters, used to threaten them, whenever they were in conflict, with the appearance of a Prophet, who would slaughter them as ‘Ād and Iram (two ancient Arab tribes) had been destroyed. When the Prophet thus talked to them about Islam, they said unto one another: O people, he is indeed the Prophet with whom the Jews have been threatening us. Do not let them forestall us in accepting him! So they answered him favourably . . .’[3]

Now, it seems clear, from the manner in which Ibn Isḥāq has described the circumstances that existed prior to the Aqabah Pledges, and which helped secure the conversion of this company of Khazraj, that the monotheistic Jews of Yathrib had exerted great influence on the political life of Yathrib. In fact, so strong was their endeavour to secure complete dominance in the city that the Khazraj and the Aws had come to regard them as a serious threat to their own independence and feared their encroachment into their agricultural and commercial interests. The very keen sense of national and cultural identity, characteristic of the Jews, suggested that there might also have been cultural, national and even racial conflicts at the bottom of the Arabs' fears and suspicions of their Jewish neighbours with whom they were ethnically related, since all of them were semitic.

However, despite their conflict with the Jews, the Arab Yathribites must have been deeply impressed with the monotheistic faith of the Jews of the city. They might even have felt inferior every time they compared it with their heathenistic idolatry. Perhaps they ascribed the latter's dominance to their superior religious faith. Therefore, they may have recognized in the new religion of Islam, and in the leadership of the Prophet, a means of redressing the cultural and religious inferiority that set them behind the Jews. Also, they saw in the doctrine of brotherhood advocated by the Prophet a way of healing the wounds of wars and revenge that had raged for many years amongst the Arab tribes of Khazraj and Aws. At any rate, whatever their real motives in espousing the cause of the Prophet, they returned to Yathrib with the thrilling news that there was a new Prophet in Makkah, that they had met him, and believed in him. The Prophet's name was constantly mentioned in Yathrib, and efforts were made to win more people to the new religion. The activities of the new Muslims of Khazraj brought increased numbers of both Khazraj and Aws to Makkah seeking to meet the famed Prophet of Banū Hāshim. Their meeting with the Prophet resulted in the momentous event of the first 'Aqabah Pledge.

The First 'Aqabah Pledge

The first 'Aqabah Pledge or the Pledge of Women *(Bay'at an-Nisā')*, involved twelve men, ten from Khazraj and two from Aws, who met the Prophet and pledged themselves to Islam and the Prophet. The terms of the pledge were as follows:

Ibn Isḥāq narrates on the authority of 'Ubādah ibn aṣ-Ṣāmit, one of the twelve men who took the pledge and who, speaking for the whole group, said:

'The Messenger of Allah has concluded with us the Pledge of

Women, that is before war was made legitimate, that we do not take a partner with Allah; we do not steal or fornicate; we do not kill our offspring. We do not slander in any way, nor do we disobey the Prophet in any matter that is righteous.' When the twelve men took this pledge, the Prophet commented that if they fulfilled its terms they would enter paradise. But if they failed in any of its terms, then to Allah belongs their future, either to punish or forgive them.[4]

Led by the celebrated As'ad ibn Zurārah, who subsequently played a leading role in spreading Islam in Yathrib, the twelve men pledged to follow the Prophet's teachings. They included all the men except Jābir ibn 'Abdullāh, who had met him the previous year. The names of the remaining seven were as follows:

From Khazraj:

Mu'ādh ibn al-Ḥārith
Dhakwān ibn 'Abd Qays
'Ubādah ibn aṣ-Ṣāmit
Yazīd ibn Tha'labah (Abū 'Abd ar-Raḥmān)
Al-'Abbās ibn 'Ubādah ibn Naḍlah

From Aws:

Abū al-Haytham ibn at-Tayyihān
'Uwaym ibn Sā'idah

The first pledge is termed *Bay'at an-Nisā'* (the Pledge of Women) because it did not involve a pledge to fight: war for defending the cause of Islam had not yet been instituted. The conversion of those seven men and their undertaking was yet another very significant development in the winning of the important city of Yathrib, which was destined to become the political capital of the first Muslim State. They were not only influential men of the sub-clans of Khazraj, but were also widely representative of the city population in that they included two men of the rival tribe of Aws. The twelve men returned to Yathrib, accompanied by Muṣ'ab ibn 'Umayr ('Abd ad-Dār), a noted Companion of the Prophet who was a leading figure in Makkan society before the rise of Islam. Handsome, of a wealthy aristocratic family, and of refined taste in his dress, Muṣ'ab was extremely popular in the aristocratic circles of Makkah. Among the initial converts to the new faith, Muṣ'ab was noted for his knowledge of the Qur'ān and his dedication to the cause of Islam. To his remarkable tact, wise diplomacy and his persistence must be attributed a great part of the credit for winning the allegiance of several of the leading men of the Khazraj and the Aws, including the famed Usayd ibn Ḥuḍayr and Sa'd ibn Mu'ādh, the latter being the foremost chief of the Khazraj.

The Second 'Aqabah Pledge

The second pledge took place a year after the first which was concluded in the eleventh year of the Prophet's mission (i.e. 621 C.E.). Thus the second pledge occurred just one year before the Prophet's *Hijrah* to Yathrib. That year, the youthful Muṣ'ab and seventy-three men and two women of the Yathrib Muslims set out for Makkah, to meet the Prophet. Men of the first 'Aqabah Pledge who also witnessed the second 'Aqabah Pledge were:

As'ad ibn Zurārah	one of those who embraced the new Faith, even before the first 'Aqabah Pledge;
Abū al-Haytham ibn at-Tayyihān	also an early Muslim;
al-Barā' ibn Ma'rūr	probably the spokesman for the group; and
Ka'b ibn Mālik	a poet on the authority of whom Ibn Isḥāq narrated some of the episodes of the events that led to the second 'Aqabah Pledge.

One of the two women was the celebrated Nusaybah bint Ka'b, wife of the noted Companion of the Prophet, Zayd ibn 'Aṣim. Nusaybah took part in the actual fighting during the *Riddah* wars (the wars of Aspostasy after the death of the Prophet). One of her hands was cut off in the fighting and she sustained many other wounds. Nevertheless she lived for many years afterwards. The other Muslim woman who witnessed and participated in the pledge was Asmā' bint 'Amr.

The Yathrib Muslims visited the Prophet at his house in Makkah, probably unnoticed due to the crowds of pilgrims entering the city. The Prophet asked them to meet him again in the valley of Minā, outside Makkah, at 'Aqabah. They were told to slip out to the meeting place after midnight, when no one was about.

Both Ibn Isḥāq and Ibn Sa'd give roughly the same account of the meeting. Both sources relate that the Prophet was accompanied only by his uncle al-'Abbās who was an unbeliever at the time. The fact that the Prophet was under the protection of the clan of Nawfal at that time, and not under that of the Hāshim, does not really prove that his clan had abandoned him by then. What probably happened was that they, following the death of Abū Ṭālib and the long banishment in the Shi'b outside Makkah, were too weak to provide him with effective protection. It is not that they were unwilling to provide such protection. They were unable owing to their prolonged hardship to express their solidarity with him.

Al-'Abbās' statement, made before the assembly of the Yathrib company, that the Prophet was well protected amongst his people, could be understood as (a) referring to the fact that the Prophet was actually enjoying some kind of protection at that time, though it was the Nawfal, rather than the Banū Hāshim that were extending it to him; (b) it could also be taken as expressing a strategy which al-'Abbās was employing in order to obtain favourable terms for his nephew, in case he decided to settle in Yathrib. Al-'Abbās was alleged to have been the first person to speak in the assembly, demanding a solid unwavering pledge for the support and protection of the Prophet. He warned them that if they were not sure that they could fulfil the terms of the pledge, and provide effective protection for him should he migrate to their city, they should refrain from taking the pledge.

Then the Prophet himself spoke, reciting some verses of the Qur'ān and explaining some of the doctrines of Islam. Then he extended his hand, saying:

'Take your pledge that you would protect me from whatever you protect your women and children.'

Al-Barā' ibn Ma'rūr took the Prophet's hand and said: 'Yes, by He who has sent you with the truth, we would most certainly protect you from what we protect our women, so take our pledge, O Messenger of Allah, for by Allah, we are the sons of war and the people of combat; we have inherited it generation after generation.'

Then Abū al-Haytham at-Tayyihān interrupted him, saying: 'O Messenger of Allah, there are links between us and the men – referring to the Jews of Yathrib – and we are going to sever them. Do you think that if we were to do that and Allah makes you victorious, you would go back to your people and abandon us?'

The Prophet smiled broadly and said: 'Nay, but (your) blood is (my) blood, and (your) war is (my) war.[5] I am of you, and you are of me: I fight whom you fight and I make peace with whom you make peace. At this point, al-'Abbās ibn 'Ubādah ibn Naḍlah came forward and said:

'O Khazraj (meaning both Khazraj and Aws), are you fully aware of what you have pledged to this man?'

'Yes,' they said.

'You are giving your pledge to fight anyone (*lit.* ruddy and the black of mankind). So if you think that if it should happen that disaster befalls you or that your chiefs were killed, that you could surrender him, it is better for you to stop now. For that (the surrender) would lead to indignity (and dishonour) in this life and the Hereafter. But if you believe that you can fulfil your pledge to him, even should your wealth dwindle and your chiefs be killed, then take it (the pledge). For by Allah, it is a blessing in this life and the Hereafter.'

Then they said: 'We will take it on the risk of losing our wealth and endangering the lives of our chiefs. O Messenger of Allah, what would be our reward if we fulfil our pledge?'

'Paradise,' he replied.

'Stretch out your hand then,' they said.

Enthusiastic hand-shaking followed, symbolizing the profound and momentous commitment that was being made.

As soon as the making of the Pledge was over, the Prophet proceeded to appoint twelve *Nuqabā'* or headmen to be responsible for the affairs of the company. They were assigned the duties of providing leadership and guidance for their respective groups. The role of the *Naqīb* (sing. of *Nuqabā'*) was a many-sided one: he was the leader of the Prayer, the Qur'ānic teacher, the judge and arbiter in disputes, adviser, and the military commander on the battlefield. It is characteristic of Islam that it integrates the affairs of man in one, unified scheme. The device of the *Nuqabā'* was the inauguration of this new style of state and social organization and education.

The *nuqabā'* had the example of Muṣ'ab ibn 'Umayr and his inspiring leadership to guide them in discharging their responsibilities as leaders of the new Muslim community at Yathrib. There were urgent matters for them to attend to. Not only was the Prophet, at least partly, motivated in devising the idea of *nuqabā'* as a method of social organization by his belief that the young Muslim community would soon have to face a war with the Quraysh; also they themselves, as was voiced by al-'Abbās ibn 'Ubādah, were quite aware of such an eventuality. Thus the second 'Aqabah pledge came to be known as the Pledge of War *(Bay'at al-Ḥarb)*. The Muslims of Yathrib were pledged to support and defend the Prophet at any cost. They were ready to go to war if that was necessary for his defence. However, the pledge of war was strictly defensive. Commitment to wage an offensive war against the Quraysh or anybody else was not even hinted at. We shall see later that when the Prophet had to wage an offensive war (Badr) against the Quraysh, he scrupulously asked the permission of the *Anṣār* (or the Muslims of Yathrib).

NAMES AND CLANS OF THE *NUQABĀ'*

Name	*Tribe*	*Clan*	*Remarks*
As'ad b. Zurārah	Khazraj	Banū an-Najjār	Played a leading role in winning the city of Yathrib. It was with As'ad that Muṣ'ab was lodging when he was deputized to Yathrib.
Sa'd b. ar-Rabī' b. 'Amr	Khazraj	Banū al-Ḥārith	Witnessed Badr, fell a martyr at Uḥud.
'Abdullāh b. Rawāḥah	Khazraj	Banū al-Ḥārith	Third commander in the battle of Mu'tah, where he fell a martyr, a sensitive poet and staunch fighter in the cause of Islam, who witnessed Badr, Uḥud and most of the battles.

Rāfi' b. Mālik	Khazraj	Zurayq	One of the six who converted even before the first 'Aqabah pledge. An advance pioneer who did much to spread Islam in Yathrib.
Al-Barā' b. Ma'rūr	Khazraj	Salimah	The spokesman of the Yathribites at the second 'Aqabah pledge, and the first to pledge himself in defence and support of the Prophet.
'Abdullāh b. 'Amr b. Ḥarām	Khazraj	Salimah	
'Ubādah b. aṣ-Ṣāmit	Khazraj	Banū Sālim	
Sa'd b. 'Ubādah	Khazraj	Banū Sā'idah	One of the paramount chiefs of Khazraj. After the death of the Prophet, Sa'd, then of advanced age, publicly aspired to become the first Caliph. However, later on he withdrew his nomination and supported Abū Bakr and his successor as ruler over the Muslim state at al-Madīnah. He was taken captive by the Quraysh after the second 'Aqabah pledge.
al-Mundhir b. 'Amr b. Khunays	Khazraj	Banū Sā'idah	

Usayd b. Ḥuḍayr	Aws	Banū al-Ashhal	One of the paramount chiefs of Aws. His early conversion by Muṣ'ab persuaded many to espouse the cause of Islam.
Sa'd b. Khaythamah		Aws	
Rifā'ah b. 'Abd al-Mundhir	Aws	'Awf b. 'Amr	

The Yathribites were fully aware that by concluding this pledge they were exposing themselves to the enmity and wrath of the Quraysh and this was made clear by the way they acted after the conclusion of the pledge: (a) first of all, al-'Abbās ibn 'Ubādah suggested to the Prophet that, should he give them permission, they were prepared to launch an offensive expedition against the Quraysh, who were then assembled in Minā, unarmed, for the purpose of Pilgrimage. The Prophet, however, pacified al-'Abbās, saying that he was not yet permitted to wage war. (b) their fear of Quraysh reprisals was evident from the discreet manner in which they slipped in and out of the meeting of the second 'Aqabah Pledge. It is also evident from their sudden departure that they feared to stay longer in case their pledge to the Prophet might become known to the Quraysh, who in any case came next morning to the Yathribites in order to investigate a rumour of the meeting and the pledge. The Muslims kept silent and the others – the polytheists – denied in good faith any knowledge of such a meeting with the Prophet. As soon as the Quraysh had departed, fairly well-assured that nothing had happened, al-Barā' and his company hastily left for their city. Their sudden departure, however, alerted the Quraysh, who then hotly pursued them. They missed al-Barā' and his group, but came across two of the *nuqabā'*, Sa'd ibn 'Ubādah and al-Mundhir ibn 'Amr, at a place called Adhākhir. Al-Mundhir managed to escape but Sa'd was taken captive to Makkah, where he was badly treated despite his high standing among the people of Yathrib. Eventually he was saved by Jubayr ibn Muṭ'im ibn 'Adī and al-Ḥārith ibn Ḥarb ibn Umayyah; Sa'd had previously done favours for both men, looking after their commercial interests when they passed through Yathrib on their way to the markets of Syria.

Shortly afterwards, the Prophet directed his persecuted followers to migrate to Yathrib, where the *Anṣār* (Helpers) of the city had already shown their willingness to give asylum and protection to the afflicted Muslims, despite the real danger of armed conflict with the Quraysh. Makkah was soon emptied of its Muslim population. Eventually only the Prophet, Abū Bakr and 'Alī were left. The Prophet awaited his Lord's permission to leave. Abū Bakr would be his travelling companion and 'Alī had a crucial mission to perform once permission to leave Makkah was received. The Quraysh became more and more apprehensive that the Prophet might escape from the city and become reunited with his followers in Yathrib. The dangers inherent in such a course of events had not been missed by the politicians of the old tribe. They thought of a very simple solution to their problem. Muḥammad would have to be killed! But they would have to find a way of killing him that would not provoke a blood-feud among the clans of the Quraysh. Eventually they agreed on an ingenious plan. A strong youth would be selected from each clan and together they would participate in killing him. His clan, Banū Hāshim and their allies, would never be able to fight the whole of the Quraysh in retaliation. They would have to settle for blood-money, which the Quraysh would gladly pay, if only they could get rid of this 'praying man' who had incited their slaves against them.

The *Hijrah* to Yathrib

Ibn Isḥāq seems to make a direct link between the legislation of war on the one hand, the conclusion of the second 'Aqabah Pledge and the particular nature of its terms (the fact that it was a pledge of war) and the Prophet's advice to his followers to emigrate to Yathrib, and finally, his own emigration to that city. Ibn Isḥāq maintains that all these steps were indispensable in preparation for a war of liberation on behalf of the persecuted *ummah* of Islam.

Such a war could not have been possible without a solid, well-organized and determined following and a secure base from which hostilities could be directed. On this territorial base, no matter how narrow, a Muslim State could be established provided it possessed certain characteristics. It would have to be a natural human settlement, capable of supporting its population with essential provisions. It must be populated with people willing and able to defend the existence of such a state. It had to be fairly remote from the enemy territory so that early warning could be received of hostile enemy movements. It had to be defensible, and the easier it was to defend the more suitable it would be. From such a base it would then be possible to launch an offensive against aggressive concentrations of the enemy. These requirements were satisfied to a reasonable degree by the oasis of Yathrib, lying as it did on the vital commercial route of the Quraysh to Syria. Allah's direction and guidance of his Prophet to turn to Yathrib and its people was indeed part of His Mercy and Divine, Loving care for His Prophet and his followers.

Before the second 'Aqabah Pledge, the persecuted Muslims in Makkah were told to withstand the trials and indignities inflicted upon them by the polytheists with patience and fortitude. They were directed to be persistent. Trials and persecutions were deemed to be the crucible in which the Muslims would be examined, and their sincerity and fortitude tested. Those who were weak or insincere would be eliminated in the course of this persecution and only those who were strong and sincere would remain. A war against the Quraysh waged by Muslims from inside Makkah would have inevitably turned into a civil and religious strife within the community itself. Perhaps such a strategy of civil strife would not have been successful in alleviating the suffering of the Muslim converts. So it would appear that the prospects of such a course for the oppressed Muslim minority must have looked very doubtful indeed.

Let us continue the narrative of the dramatic events which took place that night when a plan to assassinate the Prophet was to be carried out by the representatives of the various clans of the Quraysh. It was the night of the 2nd or 3rd of Rabīʿ al-Awwal (14th or 15th September, 622), since the Prophet having spent about ten days on the road, reached the outskirts of Yathrib (to be known henceforth as al-Madīnah or the city of the Prophet) on 12th Rabīʿ al-Awwal of the thirteenth year of his mission. According to Ibn Isḥāq, Gabriel came to Muḥammad, *ṣallā Allāhu ʿalayhi wa sallam,* and told him not to spend that night in Makkah. ʿAlī would sleep in his bed to allay suspicions that he might not still be there. 'Alī's other duty was to make sure that all the things deposited with the Prophet for safekeeping had been returned to their owners. Towards midnight, as the murderous conspirators were assembling around his house, waiting for a suitable moment to accomplish their treacherous mission of killing the man who had exhorted them to be peaceful and just, the Prophet quietly slipped out of the house. Ibn Isḥāq narrates that as he approached them he took a handful of dust and threw it at their heads, reciting verses of *Sūrah Yā Sīn* as follows:

> *Yā Sīn.*
> By the Qur'ān, full of wisdom, you are indeed of those sent on a Straight Path.
> A revelation of the Most Mighty, Most Wise.
> We have put yokes round their necks, reaching unto their chins so that they are rendered stiff-necked.
> And We have made a barrier in front of them, and a barrier behind them; thus have We blinded them so that they cannot see.[6]

Because of this event, these verses of *Yā Sīn,* even in our day, are recited by Muslims in the belief that they possess a protecting property, i.e. Allah protects whom He wills by means of this property. The spiritual properties inherent in these verses are indeed a protection but this does not in any way mean that they place a restriction upon the unlimited omnipotence of Allah, Most High, Most Mighty.

The Prophet, having escaped the besieging Quraysh, made his way to the house of Abū Bakr who had prepared two she-camels loaded with the necessary provisions and obtained the services of a trustworthy guide, 'Abdullāh ibn Arqaṭ (Banū Bakr), in readiness for the journey to Yathrib. To elude the watchful Quraysh, they slipped out of Makkah under cover of darkness and made their way southward, instead of northward, the true direction of Yathrib. Once outside the city, they headed towards Mount Thawr where they concealed themselves in a cave. Abū Bakr directed his son 'Abdullāh to bring them news of the Quraysh movements every evening, and ordered his freeman 'Āmir ibn Fuhayrah to graze the family flocks around the cave so as to remove the footmarks made by 'Abdullāh ibn Abū Bakr and

Asmā', his sister, as they came with news and fresh provisions. When the Quraysh found out that the Prophet had escaped leaving 'Alī in his bed, concealed beneath his red cloak, they became very angry. They offered a reward of a hundred she-camels to whoever brought the Prophet back. Their horsemen set out searching along every track and in every direction. They once came very close to the cave where the Prophet and Abū Bakr were hiding, but passed by when they found no sign of human footprints anywhere in the vicinity.

All the time they lay concealed in the cave, Abū Bakr was filled with anxiety for the life of the Prophet. But the Prophet pacified him, saying that Allah was with them. Meanwhile, the search for them intensified as the news of the hundred she-camel reward became known. But, three days later, the search had abated sufficiently for the Prophet and Abū Bakr to start their northward journey. They did not take the ordinary, beaten track for fear of being discovered. Instead, they chose a little-used road to Yathrib. The journey was hard and the weather oppressively hot. The only incident was when one of the pursuers, by the name of Surāqah ibn Mālik, came close to them but, overawed by the Prophetic presence, he was glad to get away safely, promising that he would not disclose the whereabouts of the Prophet and his companion.

Ever since they had heard about his setting out for Yathrib, the Yathribites had been waiting on the outskirts of the city in eager anticipation. As the Prophet spent about eleven days on his journey to the city – three concealed in the cave, and eight on the little-used road – they must have waited very patiently. A Yathribite Jew was the first to see him approaching the city. As he shouted the exciting tidings of his arrival, the city, wearing its brightest colours, was instantly transformed into one, long continuous procession of joy and celebration. Women and children shouted with excitement:

The Prophet has come!
The Prophet has come!
This is the Messenger of Allah, he has come.

Al-Barā', commenting on the Prophet's reception in Yathrib, said that he had never seen the people of the city so joyous and happy. 'Abbās ibn Mālik said that he had never seen a better or a brighter day in the city than the day of the Prophet's arrival.

It was almost midday when the Prophet and his companion reached Qubā' on the outskirts of the city. That day was 12th Rabī' al-Awwal of the thirteenth year of the Prophet's mission. A new calendar, the Islamic calendar, was inaugurated by the *Hijrah* of the Prophet to Yathrib, henceforth to be known as al-Madīnah. A new era had begun.

Notes and References

1. Slight variations of this version are given in many sources. See for example, Ibn Hishām, Vol. I, p. 406 and Ibn Sa'd, Vol. I, p. 215.
2. Parentheses added.
3. Ibn Hishām, Vol. I, p. 428f.
4. *Ibid.*, p. 433.
5. Ibn Hishām maintains that the expression *'Ad-dam ad-dam wa-l hadm al-hadm'* means 'Your pledge is my pledge and your taboo is my taboo (or your inviolability is my inviolability).
6. Qur'ān, 26 *(Yā Sīn)*: 1–9.

Appendix 1

The *Isrā'* and *Mi'rāj*, A Fuller Account of an Epoch-Making Event

The Story as told in the Original Sources

1. *Ibn Hishām's Account*

Drawing on *Sīrat Rasūl Allāh,* by Muḥammad ibn Isḥāq, Ibn Hishām's account of *Isrā'* and *Mi'rāj* is based on the authorities of (1) 'Ā'ishah, wife of the Prophet, (2) Ibn Mas'ūd, Mu'āwiyah ibn Abī Sufyān and others. Largely because of this dependence on 'Ā'ishah and Mu'āwiyah, Ibn Hishām unreservedly asserted the view that both the *Isrā'* and *Mi'rāj*[1] were not experienced by the Prophet in normal, bodily wakefulness; rather the whole occasion was a true dream, in which the soul of the Prophet, but not his body, was involved. Ibn Hishām based his position on this issue on the following considerations:

(i) Both 'Ā'ishah and Mu'āwiyah stated that the *Isrā'* and *Mi'raj* were purely spiritual events, in which only the soul of the Prophet was involved; thus (*Isrā'* and *Mi'rāj*) were no more than a true, authentic dream in which the Prophet saw that he journeyed to Jerusalem and then ascended to the Heavens.

(ii) In particular, 'Ā'ishah gave her witness, decisive in Ibn Hishām's view, that the Prophet's body was not absent that night at any time.

(iii) Ibn Hishām and the authorities on whom he was relying quote the Qur'ānic verse: 'And We granted the vision which We have shown you but as a trial for mankind,

> and (also) the Cursed Tree (mentioned) in the Qur'ān . . . ' (17: 60).

Ibn Hishām and his sources believe that this verse affords excellent argument that the *Isrā'* and *Mi'rāj* were of the spirit alone. Crucial to this interpretation (of the Qur'ānic verse in question) is the use of the word *ru'yā*. Some authorities assert that this word is to be distinguished from the word *rūyah*. The former connotes vision as occurs in dreams, whereas the latter connotes ordinary physical vision. But ash-Sha'rāwī[2] rejects this point, saying that *ru'yā* is also used to connote ordinary bodily seeing when the event or sight in question is deemed strange or extraordinary. He offers in evidence quotations both from pre-Islamic *(Jāhilī)* and Islamic poetry, giving a verse by al-Mutanabbī as a representative example of Islamic poetry.[3]

2. *Ibn Kathīr's (and aṭ-Ṭabarī's) Account*

Ibn Kathīr[4] partially bases his account on that of aṭ-Ṭabarī. He explicitly rejects Ibn Hishām's account as unfounded. Ibn Kathīr's discussion of *Isrā'* and *Mi'rāj* is most comprehensive. He begins with the mention of *Isrā'* in *Sūrah Banī Isrā'īl* in the Qur'ān. He goes on to cite all the *aḥādīth* narrated on the issue, even those whose authentication is not sufficiently sound, and after a thorough discussion, concludes by rebutting Ibn Hishām's version and giving his own instead. Ibn Kathīr's position is that the *Isrā'* and the *Mi'rāj* were of both body and soul. His account is as follows:

'In truth, the Prophet, *ṣallā Allāhu 'alayhi wa sallam,* was taken in a night journey, quite awake, from Makkah to Jerusalem, riding *al-Burāq*. Arriving at the Aqṣā Mosque, he fastened his mount at the door and entered, performed two *rak'ahs* of prayer and accepted, as hospitality a glass of milk (preferring it to water and wine) when this was offered to him by the Archangel Jibrīl (Gabriel). Then he was presented by *al-mi'rāj* which is a being that looked like a ladder or a staircase, and he ascended to heaven using that *mi'rāj*. He reached the first heaven, spoke to Adam, whom he found in the company of the souls of the dead, divided in two groups, good and bad. In the second heaven, he met 'Īsā (Jesus) and his cousin Yaḥyā (John [the Baptist]). In the third heaven, he met Yūsuf (Joseph), looking like a full moon in the striking radiance of his beauty. In the fourth heaven, he met Idrīs (Enoch); in the fifth heaven, he met Hārūn (Aaron), the handsomest old man he ever saw, with silver white hair, and a great long, white beard; in the sixth heaven, he met with Mūsā (Moses), and in the last heaven he met Ibrāhīm (Abraham), leaning with his back against *al-Bayt al-Ma'mūr* which is the celestial analogue of *al-Ka'bah.*'

Ibn Kathīr also explains that the Prophet met the Angel Ismā'īl who guards the doors of Heaven and the Angel Mālik, custodian of Hell. Whereas Ismā'īl was of smiling countenance before the Prophet, Mālik maintained a stern attitude, never offering to smile. The Prophet was vexed by this and looked to Jibrīl for an explanation.

'This is Mālik, the custodian of Hell; who never smiles. If he could smile at all, he would smile to you, O Muḥammad!' Hearing this, the Prophet asked to see Hell and Paradise, and was shown both. In Paradise, he was shown his future lodging therein, that of 'Umar, the station of Bilāl and the wife-to-be of Zayd ibn Ḥārithah, the adopted son of the Prophet.

2.1 *Terrible Sights*

Then the Prophet was shown some terrible sights:

(1) Those who unlawfully acquire and spend the wealth of orphans were seen swallowing balls of fire, which entered at the mouth and came out from their posterior to be swallowed again and again.
(2) Those who deal in usury *(ribā)* were seen with bellies the size of big rooms filled with blazing fires.
(3) Those who engage in slurs and slanders, defame others by spreading false and vicious rumours about them, were seen eating rotten human flesh.
(4) Married fornicators were seen eating rotten meat and avoiding cooked fresh meat.
(5) Married women who entered strangers in the lineage of their husbands, by bearing and giving birth to the children of other men, were seen tortured by being hung by their breasts.

2.2 *Some Wondrous Sights*

The consoling sights the Prophet was shown by far outnumbered the terrible ones!

To begin with he saw the *Burāq,* the *Mi'rāj* and the Aqṣā Mosque in Jerusalem. He saw Jibrīl in his true form, with six hundred beautiful wings of vast dimensions, covering the whole horizon and adorned with shining, precious rubies, emeralds and pearls.

He saw the Angel Ismā'īl, the Grand Keeper of the Doors of Heaven with radiant face and smiling eyes.

He saw the indescribable wonders of Paradise, and some of the abodes allocated for him and his companions. He saw and met the Prophets Adam, Jesus, John, Joseph, Idris, Aaron, Moses and Abraham. He was shown *al-Bayt al-Ma'mūr* (the Oft-visited House), and many other wondrous sights.

3. *The Lotus Tree (Sidrat al-Muntahā)*

The *Sidrat al-Muntahā* (literally Nabk tree (or Christ-thorn or lotus tree) stationed at the last extremity of the cosmos) is mentioned in the Qur'ān:

'1. By the Star when it falls,
2. Your Companion errs not, nor is he deceived,
3. Nor does he speak out of (his own) desires,
4. It is naught save a *Waḥy* (Revelation)[5] that is inspired,
5. Which One of mighty powers has taught him,
6. One vigorous, that was firmly established,
And he was on the uppermost horizon,
7. Then he drew nearer and came down,
8. Till he was (at a distance of),
9. Two bows' length or even nearer,
10. And He revealed unto His servant that which He revealed.
11. The heart lied not (in seeing) what it saw,
12. Will you then dispute with him concerning what he saw?
13. And surely he saw him yet another time!
14. By the Lote-tree of the utmost boundary!
15. Near unto which is the Garden of Abode!
16. When that which shrouds the lote-tree did shroud it!

17. The eye turned not aside nor yet was overbold!
18. Surely, he saw some of the greater revelations (signs) of his Lord!' (*an-Najm* 53: 1–18)

This English rendering of *Sūrah an-Najm* (the Star), pre-supposes that Muḥammad, *ṣallā Allāhu 'alayhi wa sallam*, actually saw his Lord on his *Mi'rāj* (ascent to heaven). This view has adherents among old as well as recent authorities. Leading among the recent authorities is Shaikh Muḥammad Mutawallī ash-Sha'rāwī, of Egypt. In his work on *Isrā'* and *Mi'rāj* referred to above, ash-Sha'rāwī advances the following reasons to support his view:

1. *Sūrah an-Najm* (the Star) refers to the source of *waḥy*. This is Allāh, *subḥānahū wa ta'ālā*. Jibrīl is not the source of revelation, but the mere conveyer of it.
2. The verses of *Sūrah an-Najm* refer to the Prophet as *'abdihī* (i.e. His slave) indicating that the Prophet stands (*vis-à-vis* the source of *Waḥy*) in the relation of slave to master. Thus the source of the *Waḥy* in question cannot be Jibrīl, because the Prophet Muḥammad, *ṣallā Allāhu 'alayhi wa sallam,* could never be said to be a slave of Jibrīl.
3. The verses of *Sūrah an-Najm* mention the fact that the polytheists among the Quraysh did not believe the Prophet's report of *Isrā'* and *Mi'rāj*. The vision of Jibrīl or lack of it was never the theme of that disputation. Rather it was the visiting of Jerusalem during the ascent to heaven and the seeing of Allāh, *subḥānahū wa ta'ālā*.
4. The Qur'ānic assurance – that the heart of the Prophet Muḥammad, *ṣallā Allāhu 'alayhi wa sallam,* did not deceive him, nor his vision turn aside nor yet was it overbold (transgressing its limits) – strongly suggests that the seeing in question was that of Allāh, *subḥānahū wa ta'ālā*.
5. Finally, how could the seeing be that of Jibrīl, whereas the Prophet had actually seen him, since Ḥirā', a number of times, and he was his companion all the way from Makkah to Jerusalem and during his ascent to the heavens, thus throughout his *Isrā'* and *Mi'rāj*. He had

even seen him in his true shape, before the event of *Isrā'* and *Mi'rāj* (probably in Makkah, before the *Hijrah*).

4. *Training and Preparation of the Prophet for Isrā' and Mi'rāj*

It must be remembered that since boyhood Muḥammad, *ṣallā Allāhu 'alayhi wa sallam,* had been carefully prepared and nurtured by Allah, *subḥānahū wa ta'ālā,* for his future role as Prophet and Apostle. An important aspect of this training was the spiritual operation which he had undergone, when he was a child of no more than four years, staying with his bedouin wet-nurse Halīmah as-Sa'diyah. Ibn Kathīr reports accounts of *Isrā'* and *Mi'rāj* which relate that Jibrīl performed another spiritual operation in which the heart of the Prophet was cleansed with the water of Zamzam, and his belly was stuffed with wisdom and illumination. This second operation and training qualified the Prophet to withstand the rigours and trials of *Isrā'* and *Mi'rāj.* His ordinary human perceptive and cognitive powers would not have been able to withstand the power and illumination of Allah, *subḥānahū wa ta'ālā*.

5. *The Prophet's Vision of God*

When Muḥammad, *ṣallā Allāhu 'alayhi wa sallam,* reached the lote-tree, Jibrīl still accompanying him, he stopped, saying he could not proceed any further, and quoted the Qur'ānic verse: 'There is no one of us but has his appointed place (or rank)!' (*aṣ-Ṣāffāt* 37: 164)

The Archangel said: 'If I were to proceed one step (the size of an ant) further, I would burn . . . but if you were to proceed, O Muḥammad, you would pass through . . . '

The Prophet asked: 'O Jibrīl, do you need anything from your Lord?'

Jibrīl replied: 'Yes. If you reach where no one has ever reached, and it is said to you, here you are and here I am, then mention me to your Lord!'[6]

It is reported that Jibrīl pushed the Prophet forward who was thus pushed through 70,000 barriers of light to find himself prostrating in front of the Throne and the Chair of his Lord. He felt very much his isolation and was troubled and most apprehensive. It was the first time, since the beginning of *Isrā'* and *Mi'rāj* that he found himself alone, unaccompanied by Jibrīl. His protestation to Jibrīl was of no avail. The Prophet said to his companion before he was pushed forward:

> 'O Jibrīl, I am your guest this night. Is it befitting for the host to abandon his guest? Is this a place where a friend will abandon his friend?'

To this passionate plea, Jibrīl advanced his acceptable excuse, quoted above. The Prophet knew that from then on he must be on his own, absolutely alone.

Then he was wrapped and carried in the mist of a mighty cloud, traversing immense, indescribable distances, at the end of which he found himself prostrating in front of the Throne of his Lord. Here he was greeted by Allah, *subḥānahū wa ta'ālā,* and he responded with the words which are repeated by every Muslim in his daily prayer (when sitting after performing the second *rak'ah): at-taḥīyātu lillāhi wa'ṣ-ṣalāwātu wa'ṭ-Ṭayyibātu . . . wa 'alā 'ibādillāh aṣ-ṣāliḥīn.*

6. *Between the Prophets Ibrāhīm and Muḥammad*

The Prophet Ibrāhīm is the paternal ancestor of the Prophet Muḥammad, *ṣallā Allāhu 'alayhi wa sallam,* and for that matter, all Quraysh, the tribe of the Prophet. Thus Ibrāhīm parented two great nations, the Quraysh Arabs and the Israelites (sons of Ya'qūb, son of Isḥāq, son of Ibrāhīm). The lineage of the Prophet Muḥammad, *ṣallā Allāhu 'alayhi wa sallam,* goes back to Ibrāhīm via Ismā'īl adh-Dhabīḥ (the one spared from slaughter by God). The Muslims in general (Arabs or non-Arabs) are spiritually related to Ibrāhīm by the Qur'ān, which describes him as the spiritual ancestor of all Muslims:

'And strive in (the cause) of Allah as you ought to strive (with endeavour, sincerity and discipline). It is He Who has chosen you and has not laid down upon you in religion any hardship, the faith of your father Abraham. It is He Who has named you Muslims, both before and in this (Revelation) that the Messenger may be a witness for you, and you be witnesses for mankind . . . ' (*al-Ḥajj* 22: 78)

The Prophet Muḥammad, *ṣallā Allāhu 'alayhi wa sallam,* reported his meeting with Abraham on the seventh and last of the heavens. Thus Abraham's status surpasses that of all Prophets, including Adam and Moses, who occupied the first and the sixth heaven respectively. The Prophet said he was struck by the physical similarity that existed between him and the Semitic Patriarch Ibrāhīm. As the closest friend of God *(Khalīlullāh),* it is quite logical that Ibrāhīm should occupy the Heaven immediately next to the Throne of God.

7. *Between the Prophets Moses and Muḥammad* (The Ordinance of *Ṣalāt*)

Accounts of the *Isrā'* and *Mi'rāj* are strongly suggestive of a very special relationship between the Prophets Muḥammad and Moses:

(1) For one thing, Muḥammad, *ṣallā Allāhu 'alayhi wa sallam,* described the physical appearance and complexion of Moses as one most comparable to that of the men of the Arabian tribe of Shanū'ah. In another place the Prophet compared the physical appearance of Moses to that of the men of the Azd of Oman. The Azd were originally of the Arabs of Yemen, who migrated northward to Oman and other regions of the Northern Arabian Peninsula. They are typically tall and dark brown of complexion, and very fierce and powerful of physique. This description implies an ethnic affinity between Arabs and Israelites.

(2) Secondly, when Muḥammad, *ṣallā Allāhu 'alayhi wa sallam,* received the ordinance to establish fifty prayers a day, Moses strongly intervened to lessen the number. He strongly urged the Prophet to go back to his Lord a number of times, until the number of the obligatory performances was reduced from fifty to only five.

This incident of Moses' intervention on behalf of the Muslims is reported in almost all the authentic sources of the *Isrā'* and *Mi'rāj*. It forcefully argues Moses' friendship and sympathy for the Prophet Muḥammad, *ṣallā Allāhu 'alayhi wa sallam,* and all Muslims. Moses is also reported, in these sources, to have sobbed in compassion and sorrow for the Jews because the followers of Muḥammad, *ṣallā Allāhu 'alayhi wa sallam*, will enter Paradise in greater numbers than his own. Al-Ghazālī[7] said that through the *Isrā'* and *Mi'rāj,* the Prophet Muḥammad's surpassing Moses is well-confirmed: while Moses was granted the status of *Kalīm ar-Raḥmān* (the one who talked to God) Muḥammad, *ṣallā Allāhu 'alayhi wa sallam,* was granted the vision of God.

7.1 *Moses and the Muslim Prayer (Ṣalāt)*

The ordinance of Muslim prayer *(ṣalāt)* was one of the cardinal objectives of *Isrā'* and *Mi'rāj*. Perhaps it comes next only to the objective of honouring the Prophet, and his consolation by God Almighty after the loss of his beloved wife, the great Khadījah, and then of his protector Abū Ṭālib. This tour in the Realm of the Divine was certainly the foremost purpose of *Isrā'* and *Mi'rāj*: these events were meant by God 'So as to show him Our major signs'. (*al-Isrā'* 17: 1)

When Muḥammad, *ṣallā Allāhu 'alayhi wa sallam*, saw something of the portents or tokens of his Lord, his heart was consoled and his anxieties about the fate of his call to Islam were allayed, since he was shown evidence of the decisive victories of Islam to come. He was shown signs of his Lord's most consummate omnipotence and grandeur; he was further granted within the eye of his heart a vision of the Divine Himself. These objectives being realized, the most practical objective was the ordinance of *ṣalāt*.

It may be asked, at this juncture, why of all the religious obligations, was *ṣalāt* uniquely ordained, not on the earth but in Heaven, and by the Almighty Himself in person, and not through the Archangel Jibrīl?

The answers to these questions highlight the supreme, central significance of *ṣalāt* in Islam. It is (1) the *'Imād ad-Dīn,* the archcolumn of Islam, (2) the first deed to be assessed and judged on the Day of Reckoning. (3) *Ṣalāt* is the daily *Mi'rāj* or spiritual ascent of the Muslim. It is his chief instrument of worship and of sharing in the labour of the Angels, namely the singing of the praises of the Lord and of affirming servanthood and submission to His Will. (4) *Ṣalāt* is the means of bringing the Muslim closest to his Lord, Sovereign and Sustainer of the Heavens and the earth and everything therein. When a Muslim is close to his Lord, his prayers will be answered, his worthy hopes and well-meant desires will be granted. (5) Also *ṣalāt* can shield the Muslim from the malevolence of Satan and his evil agents, from vice and lewdness. Of course, this shielding is not automatic. Only if the Muslim is determined to resist evil and lewdness does *ṣalāt* become a potent weapon:

> Surely *ṣalāt* forbids lewdness and wrong and is the cardinal method of the remembrance of Allah . . . (*al-'Ankabūt* 29: 45)

The Qur'ān also repeatedly commends *ṣalāt* as the cardinal weapon of the Muslim, especially in times of hardship and distress:

> And be aided by patience and *ṣalāt* (avail yourself of *ṣalāt*) and surely it (*ṣalāt*) is a heavy duty except for those who are pious. (*al-Baqarah* 2: 45)

As mentioned above, Moses is reported to have been instrumental (out of compassion for Muḥammad, *ṣallā Allāhu 'alayhi wa sallam,* and his *Ummah*) in reducing the number of prayers from fifty during one day and night, to only five. He repeatedly advised Muḥammad, *ṣallā Allāhu 'alayhi wa sallam,* to go back to his Lord, and ask for a reduction in the number. He told Muḥammad, *ṣallā Allāhu 'alayhi wa sallam,* that he had experience in this matter with the Israelites who found it very difficult to perform only two prayers, one at dawn and one at sunset. This incident indeed underlines the affinity that ought to exist between true, genuine followers of Moses, if they exist, and true Muslims. But alas! Witness the notorious enmity and conflict that nowadays divide Muslims and Jews in Palestine.

7.2 *Ṣalāt and the Rationale of Religion*

Ṣalāt (prayer in general for that matter) is intimately related to the rationality of religious life. If one believes that one is created by God the Almighty, Who is at the same time the Benevolent source of the blessings of life, then to pray to Him is the rational thing to do. It is only natural to be grateful to one's Creator and Sustainer. Praying and performing *ṣalāt* is the ritual expression of this gratitude. A person of a naturally wholesome and noble disposition, whose native common sense has not been spoilt by arrogance and false pride, will find it rational as well as commendable to pray, especially in times of hardship. At the same time, the disciplines of *ṣalāt,* listening and following strictly the *imām* leading the prayer attaches the Muslim inwardly to the values of obedience, discipline and socio-political consciousness.[8]

8. *The Prophet Prefers Milk to Wine*

It is reported, by Ibn Kathīr and others, that on arriving at Jerusalem, Jibrīl offered the Prophet two glasses, one containing milk, the other wine. The Prophet chose the milk. Jibrīl commented: 'You have been rightly guided to the natural choice! Had you chosen wine, your *Ummah* would be greatly tempted by it.'

The choice of milk symbolizes an important characteristic of the faith of Islam, namely that it is the natural religion for man, in total harmony with the original, normal disposition of human nature. The Qur'ān calls this original disposition the *fiṭrah*.

'According to the Qur'ān, an Islamic world-view, the human being – man and woman – is created by God in a naturally good and pure state, free from sin. This is called the state of *fiṭrah.* A baby at birth is totally innocent. He does not bear the sin or guilt of his parents or his ancestors. He starts off with a clean slate . . .'[9]

The Qur'ān states:

> So set your face (O Muḥammad) for the religion of the naturally upright, (turning away from all that is false) in accordance with natural disposition (*fiṭrah*) in which God has originally created man.
> No alteration (let there be) in what God has created.
> That is the religion upright, but most men know not . . . (*ar-Rūm* 30: 30)

According to Islam, though man is born with this original *Fiṭrah* it is corruptible by upbringing, education and environment. For this reason, the Almighty has sent Prophets and Messengers to remind man of his natural disposition and to help guide him in accordance with it, teaching him to resist the temptations of Satan, whose main business is to distract man from his pristine innocence by beautifying evil and making rebellion against the Almighty appealing. However, all the Scriptures brought by the Prophets and Messengers before Islam have been tampered with and forgeries introduced into them. Only the Qur'ān has been most perfectly preserved by the Almighty in the original form in which it was received by the Prophet Muḥammad, *ṣallā Allāhu 'alayhi wa sallam.*

9. *Prophethood Transferred from the Israelites to the Arabs*

Ever since Jacob (Israel) Prophethood in the region now called the Middle East remained in the house of the Israelites, descendants of Prophet Jacob, son of Isaac, son of Abraham, the Patriarch of the Semitic peoples. Jacob, Joseph and his brothers, then Moses, Aaron, John (the Baptist) and Jesus son of Mary, are but a few of the great names. With the coming of Muḥammad, *ṣallā Allāhu 'alayhi wa sallam,* Prophethood switched from the Israelites to the Arabs, descendants of Ishmael, son of Abraham by Hagar, the Copt. This change is symbolized in the act in which the Prophet, ushered by Gabriel, led the prayer, in the Aqṣā Mosque, with all the Prophets, including Adam and Abraham lined up behind him. The Qur'ān gives the reasons for this change. The Israelites were initially favoured by God over mankind. They succeeded in the holy land of Palestine after the Canaanites, but they did not honour the favour done to them. Rather, they turned against their Prophets and rebelled against God. They changed and falsified their Scriptures, and killed their Prophets.

In the history of Islam, this change in the fortunes of the Israelites was also symbolized by the change of the *qiblah* from Jerusalem to Makkah, an event which marked the beginning of the end of friendship and alliance established between the Muslims and Jews of Madinah by the pact of *Ṣaḥīfah.*[10]

According to the Qur'ān, the Banī Isrā'īl are no longer the 'chosen people'. The Muslims are the best people if they fulfil the conditions of being true to the mission of Islam:

> You are the best nation (*Ummah*)
> brought forth to mankind.
> You enjoin the good
> and forbid the wrong
> and you believe in (the One True God) – Allah . . .
> (*Āl 'Imrān* 3: 110)

The link between *Isrā'* and *Mi'rāj* and the story of the children of Israel is not arbitrarily established by this study. Rather it is found in the Qur'ān itself. First of all, the *Sūrah* of *Isrā'* (night journey) is alternatively known as the *Sūrah of Banī Isrā'īl*. Secondly, the opening verse of this *sūrah* is immediately followed by the mention of Moses and Banī Isrā'īl, in the following way:

'We gave unto Moses the scriptures and appointed it a guidance for the children of Israel, saying: Choose no guardian beside Me'. (*al-Isrā'* 17: 2)

This *Sūrah* of the children of Israel tells about the fate of the ancient Kingdom of the Israelites, after Moses; how they spread corruption and arrogance on two occasions, and how the Almighty twice destroyed them, once by the Persians and once by the Romans. Thereafter they were dispersed on the earth (the diaspora). The *Sūrah* goes on to set out a rule for the Israelites:

'If you return (to the crime of corruption and arrogance), We will return (with Our chastisement).' (*al-Isrā'* 17: 8)

What is curious about that verse (the eighth of this *Sūrah*) is that it implies that Allah will give the Israelites a period of grace after their destruction by the Persians and the Romans:

'It may be that your Lord will have mercy on you, but if you return (to your crime) We will return (with Our punishment) . . .'

10. *Socio-Political Dimensions of Mi'rāj and Isrā' as Outlined by Mawdūdī*

For Mawdūdī the event of *Mi'rāj* marks a watershed in the mission and message of Islam, in the career of the Prophet Muḥammad, *ṣallā Allāhu 'alayhi wa sallam*, and in the nascent Islamic history.

The Prophet's *Mi'rāj* fits in well with the divine scheme in that earlier Prophets – Ibrāhīm and Mūsā too – had undergone a similar experience. Like the Prophet Muḥammad, *ṣallā Allāhu 'alayhi wa sallam,* they too, were provided with an opportunity to gain first-hand knowledge of the divine working and secrets of the kingdom of the heavens and the earth (*al-An'ām* 6: 75). How Allah grants life to the dead was vividly demonstrated to the Prophet Ibrāhīm (*al-Baqarah* 2: 260). Also the Prophet Mūsā saw Allah's glory on the Mount (*al-A'rāf* 7: 143) and was granted a unique opportunity to appreciate the divine knowledge (*al-Kahf* 18: 65).

Mi'rāj signifies a Messenger's elevation to higher ranks and a manifold increase in his responsibilities. After having carried out the mission of Islam for twelve years, the Prophet Muḥammad, *ṣallā Allāhu 'alayhi wa sallam,* was eventually granted *Mi'rāj.* By this time he had preached his message in almost the whole of Ḥijāz and the neighbouring country of Abyssinia. It was time for his mission to enter the next phase. He was soon to move from the hostile Makkah to Madinah, which was ready to greet his message. Since it was to be a consequential move, transforming the Islamic movement into the Islamic State and exposing Islam to other nations, Allah summoned the Prophet Muḥammad, *ṣallā Allāhu 'alayhi wa sallam,* for special instructions. This marvellous journey happened, significantly enough, only a year before the Prophet's *Hijrah* (migration) to Madinah.

Why the Prophet was summoned for *Mi'rāj* is set out quite clearly in the *Sūrah al-Isrā'* or Banī Isrā'īl. In one part of the *Sūrah* the Makkan unbelievers are warned that if they continue persecuting Muslims and force the Prophet into migration, it would ruin the fate of Makkan unbelievers (*al-Isrā'* 17: 71–7). So the Israelites, who were to interact with the Prophet in Madinah, were told that it was their last chance to mend their ways in that they had already wasted earlier opportunities (*al-Isrā'* 17: 4–8). The main thrust of the *Sūrah,* however, consists in laying down the following fourteen fundamental principles which should lie at the heart of human conduct, morals and culture:

(1) Allah alone is to be worshipped and no partners be ascribed to Him (17: 23).
(2) The family should hold pride of place in the society. Children should be obedient to parents and due rights be rendered to the kindred (17: 24–6).
(3) The poor, the wayfarer and the needy be helped (17: 26).
(4) One should not squander his wealth. For spendthrifts are brothers of the Devils (17: 27).
(5) One should be moderate in his expenditure in that one should be neither spendthrift nor miser. For it puts others to hardship, too. (17: 27 and 29).
(6) Man should not disturb the divine arrangement for distributing sustenance. Man does not have the capability to do this job (17: 30).

(7) One should not kill one's children for fear of want. For Allah will provide sustenance for them as He does for us (17: 31).
(8) Illicit sex is an abhorrent way of fulfilling one's desire. Not only should one shun it as a sin, any approach or temptation to it should be avoided as well (17: 32).
(9) Allah has sanctified human life. No one should therefore be killed except for a just cause. Nor should anyone commit suicide (17: 33).
(10) The orphans' interests should be carefully safeguarded until they come of age (17: 34).
(11) One should keep his word in that one is accountable to Allah for all his deeds (17: 34).
(12) One should give just measure and weight (17: 35).
(13) Idle curiosity and following one's whims are to be avoided. One will have to answer how he has used his abilities and power (17: 36).
(14) Arrogance, insolence or pride is to be shunned. For it is the first step to many evils (17: 37).

Far from being mere moral precepts, these fourteen principles, revealed to the Prophet Muḥammad, *ṣallā Allāhu 'Alayhi wa sallam,* on the *Mi'rāj* night, were to serve as the very manifesto of Islam. They signified the foundation of the Islamic order of life. The Prophet was provided with this set of guidelines at the time his mission was about to assume the role of political power and state. Understandably, he was instructed in advance on what principles the society was to be built. In addition to this guidance, Allah enjoined upon all Muslims to pray five times a day in order to strengthen morally and spiritually those entrusted with following this guidance. Prayers were prescribed for them lest they became oblivious of Allah. For Prayers would keep them ever-conscious of their limited role as servants of Allah, answerable to Him for all their deeds.[11]

11. *Approval and Misgivings about Isrā' and Mi'rāj*

When the Prophet broke the extraordinary news of the *Isrā'* and *Mi'rāj,* the people of Makkah were divided in their response. The faithful, led by Abū Bakr, were very impressed and rejoiced.

The tremendous events gave fresh, immeasurable confirmation of their faith. It gave good tidings of things yet to come, of glory and succour, after persecution and oppression. When the news was first broken to Abū Bakr, he asked:

- Did he (the Prophet) really tell of these things?
- Yes, they said.
- If he reported this news, then he has told the truth, because he never tells a lie.

Because of this response, Abū Bakr was given the honorific title of *as-Ṣiddīq,* the sincere believer.

On the other hand, those Makkans of the Quraysh who did not believe became wildly mocking and derisive:

- Did he really say that he went to Jerusalem and came back in a single night, whereas it takes us a whole month (exhausting our camels to the point of death) to get there.

It was said: When faced with these misgivings and the fresh campaign of slight and slander that broke in its wake, the Prophet gave many proofs of the factuality and truth of his account. He told them of a caravan he had met on the road to Jerusalem, of a stray camel of theirs and how he had directed them as to where it was. He told them of another caravan, which he visited while they were asleep, and how he drank of their water, not forgetting to put the lid on afterwards. When the people of the Quraysh challenged the authenticity of this information the Prophet responded by describing the Aqṣā Mosque in detail, then told them the exact date and time when the caravan he had met on the road would return to Makkah, namely at sunrise, with a camel of a certain description at its head, that is, an *Awraq* (an elegant, quick-paced camel). On that day, the Quraysh were up very early in the morning and went to the outskirts of the city in the direction of Jerusalem.

'Behold the sun has risen' shouted a Quraysh of the unbelievers. 'And behold, the caravan has arrived, with the *Awraq* at their head,' shouted another, 'just exactly as Muḥammad foretold.'

After a few days, the heated controversy about *Isrā'* and *Mi'rāj* was overwhelmed in the great events that were taking shape. The Muslims began to migrate, in ones, twos and threes, to Yathrib.

The Quraysh, very disturbed about their exodus from Makkah, sought to block it as much as they could. Then they became preoccupied in a conspiracy to kill the Prophet, *ṣallā Allāhu 'alayhi wa sallam*. That conspiracy failed miserably. The Prophet managed to get away, and made the fateful *Hijrah* that was destined to change the history of Islam, of Arabia, and in great measure, of the world at large.

12. *Epilogue*

The event of *Isrā'* and *Mi'rāj* had a deep and lasting impact on the thought and life of Muslim peoples, and was echoed by writers and philosophers far afield. Countless poets and story-tellers have eternalized the event. In the Muslim world, to this day, the *Isrā'* and *Mi'rāj* are commemorated in festivals, feasts and sessions of religious teaching about its significance. The poet-philosopher, Abu'l A'lā al-Ma'arrī, wrote his celebrated *Risālah al-Ghufrān* expressing his impressions of the fantastic sights the Prophet beheld during his ascent to the heavens, in particular the terrible torments of the people of Hell, and the fantastic bliss of the people of Paradise. The poet-mystic Ibn al-Fāriḍ wrote beautiful verses about the elevation of Muḥammad, *ṣallā Allāhu 'Alayhi wa sallam,* how he drew near to his Lord, surpassed all angels and Prophets. Ibn 'Arabī wrote 'Shajarat al-Kaun', i.e. The Tree of Cosmos. European poets and writers were also drawn to the fascination and extraordinary beauty of the event – the best known of whom is Dante who is said to have drawn upon it for his 'Divine Comedy'.

For the Muslims at large, the *Isrā'* and *Mi'rāj* signify above all the Lord's bestowal of grace on His Prophet and servant Muḥammad, *ṣallā Allāhu 'alayhi wa sallam,* and his confirmation as the *Imām* and leader of the spiritual realm, of angels as well as Prophets. Al-Buṣayrī (of Yemen), the poet, composer of the famous poem *Al-Burdah,* said in this respect:

> You journeyed by night from a sacred mosque to a sacred mosque as a moon steals its way in the darkest of nights – ascending, ascending till you reached such heights, so nearest to the Divine as none had attempted before . . .

A Sudanese poet – Wad Sa'd (song by Wad min al-Allah)

comparing the station achieved by Muḥammad, *ṣallā Allāhu 'alayhi wa sallam,* through the *Isrā'* and *Mi'rāj,* and that achieved by Moses, when God Almighty spoke to him at Sinai, said:

> The son of 'Imrān (i.e. Moses) traversed a sea seen by the naked eye, but the Chosen One (Muḥammad) traversed the sea of heaven, closely guarded and surrounded (by Angels).

I conclude this epilogue with the prayer:

> *Subḥānaka Allāhumma wa biḥamdika, Ashhadu an Lā ilāha illā anta, Astathfiruka wa Atūbu ilayka!*
> *Wa nuṣallī wa nusallim 'alā sayyidinā Muḥammad, Ṣallā Allāhu 'alayhi wa Sallam.*

Al-Ain (U.A.E.) **Zakaria Bashier**

Notes and References

1. *Isrā'* (Arabic) here means the night journey from the Haram Mosque of Makkah to the Aqṣā Mosque in Jerusalem. The *Mi'rāj* (Arabic) signifies the Prophet's ascent to heaven.
2. Ash-Sha'rāwī, Muḥammad Mutawallī *Al-Isrā' wa al-Mi'rāj,* edited by Riyād 'Abdullāh, Dār al-'Ālam, Beirut, 1985, p. 29.
3. The pre-Islamic poet quoted by ash-Sha'rāwī is Ar-Ra'z al-Numayrī.
4. Ibn Kathīr: *Tafsīr ibn Kathīr,* Vol. 1, Dār al-Ma'rifah, Beirut, pp. 1–24.
5. The Arabic word *Waḥy* signifies inspiration in the case of Divinely ordained Prophets and Messengers. Other types of inspiration, such as received by good saintly people or geniuses, is referred to in Arabic by special words, such as *Ilhām.*
6. Shaikh Muḥammad M. ash-Sha'rāwī: *Isrā' wa al-Mi'rāj,* p. 52. Ash-Sha'rāwī is here drawing on Muhyiddīn ibn 'Arabī: *Shajarat al-Kaun,* p. 95.
7. Al-Ghazālī: *Mishkāt al-Awār,* Dār al-Kutub al-'Ilmiyah, Beirut, 1986, p. 46.
8. (i) Ḥasan at-Turābī, *Aṣ-Ṣalāt 'Imād ad-Dīn,* Kuwait, 1968.
   (ii) Shaikh Muḥammad Mutawallī ash-Sha'rāwī, *Al-Isrā' wa al-Mi'rāj,* edited by Riyād 'Abdullāh, Dār al-'Ālam, Beirut, 1985.
9. Abdul Wahid Hamid, *Islam the Natural Way,* MELS, London, 1989, p. 27.
10. Zakaria Bashier, *Sunshine at Madinah,* Islamic Foundation, Leicester, 1990, Chapter 2.
11. Sayyid Abul A'lā Mawdūdī, *Nashrī Taqrīren* (Radio talk), (Urdu) Islamic Publications Ltd., Lahore, 1976, pp. 39–71.

The 'Satanic' Verses and the Orientalists*

(A note on the authenticity of the so-called Satanic verses)

M.M. Ahsan

A number of leading Orientalists have made special studies of the Qur'ān and some of them have translated it into European languages. On the whole the attitude of such scholars of the Occident has been unsympathetic and sometimes hostile. There are a few who still regard the Qur'ān as the writing of the Prophet, *ṣallā Allāhu 'alayhi wa sallam*, and not, as the Muslims regard it, the word of God revealed through the angel Gabriel. Many take pains to point out the alleged borrowing of the Qur'ān from Judaeo-Christian sources. Such erroneous assertions have taken on a formulaic significance and echoes of it are too often heard even after new researches have shown otherwise.[1]

A reader of secondary writings of Islam becomes puzzled when he finds two diametrically opposed conclusions reached by Orientalist and Muslim writers using the same sources and materials. It seems that Muslims are not far wrong when they allege that the Orientalists build their edifice on the foundations of so-called objectivity, using the tools of analytical research and critical examination which leads to interpretations not necessarily based on facts but pure speculation, hypothetical assumption and that sometimes a deliberate attempt has been made by many Orientalists to cast doubt on the teachings of Islam by challenging the authenticity of the Qur'ān and the *Sunnah*. Christian, Marxist

---

*This is a revised version of the article that appeared in *Hamdard Islamicus,* Vol. 5, No. 1, Spring 1982, pp. 27–36.

and Jewish Orientalists have quite often tried to prove, directly or indirectly, that at least some portions of the Qur'ān and *Ḥadīth* are fabricated or inconsistent and are, therefore, unreliable sources for the Islamic way of life. However, such Orientalists have based their attack on the flimsiest of intellectual grounds. In this paper, an attempt has been made to analyse the Orientalists' allegations about the incorporation of the so-called Satanic verses[2] in the Qur'ān – a theme discussed with relish by almost all Western writers on the life of the Prophet.

This theme also inspired the heretic Salman Rushdie to compile his most outrageous and blasphemous novel, *The Satanic Verses* (Viking/Penguin, London, 1988) in which he not only ridiculed Islam and its Prophet but made gratuitous and venomous attacks on Islam, Muslim history, Islamic institutions and everything held sacred in Islam. The publication of this sacrilegious book not only caused uproar, indignation and revulsion in the Muslim community all over the world, but brought the deaths of over thirty Muslim protesters in the Indo-Pak subcontinent and injury to hundreds of innocent Muslims. The Iranian leader, Ayatollah Khomeini, also issued a *fatwah* (14th February, 1989) condemning the author as *murtad* (apostate) and passing a death sentence which obliged the author to go into hiding under the protection of the British government, who have since spent millions of pounds ensuring his comfort and safety. Although the book was banned in most Muslim and several non-Muslim countries, the British government and the publishers refused to entertain the Muslim community's demand, submitted by the U.K. Action Committee on Islamic Affairs and other organizations, to withdraw the book from circulation. In the U.K. and the U.S.A. where the main campaign against the book was launched and sustained, a hysterical campaign against Islam and Muslims was launched by print and electronic media. The simple issue of blasphemy and profanity was turned into a clash of Muslim and Western liberal culture, a confrontation between freedom of expression and censorship. The Rushdie affair also occasioned the publication of more than a dozen books and over 100 articles in different journals and periodicals (for an annotated bibliography on the literature on the Rushdie affair, see M.M. Ahsan and A.R. Kidwai, *The Satanic Saga: Muslim Perspective on the Satanic Verses Affair*, The Islamic Foundation, 1991).

Before proceeding further, let us look at the story of the so-called 'Satanic' verses[3] which Orientalists like William Muir, Theodor Nöldeke, among earlier writers, and W. Montgomery Watt among contemporary 'biographers' of the Prophet, narrate with their usual 'masterly' comments.[4] These writers apparently base the story on some historical sources which, at first sight, seem quite weighty but on critical investigation fail to satisfy the criteria of historical criticism.[5] Muslim writers in the past such as Ibn Isḥāq, Ibn Hishām, al-Suhaylī (the commentator of Ibn Hishām and the author of *Rawḍ al-Unuf*), Ibn Kathīr, al-Bayhaqī, Qāḍī 'Iyāḍ, Ibn Khuzaymah, ar-Rāzī, al-Qurṭubī, al-'Aynī, al-Shawkānī, etc., as well as contemporary and near contemporary writers like Abul A'lā Mawdūdī, Sayyid Quṭb, Muḥammad Ḥusayn Haykal, etc., have all rejected the story as preposterous and without foundation.[6]

Aṭ-Ṭabarī, Ibn Sa'd and some other Muslim writers have mentioned (though they vary considerably in matters of detail) that the Prophet Muḥammad, *ṣallā Allāhu 'alayhi wa sallam*, under Satanic inspiration added two verses to *Sūrah an-Najm* (53), which are as follows:[7]

تِلْكَ الْغَرَانِيقُ الْعُلَى ، وَإِنَّ شَفَاعَتَهُنَّ لَتُرْتَجَى ،

[These are the high-soaring ones (deities), whose intercession is to be hoped for!]

The Prophet, it is alleged, recited these along with other verses of *Sūrah an-Najm* in the prayer. The idolaters of Makkah who were present in the Ka'bah at that time joined him in the prayer because he praised their deities and thus won their hearts. The story afterwards reached Abyssinia where the Muslims persecuted by the Makkan infidels had earlier migrated and many of them returned to Makkah under the impression that the disbelievers no longer opposed the Prophet and the Islamic movement. The story also says that the angel Gabriel came to the Prophet the same evening and told him about the mistake he had committed by reciting verses which were never revealed to him. This naturally worried the Prophet and made him apprehensive. Then, 'admonishing' the Prophet, God revealed the following verses of *Sūrah Banī Isrā'īl,* which read:

وَإِن كَادُوا لَيَفْتِنُونَكَ عَنِ الَّذِي أَوْحَيْنَا إِلَيْكَ لِتَفْتَرِيَ عَلَيْنَا غَيْرَهُ -
وَإِذًا لَّاتَّخَذُوكَ خَلِيلًا - وَلَوْلَا أَن ثَبَّتْنَاكَ لَقَدْ كِدتَّ تَرْكَنُ إِلَيْهِمْ
شَيْئًا قَلِيلًا - إِذًا لَّأَذَقْنَاكَ ضِعْفَ الْحَيَاةِ وَضِعْفَ الْمَمَاتِ ثُمَّ
لَا تَجِدُ لَكَ عَلَيْنَا نَصِيرًا - (بنى اسرائيل - ٧٣ - ٧٥)-

They were constantly trying to tempt you away from that which We have revealed to you, so that you may substitute in its place something of your own, in which case they would have actively taken you as a friend. And if We had not made you firm, you might have indeed inclined to them a little. Then We would have made you taste a double punishment in this life and a double punishment after death and then you would not have found any helper against Us. (17: 73–5)

This made the Prophet feel very guilty until God revealed the following consoling verse of *Sūrah al-Ḥajj*:

وَمَا أَرْسَلْنَا مِن قَبْلِكَ مِن رَّسُولٍ وَلَا نَبِيٍّ إِلَّا إِذَا تَمَنَّىٰ أَلْقَى
الشَّيْطَانُ فِي أُمْنِيَّتِهِ - فَيَنسَخُ اللَّهُ مَا يُلْقِي الشَّيْطَانُ ثُمَّ يُحْكِمُ
اللَّهُ آيَاتِهِ - وَاللَّهُ عَلِيمٌ حَكِيمٌ - (الحج - ٥٢)-

Whenever We sent a Messenger or a Prophet before you and he framed a desire, Satan put obstacles in it. Then Allāh removes the obstacles placed by Satan and He firmly establishes His signs. (22: 52)

This is the gist of the story mentioned by aṭ-Ṭabarī and some other writers which has been used by the Orientalists to reinforce their views on the Qur'ān. The story would, among other things, imply that the Prophet and his Companions took the 'Satanic' verses as a true revelation from God, otherwise nobody would have accepted them.

Let us now examine the story and its contents in the light of internal and external evidence and evaluate it on the basis of criteria of historical criticism. In doing so, first of all one has to find out the chronological sequence in the story and establish whether or not all its details relate to one period and are interconnected. Special attention should also be devoted to determining the periods of revelation of the three verses mentioned in the report which will validate or falsify the episode.

It can be easily gleaned from the story that the incident of reciting the 'Satanic' verses and the consequent prostration of the disbelievers in the Ka'bah happened after the first batch of Muslims had migrated to Abyssinia. This emigration, according to all reliable historical sources, occurred in the month of Rajab of the fifth year of the Prophetic call or about eight years before the *Hijrah* to Madinah. Therefore, the incident must have happened close to this date and not long after the migration to Abyssinia.

The verses of *Sūrah Banī Isrā'īl* (17: 73–5) which were revealed, according to the story, to 'admonish' the Prophet for allegedly reciting the 'Satanic verses', in fact were not revealed until after the event of the *Mi'rāj*. The *Mi'rāj* or the Ascent of the Prophet, according to historical sources, occurred in the tenth or eleventh year of the Prophetic call, i.e. about two or three years before the *Hijrah* to Madinah. If this is so, then it implies that the 'Satanic' verses were not detected or for some reason no mention was made about the alleged interpolation of the verses for five or six years and only afterwards was the Prophet admonished for it. Can any sensible person, asks Abul A'lā Mawdūdī, believe that the interpolation occurs today, while the admonition takes place six years later and the abrogation of the interpolated verses is publicly announced after nine years (cf. *Sīrat-i Sarwar-i 'Ālam,* Vol. 2, p. 574). The relevant verse of *Sūrah al-Ḥajj* (22: 52) according to the commentators of the Qur'ān was revealed in the first year of the *Hijrah,* i.e. about eight to nine years after the incident and about two and a half years after the so-called admonition of the Prophet (17: 73–5).[8] Could anybody who knows about the Qur'ān, its history and revelation, understand and explain how the incident of interpolation was allowed to be tolerated for six years and also why the offensive 'verses' were not abrogated until after nine years? Watt's theory is that 'the earliest versions do not specify how long afterwards this (abrogation) happened; the probability is that it was weeks or even months'[9] is nothing but a hypothesis. Had he investigated the chronology of the three revelations relative to the story, he could not possibly have missed the facts related above.

Let us now turn to some internal evidence. It has been said in the story that the 'Satanic' interpolation occurred in *Sūrah an-Najm* (53: 19f.) which delighted the idolaters present in the Ka'bah and as a gesture of friendship and good-will, they all bowed down with the Prophet. In order to comment on the story it would seem necessary to read the verses in the Qur'ān, adding the two alleged 'Satanic' verses, and find out what is actually meant to be conveyed here. It would read as follows:

أَفَرَءَيْتُمُ اللَّتَ وَالْعُزَّىٰ - وَمَنَوٰةَ الثَّالِثَةَ الْأُخْرَىٰ - أَلَكُمُ
الذَّكَرُ وَلَهُ الْأُنثَىٰ - تِلْكَ إِذًا قِسْمَةٌ ضِيزَىٰ - إِنْ هِيَ إِلَّا أَسْمَاءٌ
سَمَّيْتُمُوهَا أَنتُمْ وَآبَاؤُكُم مَّا أَنزَلَ اللَّهُ بِهَا مِن سُلْطَٰنٍ إِن
يَتَّبِعُونَ إِلَّا الظَّنَّ وَمَا تَهْوَى الْأَنفُسُ - وَلَقَدْ جَاءَهُم مِّن
رَّبِّهِمُ الْهُدَىٰ - (النجم - ١٩ - ٢٣) -

Have you considered al-Lāt and al-'Uzzā and Manāt, the third, the other! *These are the high-soaring ones (deities) whose intercession is to be hoped for!* Are the males for you and for Him (God) the females? This indeed is an unjust division. They are but names which you have named, you and your fathers, for which God has revealed no authority. They follow but conjecture and what (their) souls desire. And now the guidance has come to them from their Lord. (53: 19–23)

If one reads the italicized part of the alleged Satanic verses quoted above, one fails to understand how God on the one hand is praising the deities and on the other discrediting them by using the subsequent phrases quoted above. It is also difficult to see how the Quraysh leaders drew the conclusion from this chapter that Muḥammad, *ṣallā Allāhu 'alayhi wa sallam*, was making a conciliatory move and was adopting a policy of give and take.

Drawing conclusions from various reports connected with the story, Watt suggests that 'at one time Muḥammad must have publicly recited the Satanic verses as part of the Qur'ān; it is unthinkable that the story could have been invented later by Muslims or foisted upon them by non-Muslims. Secondly, at some later time Muḥammad announced that these verses were not really part of the Qur'ān and should be replaced by others of a vastly different import'.[10] Watt's suggestion that Muḥammad replaced the 'Satanic' verses with some others of a vastly different import is pure speculation. If one takes the 'Satanic verses' to be true, it would imply that the verses to be found in 53: 19f. were not revealed in the same period. Watt's suggestion also implies that Muḥammad and his followers read the 'Satanic' verses in place of or in addition to the verses found in the Qur'ān for 'weeks and even months' and that when Muḥammad later realized that these verses could not be correct, then the true version and continuation of the passage was revealed to him. This supposition is again pure speculation and is not based on any historical data. The story which we have summarized in the beginning suggests that Muḥammad did not realize his fault until God admonished him *six years later* and that the matter was rectified perhaps *another two and a half years* after.

It is obvious that Watt and other Orientalists accept part of the story and reject the other parts apparently because they are unable to find any link or sequence. Had there been any element of truth in the story, it could have caused a scandal against Islam and the Prophet and every detail must have found its place in the *Ḥadīth* literature. Why is the authentic *Ḥadīth* collection (namely the *Ṣiḥāḥ Sittah*) conspicuously silent about the *scandalous* part of the story? Does it not lead to the conclusion, contrary to the established fact, that *Ḥadīth* literature itself is very defective as it failed to record such an important event which led the Prophet and his Companions to read 'Satanic' verses for weeks, months or perhaps even years without realizing their error? In fact, al-Bukhārī, Muslim, Abū Dāwūd, Nasā'ī and Aḥmad b. Ḥanbal all record the story but only to the extent that was true. They all mention that the Prophet did recite *Sūrah an-Najm* and, at the end when he prostrated, the idolaters present were so overawed that they also joined him in prostration. These leading *Muḥaddithūn* do not mention the blasphemous story which other sources have recorded. The fact that the idolaters became overawed and joined Muḥammad in prostration is not difficult to believe as they all knew what magical effect the Qur'ān exercised on the listeners which was one of the reasons why they called the Qur'ān a *magic* قَالُوٓا إِنَّ هَٰذَا لَسِحْرٌ مُّبِينٌ (يونس ـ ٧٦)ـ and the Prophet a *magician* (يونس ـ ٢) قَالَ الْكَافِرُونَ إِنَّ هَٰذَا لَسَاحِرٌ مُّبِينٌ ـ ١ There is much historical data to substantiate the validity of this statement. It will suffice to retell the story of the acceptance of Islam by 'Umar I and the listening to the Qur'ān by the *jinns* ...قُلْ أُوحِىَ إِلَىَّ أَنَّهُ اسْتَمَعَ نَفَرٌ مِّنَ الْجِنِّ فَقَالُوٓا إِنَّا سَمِعْنَا قُرْآنًا عَجَبًا (الجن ـ ١)ـ (72: 1). It is quite likely that after their prostration the Quraysh were very ashamed and tried to hide their shame by inventing the story that they heard Muḥammad praising their deities which made them join him in prostration. The news of the idolaters and Muslims prostrating together spread quickly and it even reached Abyssinia with the additional rumour that Muḥammad had reconciled with the Quraysh and that hostility no longer existed between them.

Apart from the absurd nature of the story and the external and internal criticism which it cannot stand, there is another criterion of evaluation which one should not lose sight of. The Muslim traditionists quite often evaluate *Ḥadīth* on the basis of *riwāya* (the statement or the news based on the chain of narrators and the text of the *Ḥadīth*) as well as *dirāya* (credibility of the statement). It means that if something has been attributed to the Prophet of Islam through apparently sound *Ḥadīth*, it will not automatically be accepted if it goes against the Qur'ān and other established traditions and cannot be justified by reasoning.[11] It is here that even if one regards the story of the 'Satanic verses' to be sound on the ground that it has been narrated by a number of Muslim scholars or because it conforms to the requirements of a true narration (which it lacks), no Muslim traditionist will accept this story because it stands in clear contradiction to the established beliefs of the Muslims. The first few verses of *Sūrah an-Najm* themselves very clearly say:

وَالنَّجْمِ إِذَا هَوَىٰ ـ مَا ضَلَّ صَاحِبُكُمْ وَمَا غَوَىٰ ـ وَمَا يَنطِقُ عَنِ الْهَوَىٰ ـ إِنْ هُوَ إِلَّا وَحْىٌ يُوحَىٰ ـ عَلَّمَهُ شَدِيدُ الْقُوَىٰ. (النجم ـ ١ـ ٥)ـ

By the star when it sets; your companion errs not, nor does he deviate; nor does he speak out of desire. It is nothing but revelation that is revealed – One Mighty in power has taught him. (53: 1–5)

In *Sūrah al-Jinn* (72: 26–8), it is further declared:

... فَلَا يُظْهِرُ عَلَىٰ غَيْبِهِ أَحَدًا - إِلَّا مَنِ ارْتَضَىٰ مِن رَّسُولٍ فَإِنَّهُ يَسْلُكُ مِن بَيْنِ يَدَيْهِ وَمِنْ خَلْفِهِ رَصَدًا - لِّيَعْلَمَ أَن قَدْ أَبْلَغُوا رِسَالَاتِ رَبِّهِمْ - (الجن ٢٦ - ٢٨) -

He reveals not His secrets to any, except to him whom He chooses as a Messenger; for surely He makes a guard to march before him and after him, so that He may know that they have truly delivered the Message of their Lord.

These and other verses make it clear that it is not possible for the Prophet to accept anything in the Qur'ān from any external source. If this is so, then how can one take seriously, let alone believe in the so-called story of the 'Satanic revelation'? This is why the leading traditionists and exegetists in Islam have regarded the story as malicious and without foundation. It is unfortunate that an eminent historian like aṭ-Ṭabarī mentioned this story in his *Ta'rīkh* and did not make any comment on it. It is to be noted that early Muslim historians although meticulous in their *isnād* sometimes acted like a 'tape-recorder', recording anything that came to their knowledge from a sound and apparently reliable source. In a bid to remain objective and convey the message in pure form they seldom gave their own opinion and refrained from analysing the events thereby guiding the reader to their authenticity or otherwise. Aṭ-Ṭabarī was no exception. This he makes very clear at the outset in the following words: 'This book of mine may [be found] to contain some information, mentioned by us on the authority of certain men of the past, which the reader may disapprove of and the listener may find detestable, because he can find nothing sound and no real meaning in it. In such cases, he should know that it is not our fault that such information comes to him, but the fault of someone who transmitted it to us. We have merely reported it as it was reported to us'.[12] Although there is great advantage in such a methodology there are also risks.

Unscrupulous people may take advantage of this and try to concoct something as they did indeed in the fabrication of the malicious story of the so-called 'Satanic Verses'. This is why more cautious historians of a later period such as Ibn al-Athīr criticized aṭ-Ṭabarī for his bad historical and literary judgement with regard to some of the material contained in his book. The fact that aṭ-Ṭabarī, Ibn Sa'd and some other historians and scholars recorded this story in their works does not prove that the story itself is true. Modern researchers know that there are a number of reports and events which have been proved incorrect in the light of historical criticism and other available facts. One may refer, for instance, to the article *'Abbāsa* in the new edition of the *Encyclopaedia of Islam,* where aṭ-Ṭabarī's report that Hārūn ar-Rashīd's sister 'Abbāsah was secretly in love with Hārūn's vizier, has been proved incorrect and misleading.[13]

Notes and References

1. There have been very few scholarly writings by Muslims in the English language about Orientalists' views on Islam in general and on the Qur'ān in particular. For a survey of literature on Orientalism, see my bibliography entitled 'Orientalism and the Study of Islam in the West – A Select Bibliography' published in the *Muslim World Book Review,* Vol. 1, No. 4, 1981, pp. 51–60. To this list, *Orientalism, Islam and Islamists* edited by A. Hussain, R. Olson and J. Qureshi (Amana Books, 1984) may be added.
2. In Muslim sources the whole saga is known as *Ḥadīth al-Gharānīq* or the tradition of *Gharānīq,* the high-soaring ones. William Muir was perhaps the first Orientalist to name them 'Satanic verses'. A recent Jewish researcher of Islam regards the episode as 'one of the most striking instances of "abrogation" and "substitutions" ' and suggests that it is called 'Satanic' because of its pagan connotation. Cf. Ilse Lichtenstadter, 'A Note on the Gharānīq and Related Qur'ānic Problems', *Israel Oriental Studies,* 5 (1975), pp. 54–61.
3. This article has been inspired by the writings of Mawlānā Abul A'lā Mawdūdī and is based, among other sources, on his monumental Qur'ānic exegesis, *Tafhīm al-Qur'ān* and his study on the life of the Prophet entitled *Sīrat-i Sarwar-i 'Ālam,* both in Urdu. It is unfortunate that, due to his death in September, 1979, Mawlānā Mawdūdī could not complete his critique of the Orientalists' writings on the *Sīrah* of the Prophet – a desire which his predecessor, 'Allāmah Shiblī Nu'mānī (1857–1914) the celebrated author of the *Sīrat an-Nabī,* also took to the grave and was not able to accomplish during his lifetime for various reasons.
4. Watt devotes more than eight pages in his *Muhammad at Mecca*, Oxford, 1960, pp. 101–9, to narrating and evaluating the story. A summary of this

also appears in his 1968 publication *What is Islam?*, Longman and Librairie de Liban, pp. 42–5; the new edition of this book (1979) also retains the story without any change. See also, *The Introduction to the Qur'ān*, originally written by Richard Bell, but revised by him, Edinburgh, 1970, pp. 55–6. For similar far-fetched arguments and analysis of the story see Michael M.J. Fischer and Mehdi Abedi, 'Bombay Talkies, the Word and the World: Salman Rushdie's *Satanic Verses*', *Cultural Anthropology*, Washington, Vol. 5, No. 2, 1990, pp. 107–59, in particular pp. 124–30. Note their curious argument. 'The story that Muḥammad could have used the Satanic suggestion is rejected by almost all exegetes, but the fact that the story persists as a subject of exegetes' discussions is testimony to the reality of the temptation both for Muḥammad and for later Muslims in their own struggles with such 'Babylons' as London, New York, Paris, or Hamburg' (p. 127).

5. This is why some of the more discerning scholars in the West such as the Italian L. Caetani and the Briton John Burton have rejected the story as baseless and suggested different motives for the concoction of the outrageous tale (cf. L. Caetani, *Annali, dell' Islam* (Milan, 1906), No. 1, pp. 279–81; J. Burton, 'Those are the High-Flying Cranes', *Journal of Semitic Studies*, Vol. 15, No. 2, 1970, pp. 246–65).

6. Abul A'lā Mawdūdī in his Urdu Qur'ānic exegesis, *Tafhīm al-Qur'ān*, Lahore, 1972, Vol. 3, pp. 238–45, and *Sīrat-i Sarwar-i 'Ālam*, Lahore, 1979, Vol. 2, pp. 572–8, critically examines all the aspects of the story and evaluates the writings of early Muslim scholars on the subject quite thoroughly. See also, among others, Sayyid Quṭb, *Fī Ẓilāl al-Qur'ān*, Beirut, 1974, Vol. 4, pp. 2431–3; M.H. Haykal, *The Life of Muḥammad*, translated into English by Ismā'īl R. al-Fārūqī, North American Trust Publications, 1976, pp. 105–14, and Zakaria Bashier, *The Meccan Crucible*, London, 1978, pp. 180–6.

7. Several variants of these two spurious verses have been quoted which are as follows:

الغَرانِقَةُ العُلَى . اِنّ شَفَا عتَهُنّ تُرتَجَى -

إِنَّهَا لَهِىَ الغَرَائِقُ العُلَى .

وَاِنَّ هُنّ نَهُنّ الغَرَانِقَ العُلَى وَ اِنّ شَفَا عتَهُنّ نَهِىّ الّتِى تُرتَجَى -

..... اِنّ شَفَا عتَهُنّ تُرجَى - (بِدُرُنِ اَخِفَهُ الاوُلَى الغَرَانِيقُ أوِالغَرَانِقَةُ)

(- الرّئِيسِ التَّحرِيب-)

8. For a fuller discussion of this argument see the Urdu biography (incomplete) of the Prophet by Abul A'lā Mawdūdī entitled *Sīrat-i Sarwar-i 'Ālam*, Lahore, 1979, Vol. 2, pp. 573–7.

9. W. Montgomery Watt, *Muhammad at Mecca*, Oxford University Press, 1960, p. 103.

10. *Ibid.*

11. *The History of aṭ-Ṭabarī (Ta'rīkh al-Rusul wal-Mulūk),* Vol. I, *General Introduction and from the Creation to the Flood,* translation and annotation by Franz Rosenthal, New York, 1989, pp. 170–1.
12. Cf. *Encyclopaedia of Islam,* s.v. *'Abbāsa* (by J. Horovitz).

Index